Father–Daughter Incest in Twentieth-Century American Literature

Father–Daughter Incest in Twentieth-Century American Literature

The Complex Trauma of the Wound and the Voiceless

Christine Grogan

FAIRLEIGH DICKINSON UNIVERSITY PRESS
Madison • Teaneck

Published by Fairleigh Dickinson University Press
Copublished by The Rowman & Littlefield Publishing Group, Inc.
4501 Forbes Boulevard, Suite 200, Lanham, Maryland 20706
www.rowman.com

Unit A, Whitacre Mews, 26-34 Stannary Street, London SE11 4AB

British Library Cataloguing in Publication Information Available

Library of Congress Cataloging-in-Publication Data

Library of Congress Cataloguing-in-Publication Data Available

ISBN 978-1-61147-967-6 (cloth : alk. paper)
ISBN 978-1-61147-968-3 (electronic)

Printed in the United States of America

To Rob: for taking me away and then bringing me back

Contents

Acknowledgments

This project sprang from a curiosity to better understand what kind of society produces fathers who rape their own daughters. I can articulate that question today, but seven years ago, when I first started thinking about this book, I was unable to put to words what I was trying to say. As the research unraveled, my long-suspected hunch was confirmed: the construction of femininity in a patriarchal society such as the one in which we live is itself traumatizing. It was Elizabeth Hirsh, the first reader of this material, who told me that I can say that and more importantly that I should say that, as she gave me the confidence to do so.

As I'm sure with any long project, there were days I found it difficult to maintain the momentum to do justice to this one, and I'd like to thank the following people for helping see this book to completion. Thanks to *Feminist Studies in English Literature* and *EAPSU Online: A Journal of Critical and Creative Work* for granting me permission to reprint the essays that became chapters 2 and 4 of this book.[1] I appreciate the advice from David Brunell, especially for his help with chapter 6. He read entire drafts of early iterations. I'd also like to thank the faculty and staff of the University of South Florida's English department, including Laura Runge, Gary Lemons, Gurleen Grewal, and Lee Davidson, along with my Katherine Anne Porter Society family, Beth Alvarez, Darlene Unrue, Thomas Austenfeld, Jerry Findley, and Alexandra Subramanian. Many thanks to my parents for their continued support and to my students for their willingness to explore incest narratives and to those who were generous enough to share their own personal stories with me during my office hours. I'm grateful to Grace-Carol Hoyte, who volunteered her time to work as my unofficial research assistant. Dr. Corinne Wolf has always encouraged me and taught me how to drive a hard bargain. I'd like to thank Sarah Namulondo, "my dear," whose conversations about the importance of feminism echo throughout my work and life and whose memory infuses every page of this book. To my furry four-legged friends, Logan, Cora, and Willard, who spent long days at the foot of my desk, more patient with my work some days than I was. And, finally, I'd like to thank the writer I most admire: Robert Alderman, who read and commented on the entire manuscript, even when he had his own book to write. I'd like to thank him for believing in me enough to leave everything he's known, for bringing me closer to the One who makes all things possible, and for not letting this book stay buried at the bottom of my closet.

NOTE

1. Chapter 2 was reprinted by permission of *Feminist Studies in English Language,* which published a version of this chapter in its April 2013 edition. Chapter 4 was reprinted by permission of *EAPSU Online: A Journal of Critical and Creative Work,* which published a version of this chapter in its fall 2014 edition.

Introduction

The Wound and the Voiceless

February 1, 2014, marks the first time Dylan Farrow, now called Malone, publicly wrote about the sexual abuse she suffered at the hands of her adoptive father, Hollywood hero Woody Allen, the same man who married her sister, Soon-Yi Previn. In her open letter published in *The New York Times*, Farrow presents a harrowing tale of father–daughter incest when, on August 4, 1992, at the age of seven, she was taken by the hand, led into a tight attic of her mother's Connecticut home, told to lie on her stomach and play with her brother's electric train set as Allen sexually assaulted her. Other incidents are mentioned—times when he stuck his thumb in her mouth, forced her into bed with him wearing only his underwear, and placed his head in her naked lap, inhaling and exhaling.

These secrets first went public in 1993 as a result of the split between Woody Allen and long-term girlfriend Mia Farrow. In January 1992, Mia discovered that Allen was having an affair—with their adopted daughter, Soon-Yi. The proof was in the Polaroids, explicit, nude shots Allen had taken and displayed on his fireplace mantle, effectively ending their twelve-year relationship and wrecking a family of eight children whose former sister was "promoted" to stepmother. By the summer of that year, Allen turned his gaze to his other daughter, Dylan. Upon learning of the abuse, Mia videotaped Dylan's disclosure and took her to the doctor that same day. The family pediatrician, bound by law, alerted the authorities. The Connecticut police launched a criminal investigation, which included an independent review by the Yale-New Haven Sex Abuse Clinic. On August 13, 1992, slightly more than a week after the molestation, Allen, in a strange move, sued Mia in the New York state court for custody of Dylan, along with adopted son, Moses, and his presumed biological son, Satchel, now named Ronan.

After a six-month inquiry, which included medical examinations, the criminal investigative team from Yale-New Haven Hospital concluded that Dylan was not molested. Conveniently, the three doctors who made up the team did not testify in court, other than through the sworn deposition of team leader, John M. Leventhal. In the statement, Leventhal recorded the theory held by Allen's lawyer, Elkan Abramowitz, which many others would echo two decades later: Dylan either invented the story or had the memories planted in her mind by her mother. Curiously, the investigative team destroyed their collective notes before submitting their report. The records of the 1993 trial are sealed.

When Mia came forward, the time was rife with fears of children fabricating stories of sexual abuse. In 1992, the False Memory Syndrome Foundation (FMSF) was established to defend the patriarchal family—to support parents believed to be falsely accused and to study ways memory may be manufactured. Whatever its merits, the well-funded FMSF furthered its conservative social agenda by making it okay to again discredit the stories of survivors. It is therefore not surprising that the panel of psychiatrists sided with Allen. The custody judge, Justice Elliott Wilk, however, ruled in favor of Dylan and Mia. Finding probable cause, the State of Connecticut denied Allen visitation rights—even supervised ones—of his three children. However, Mia did not pursue criminal charges "due to, in the words of the prosecutor, the fragility of the 'child victim.'"[1] In other words, the prosecution party wanted to save the young girl from more distress. And so, Allen was neither prosecuted nor convicted of any crime. Legally, he was cleared of everything. Because the statute of limitations ran out at least 15 years ago, Allen could no longer be charged today, even if conclusive evidence was found.

Not only does Dylan recount the alleged abuse in her open letter, she also describes the traumatic aftermath: doctors gaslighted her and experts attacked her credibility. She directs her attention to Hollywood's A-listers and famous actors, many who knew her as a little girl, naming Diane Keaton, Cate Blanchett, Alec Baldwin, Emma Stone, and Scarlett Johansson. She questions why they turned a blind eye to her abuse. And now, releasing her letter the same day as the Writers Guild Awards, which nominated Allen for best screenplay, it seems she's questioning why anyone would award a man who would do that to a child. Toward the piece's end she writes, "Woody Allen is a living testament to the way our society fails the survivors of sexual assault and abuse."

In his prefatory note, Nicholas Kristof, a lifelong friend of Mia and one of the foremost columnists for *The New York Times*, explains why he published Dylan's letter. Simply put: we heard from countless people on all sides of this debate, but we had yet to hear from Dylan herself. At the risk of undermining his own assertion that Allen deserves the presumption of innocence, Kristof prints the letter for the world to read. It is the story of a female who becomes nauseated at the mention of Allen's name; who to this day finds it difficult to look at toy trains; who lives in a world that celebrates her tormentor.

On February 9, 2014, Allen printed his response to Dylan's letter, also in *The New York Times*. Trying to get the final word on the matter, he predictably defends himself while placing the blame squarely on Mia, painting her to be a scheming, vindictive, scorned lover who lies and lacks integrity, evident in, among other things, her refusal to take a lie-detector test back in the nineties. Allen accuses Mia of calling his sister and threatening that because Allen took her daughter, she'll take his, and of trying to get one of his former girlfriend's, Stacey Nelkin, to testify that she was underage when he dated her. Not surprisingly, Allen managed to remind his readers that a nineteen-year-old Mia dated the much older Frank Sinatra, who Mia now claims fathered Ronan (whom she led Allen to believe all these years was his). In sum, Allen concludes that "most likely a vulnerable, stressed-out, 7-year-old was coached by Mia Farrow."[2] Dylan, whom Allen thinks has come to believe the allegations, was "a pawn for revenge." Claiming Justice Wilk wrote "a very irresponsible opinion" regarding the molestation charges, Allen asserts that Wilk sided with Mia simply because he never approved of Allen's relationship with Previn.

Moreover, Allen comments on Mia's "creative flourishes," claiming that the attic setting doesn't work because he's "a major claustrophobe" and that the idea was plagiarized from the song "With My Daddy in the Attic," written by Dory Previn, the wife of André Previn, with whom Mia had an affair. "Smelling more like Mia than Dylan," the letter is questioned by Allen, who wonders how Dylan benefits from its unnecessary disclosure because she already spoke out months previously in *Vanity Fair*. In *Vanity Fair*'s October 2, 2013, edition, Dylan does give Maureen Orth her first comments on the record, but they are couched in an article titled "Mia Farrow and Eight of Her Children Speak Out on Their Lives, Frank Sinatra, and the Scandals They've Endured."[3] This is not the first-person account Dylan would pen for *The New York Times*.

Throughout his response, Allen liberally quotes Moses Farrow, his star witness, now a thirty-seven-year-old family therapist who recently renewed his relationship with an aging Allen. Moses states that Mia "drummed it into me to hate my father for tearing apart the family and sexually molesting my sister." Moreover, Allen quotes Moses as saying, "Of course Woody did not molest my sister. . . . She loved him and looked forward to seeing him when he would visit. She never hid from him until our mother succeeded in creating the atmosphere of fear and hate towards him." And, finally, Moses dismisses Mia's family, exclaiming "Knowing that my mother often used us as pawns, I cannot trust anything that is said or written from anyone in the family."

But, whereas Moses sides with Allen, Ronan defends his sister. Shortly after long-time friend and leading-lady Diane Keaton presented Allen with the Cecil B. DeMille Lifetime Achievement Award, which included a glowing televised tribute, Ronan tweeted the following: "Missed the Woody Allen tribute. Did they put the part where a woman publicly confirmed he molested her at age 7 before or after Annie Hall?" Also, a report from 1992 undermines some of what Moses said, as it highlights Allen's obsession with a young Dylan that landed him in therapy: "Allen would arrive at Mia's house at 6 a.m. (he and his lover lived on opposite sides of New York's Central Park) and sit on the end of Dylan's bed, staring at her until she woke up. He insisted that Dylan be kept up until he got back in the evening to tuck her in."[4]

The revived allegations that Allen incestuously violated Dylan when she was seven years old elicited passionate and polarized commentary. Perhaps, as Justice Wilk observed years ago, "we will probably never know what occurred" that August day in the Connecticut attic. There are rarely witnesses in sex abuse cases, after all. As JoAnn Wypijewski, writer for *The Nation* states, "The truth is, we don't know the truth." But she goes on to add, "there is nothing high-minded or radical or feminist in pretending that we do."[5] Yes, it is a case of "he said; she said." But, as Laurie Penny of *New Statesman* correctly notes, "the problem is that, in this society, 'he said' is almost always considered more credible than 'she said.'"[6] Kristof, a supporter of Dylan, mentions that Allen deserves the presumption of innocence, however, that only applies to a criminal case, and as I've stated, no trial will be taking place. We should not misuse the law to excuse our own decision to not believe Dylan. Why aren't we granting the same courtesy to Dylan, who deserves to be believed, as we are to Allen? Why is it much easier to trust that Mia would plant false memories of sexual abuse into her daughter than it is to believe that Dylan Farrow is another survivor of an epidemic of incestuous violence?

The reception of Dylan's letter indicates that our society is still hostile to survivors, full of victim shaming and blaming. We live in a culture of denial, where, even though we know one in five girls in the United States suffers at least some form of sexual molestation during childhood or that 10 percent of women have experienced serious childhood sexual abuse, the propensity is to think the girl is lying. As feminist author and activist Louise Armstrong argued in her groundbreaking work, *Rocking the Cradle of Sexual Politics: What Happened When Women Said Incest*, even our legal system colludes in punishing women who seek justice and we shouldn't be too fast to trust the criminal and medical teams: "In one case, a doctor's testimony that semen had been found in the child's vagina after a visit with a father was discounted as insufficient evidence."[7] Most believe that Mia and Dylan have an ulterior motive. But what would they have to gain? Newspaper columnist Tom Leonard states that it does make for a good story, in two centuries no less. It became something of a media phenomenon as the public weighed in on the court of popular opinion regarding the "dark goings-on in the attic of a family house."[8]

But many of Hollywood's stars remained quiet, perpetuating the conspiracy of silence that comes with disclosures of this kind and that serves to revictimize the daughter. Or they came to Allen's defense. For example, even though Leonard joked about "the likes of Scarlett Johansson and Emma Stone" having "weightier questions to answer on the red carpet than who designed their frock," Johansson said that it's "irresponsible" to involve her in the controversy. An angry Alec Baldwin tweeted, "What the f&@% is wrong w u that u think we all need to b commenting on this family's personal struggle? . . . So you know who's guilty? Who's lying? You, personally, know that? You are mistaken if you think there is a place for me, or any outsider, in this family's issue." He later deleted his posts. Moreover, Diane Keaton swore her "belief" in Allen's innocence. Barbara Walters defended him on *The View*. And, Stephen King reduced the letter to "an element of palpable bitchery," essentially calling Dylan or Mia, or both, a bitch. He, too, later deleted his tweet after hiding behind his "technical difficulties."

Why does it sound like the victim, not the perpetrator, is on trial? As Penny states, "They say women lie to damage men's reputations and 'destroy their lives.'" And yet, "popular culture is groaning with powerful men who have been accused of sexual abuse and whose lives remain distinctly undestroyed: men such as the boxer Mike Tyson and the singer R. Kelly."[9] Allen easily fits on this list as many defended the world-renowned director, the artist who pumps out a film per year on his trusty typewriter—"an unprecedented pace he's maintained since 1969."[10] As Leonard added tongue-in-cheek, Hollywood was presented with a philosophical dilemma: "Will the fact that one of its most revered icons has been accused of the most unimaginably vile behaviour result in his films being shunned at the awards?"[11] Evidently not.

As this study illustrates, we've heard these stories before; the Allen–Farrow case is not merely a sensational or random event. Rape and incest are nothing new. Exact figures are difficult to obtain, and it depends on which study one consults, but current data suggest that anywhere from one in five to one in three girls experiences sexual abuse at the hands of fathers or father figures and that 50 to 70 percent of rape victims develop post-traumatic stress disorder (PTSD).[12] These studies reflect the definition of father–daughter incest as outlined by Judith Herman and Lisa Hirschman in their 1981 *Father–Daughter Incest*: "any sexual relationship between a child and an adult in a position of paternal authority. From the psychological point of view, it does not matter if the father and child are blood relatives. What matters is the relationship that exists by virtue of the adult's parental power and the child's dependency."[13] This definition would include biological fathers, stepfathers, and mothers' boyfriends. They further define "sexual relationship" to mean "any physical contact that had to be kept a secret."[14] This definition includes any unwanted sexual activity beyond that of penile penetration, which had previously been the only act "dignified with the name of incest."[15] According to Joan Atwood's 2007 study, "The highest incidence of incest occurred between fathers and daughters, a large percentage of it occurring when the girls were under 10."[16] Nancy Fischer cites the National Center on Child Abuse and Neglect, which indicates that sexual abuse "has greatly increased since 1980," which may have something to do with the official recognition of PTSD that same year.[17] Fischer adds a caveat, stating that researchers are unsure if the increased rates "represent an actual escalation in abuse or more willingness of individuals to report suspected abuse."[18] Nonetheless, father–daughter incest is thought to be one of the most underreported crimes, and, therefore, most victims never become part of a national, anonymous statistic, and many of its effects go untreated.[19]

What is new about incest, as Penny notes, is that we are expanding our pedophile profile to include successful men with high-earning careers: "on a cultural level we are beginning to challenge the delusion that only evil men rape, that it is impossible for a man to be a rapist or an abuser of children and also, say, a great film-maker."[20] All these years, it has been much easier to side with the perpetrator, especially one held in high esteem. In the words of clinical psychologist Judith Herman, a Boston psychiatrist associated with the Harvard Medical School and one of the most important feminist experts on trauma whose clinical work and research focus for more than forty years on victims of domestic and political trauma: "All the perpetrator asks is that the bystander do nothing. He appeals to the universal desire to see, hear, and speak no evil. The victim, on the contrary, asks the bystander to share the burden of pain. The victim demands action, engagement, and remembering."[21] Likewise, Susan Pease Banitt, a child abuse prevention professional and a treater of many adult victims of childhood trauma, maintains that "contemplating that your best loved films were created by a monster creates a level of cognitive dissonance that most people cannot handle."[22] Too much is at stake in facing the truth and coming to terms with the pervasiveness of incestuous violence. It will mean, as Jessica Valenti wrote in *The Nation*, "rethinking institutions and families and power dynamics and the way we interact with each other every day."[23] Penny adds, "it will mean looking with new eyes at our most revered icons, our social groups, our friends and relatives."[24] The intensity of the responses to Dylan's letter suggests the magnitude of what is at stake: core beliefs about the protectiveness of patriarchy and the sanctity of the family.

The public nature of Dylan's disclosures should be read in the context of a larger "speaking out" movement on sexual-abuse activism most pronounced in the 1990s but with seeds planted as early as the 1930s, as this study indicates. This political act of breaking her silence to tell the truth came with many risks but also some rewards. Dylan was failed by not just her father, but by the media, medical community, and entertainment industry. On February 10, in her follow up to Allen's letter, she explains why she published her original piece in the first place: "It took all my strength and all my emotional fortitude to do what I did this week in the hope that it would put the truth out there," she said, adding "That is my only ammunition. I don't have money or publicists or limos or fancy apartments in Manhattan. All I have is the truth and that is all I put out there."[25] In a word, she did it for the sake of truth. Hopefully, that quieted those who claimed Dylan did it for the money. Moreover, she writes, "Once again Woody Allen is attacking me and my family in an effort to discredit and silence me, but nothing he says can change the truth. For 20 years, I have never wavered in describing what he did to me. I will carry the memories of surviving these experiences for the rest of my life. Woody Allen has an arsenal of lawyers and publicists, but the one thing he does not have on his side is the truth." Dylan has been encouraged by some of the responses from those with similar experiences who now aren't afraid to share their stories: "the survivors of sexual abuse who have reached out to me—to support me and to share their fears of coming forward, of being called a liar, of being told their memories aren't their memories—have given me a reason to not be silent, if only so others know that they don't have to be silent either." Silent for twenty years, Dylan, who knows more surely than others the dangers of challenging paternal authority, wanted "to put the truth on paper from a voice that was not able to speak before."

Though there has been plenty of commentary on the controversy surrounding Dylan's public disclosures, less has been said about her PTSD diagnosis. We know Dylan was diagnosed with PTSD in 2013. In the November 1992 *Vanity Fair* piece, Mia stated that Dylan "often complained of stomachaches and headaches when Woody visited: she would have to lie down. When he left, the symptoms would disappear. At times Dylan became so withdrawn when her father was around that she would not speak normally, but would pretend to be an animal."[26] Growing up, Dylan suffered from eating disorders and would cut herself, admitting to a fear of being touched by men. Perhaps Dylan did not say more about her condition because the symptoms of PTSD have been used in the media and legal system to discount the reports of victims. And yet, the brief mention of PTSD leads me to wonder if in the admirable quest to have incest recognized as a social, political problem, the pendulum has swung too far in the other direction and we have somehow forgotten incest's psychological relevance.

This study examines stories like Dylan's in which the accompanying psychological trauma, stemming from father–daughter incest, is never easily represented nor received. Dylan's letter may be classified as a trauma narrative of sorts that testifies to her psycho-cultural woundings and her subsequent struggle for survival. Unsurprisingly, "poets, dramatists, and novelists . . . were the first to record the profound impact of traumatic stressors on cognitions, feelings and behavior," state Matthew J. Friedman and colleagues in their article titled "Considering PTSD for *DSM-5*."[27] Noting that literature first registered what are now familiar aspects of trauma studies—the importance of verbalizing trauma and the need for a witness to hear the story—Friedman and colleagues proceed to mention that the medical community caught on much later. Freud was at the forefront of these efforts, and in his work, he often turned to literature for narrative recastings of traumatic events, events which have long been thought to defy linguistic representation. Because of its peculiar nature, trauma is a shattering experience that is said to distort memory and is particularly susceptible and vulnerable to problems of understanding and reporting. Thought to be based on one original event that is itself self-replicating, trauma breaks down the distinction between past and present. Even the controversial-yet-inescapable figure in the genealogy of trauma theory realized that any narrative of traumatic experience will be somehow altered, changed, transformed, modified, distorted—in a word, fictionalized. Figurative language may well be the only properly referential language to convey what is a radically non-linguistic event. And unlike case studies, literary texts bring the vulnerability of women in a male-dominated society into focus by providing the context.

The growing interest in the topic of psychological trauma within literary studies began in the 1990s, most notably with Cathy Caruth's 1996 field-defining work, *Unclaimed Experience: Trauma, Narrative, and History*. One of the most influential critics on trauma in the humanities department, whose theoretical framework still dominates trauma theory, Caruth argued for the importance of literary representations in depicting time-limited traumatic events.[28] Titling the introduction to her pioneering work "The Wound and the Voice," she revisits Freud to argue that because literature, like psychoanalysis, is interested in the problematics and estrangements of language, it is a privileged site for articulating event traumatic experiences, which are stored as sensory fragments that have no verbal components—as she puts it, "unclaimed experiences." Although trauma works to disrupt the possibility of memory and narrative, Caruth contends that, paradoxically, from a mental imprint of the wound, a human voice cries out.

Caruth's book began a critical conversation that continues today. In the Caruthian formulation of trauma, or what Michelle Balaev calls "the traditional model of trauma" in her 2012 *The Nature of Trauma in American Novels*, trauma is understood as an event that will "never be normally incorporated into consciousness, thus leading to a fragmented sense of self and producing a type of memory with pathological symptoms in which the experience is inaccessibly frozen and unrepresentable."[29] Relying on the psychological research of Herman, Caruth also employs the work of Bessel van der Kolk, one of the world's leading authorities on PTSD. They emphasize the causal relationship between trauma and dissociation, in which the traumatic experience is encoded differently from normal memories in that it bypasses perception and consciousness and is stored as sensory fragments that have no linguistic components.[30] Hence, the result is the "unspeakability" of trauma, or what van der Kolk calls the "speechless terror" of trauma (a term from his book *Psychological Trauma*). Trauma theory is much occupied with the unrepresentable nature of trauma, or at least the not-directly-representable nature of it. For this reason, Caruth and others endorse the crucial role of the literary signifier as enabling at least a possibility of bearing witness to—if never actually understanding or being able to situate precisely—the reality of the traumatized.

In his 2014 article titled "Speak, Trauma: Toward a Revised Understanding of Literary Trauma Theory," Joshua Pederson ushers in a second-wave of literary trauma theory, one built, not on Caruth's notions, but rather, on the clinical work of Richard McNally and his 2003 book *Remembering Trauma*. Pederson's opening question reads, "Do we forget the traumas we suffer, losing them in an amnesic haze, or do our moments of deepest pain remain available to us?"[31] Repudiating the work of Caruth, Geoffrey Hartman, Dori Laub, Shoshana Felman, and others of the "first wave" of literary trauma theory, Pederson answers with the latter. Refuting the claims that trauma is amnesic and unspeakable, Pederson contends, "while victims may *choose* not to speak of their traumas, there is little evidence that they *cannot*."[32] In other words, McNally and Pederson believe that traumatic memory, although altered, is not absent and can therefore be expressed in words.

In ways, this is reassuring news for literary scholars who work with written language. Caruth, along with Herman and van der Kolk, argued that trauma eluded narrative representation. Following their lead, the literary scholar was put in a difficult position—trying to read the gaps and omissions from narratives. With this new understanding that trauma is not only speakable but also that trauma may very well enhance memory—resulting in an outpouring of words—our work as literary scholars now entails focusing on the text and what it holds, not what it leaves out.

Toward the end of his article, Pederson hits on an observation that needs further exploration. He mentions that recounting stories of trauma is difficult—not because of "some psychological inability to recall or restate"—but because of the reactions they provoke.[33] He makes this comment when discussing the attempts of male soldiers to share their war stories with their loved ones. He concludes that these unnamed vets aren't *unable* to deliver accounts of trauma; they fear the results, perhaps not unlike Dylan Farrow's reluctance to share her traumatic story. There is a significant gender component to trauma, whose implications, along with those of race and class, go unexplored in Pederson's, McNally's, and even Caruth's, work.

My study builds on this body of work by exploring two additional questions about representation. First, it asks what happens when the voice of trauma is crying out from what Toni Morrison has called the "most delicate," "most vulnerable" member of society: a female child; and, second, what happens when trauma is not just a time-limited event but chronic and cumulative experiences. Trauma scholarship over the last twenty years has examined trauma outstripping our discursive and representational resources but has only begun to address the ways social identities of gender, race, and class complicate our understanding of the post-traumatic and PTSD. In other words, as Balaev correctly concludes, "In terms of responses to trauma, the difficulty of speaking about a traumatic experience is not necessarily due to the intrinsic quality of trauma to defy all representation, but due to variable factors, including individual, social, cultural factors that influence the remembrance and narration of the experience."[34] Moreover, as Balaev states and Pederson agrees, we are beginning to understand that "the 'unspeakability' of trauma claimed by so many literary critics today can be understood less as an epistemological conundrum or neurobiological fact, but more as an outcome of cultural values and ideologies."[35] Some traumatic experiences, including father–daughter incest, are culturally reduced to the untellable. In other words, the victim struggles with incest's unrepresentability: arguably what is unrepresentable within her own psyche but certainly what cannot be said aloud because of social and political repercussions. Representation in the psyche is different from representation on the page and in the public.

The last two decades have seen the birth of book-length studies of literary incest, although it has traditionally been a neglected topic among literature scholars. Otto Rank's seminal work, *Das Inzest-Motiv in Dichtung und Sage* (*The Incest Theme in Literature and Legend*), published in 1912, surveys the incest theme primarily in German novels and dramas but was not translated into English until 1992. In the first collection of scholarly essays whose title suggests its broad scope and focus, *Incest and the Literary Imagination*, Elizabeth Barnes edited fourteen essays on works that span from medieval to contemporary literature and include a variety of critical perspectives. Bringing together a range of representative works on incest, Barnes's book establishes its importance as an object of literary inquiry and paves the way for future studies. Published in reaction to the "false-memory syndrome" debate, Janice Doane and Devon Hodges's *Telling Incest: Narratives of Dangerous Remembering from Stein to Sapphire* traces historical shifts in the discourse of incest narratives, asking what narrative structures and strategies women have created to tell incest and gain hearing. Largely literary, their work does not explicitly link academic criticism with activism.[36]

Contributing to scholar-activist research, Gillian Harkins's *Everybody's Family Romance: Reading Incest in Neoliberal America* is an interdisciplinary project that reads novels, popular media, legal proceedings, and other material of the 1980s and 1990s to examine why the prominence of father–daughter incest became a debated issue during a time of neoliberalism. She is primarily interested in how gender-based violence is coopted by or resistant against the neoliberal context of politics, economics, and culture. In *Patriarchy and Incest from Shakespeare to Joyce*, Jane M. Ford traces the incest theme in the works of Shakespeare, Dickens, James, Conrad, and Joyce, arguing that most or all of the fathers are sexually attracted to or fixated on their daughters. Selecting an early, middle, and late work by these authors, Ford is primarily concerned with analyzing not actual, but covert, incest in the father–daughter suitor triangle. The breadth of Ford's representative authors suggests the ubiquity of the incest theme. Ellen Pollak's *Incest and the English Novel, 1684–1814* explores the prevalence of incest or threatened incest in eighteenth-century British novels. Taking a feminist-historicist approach, Pollak rereads eighteenth-century narratives to reveal the masculine privilege, linking the proliferation of cultural discourses about incest to broad changes in family structure, class dynamics, and gender differences. Her important work indicates that the representation of incest in fiction has social and political significance, more so than for which it has received credit.

Drawing on this body of work, this book reads literary form as social commentary and is centrally concerned with how the study of twentieth-century American literature can help develop an approach to trauma that foregrounds its status as a social and political issue, as well as a personal, psychodynamic one. In 1980, thanks in large part to the efforts of feminist activists and Vietnam veterans, psychological trauma became an official diagnosis. Included in the *Diagnostic and Statistical Manual of Mental Disorders (DSM)-III,* the long overdue category of PTSD entered the American Psychiatric Association lexicon. It was the first time the American Psychiatric Association acknowledged "that a psychiatric disorder could be wholly environmentally determined and that a traumatic event occurring in adulthood could have lasting psychological consequences."[37] PTSD was originally identified as an anxiety disorder with four diagnostic criteria: traumatic event, reexperiences of the event, numbing phenomena, and miscellaneous symptoms. At this time, the traumatic event was "vaguely defined as an event that is 'generally outside the range of usual human experience,' and as involving a 'recognizable stressor that would evoke significant symptoms of distress in almost everyone.'"[38]

Studies have shown that "interpersonal violence tends to produce PTSD at higher rates than does other trauma."[39] Even though framing sexual abuse in terms of PTSD reassured many patients that abuse, not something intrinsic in them, caused their problems, the PTSD model has never properly fit the problem of incest. As Joseph E. Davis notes in *Accounts of Innocence: Sexual Abuse, Trauma, and the Self,* accounting for sexual abuse, let alone incest, within the PTSD model "was by no means obvious."[40] Defined by a group of symptoms rather than an explanation of how these symptoms develop, Davis adds that many researchers, namely David Finkelhor, found that, although it helped account for some cases of stranger rape, it was an ill fit to represent sexual abuse, especially the paradigm case of incest. The PTSD diagnosis is an umbrella category under which many traumatized people could be scientifically grouped. As early as 1992, Herman and other clinicians recognized that the current formulation of PTSD does not adequately serve as an explanation for multiple traumas, and they called for complex post-traumatic stress disorder (CPTSD) to be included in the *DSM-5*.

Their thinking was informed by the feminist psychotherapist Maria Root, who rendered a powerful feminist intervention into the politics of trauma through her conceptualization of "insidious trauma," a term that refers to the cumulative degradation directed toward individuals whose aspects of identity, such as gender, color, and class, differ from those in power. Complex trauma provides a useful framework for understanding the long-term consequences of many types of institutionalized sexism, racism, and classism, as illustrated in the six texts this book closely examines. Contrary to current medical definitions of psychological trauma and PTSD, most traumatic experiences of women and those economically deprived and racially othered, are not time-limited, singular "events." Rather, they are current, cumulative, and quite common. Because of patriarchal structures, "women are more likely than men to be exposed to trauma that is sustained, repeated, and more damaging in type and severity."[41]

My interdisciplinary study challenges our narrow definition of trauma and what has been clinically termed PTSD by rereading six American literary texts published in the last hundred years—*Tender Is the Night, Invisible Man, The Bluest Eye, Bastard Out of Carolina, The Kiss,* and *Redemption: A Story of Sisterhood, Survival, and Finding Freedom Behind Bars*—in terms of what they tell us about the complex trauma of father–daughter incest. The term *complex trauma* is used in the medical community to describe the effects of exposure to multiple traumatic experiences, often of an insidious, yet invasive and interpersonal, nature. Herman and others noted that the current diagnostic formulation of PTSD accounts for relatively circumscribed traumatic events, not for a spectrum of features.[42] Herman defines CPTSD as a syndrome observed in survivors of prolonged, repeated trauma. The PTSD construct, she argues, is problematic in that it fails to include the complex sequelae of chronic trauma, examples of which include patients who endured prisons, concentration camps, slave labor camps, religious cults, brothels, "other institutions of organized sexual exploitation," and as Herman states, "some families."[43] The victim's extended contact with the perpetrator creates "a special type of relationship, one of coercive control," and one that's too damaging to readily fit into the existing concept of traumatic neurosis.[44] Survivors of childhood abuse, particularly, call attention to the limitations with the existing model. The survivors often present with "chronic depression complicated by dissociative symptoms, substance abuse, impulsivity, self-mutilation, and suicidality."[45] They often engage in reenactment and revictimization. Commenting on childhood abuse, Herman states, "A history of abuse, particularly in childhood, appears to be one of the major factors predisposing a person to become a psychiatric patient."[46]

CPTSD appears to have two symptoms that distinguish it from PTSD: a significant change from previous personality and a loss of previously sustaining beliefs. Herman observes, "While the victim of a single acute trauma may say she is 'not herself' since the event, the victim of chronic trauma may lose the sense that she has a self."[47] Moreover, Herman questions the treatments given to those suffering from chronic, early, and interpersonal distress, stating, "Treatments proven to be effective for PTSD alone may be inadequate, or possibly even harmful, for CPTSD."[48]

Complex trauma is not a new idea in psychology, but this is the first book to examine this concept in relation to literary texts. In addition to the legacy of blaming the victim and denying or minimizing the harmful effects of sexual abuse, we've yet to validate the insidious and polymorphous forms of harm. Today questions remain about the uncertain place of CPTSD in the field of traumatic stress. As Herman writes, "Naming the syndrome of complex post-traumatic stress disorder presents an essential step toward granting those who have endured prolonged exploitation a measure of the recognition they deserve."[49]

Like Caruth, who argues for the importance of literary representations in depicting time-limited traumatic events, I hope to indicate that literature can be a privileged place for illustrating complex trauma because it provides a wide-ranging view of the personal, political, and social. In this book, I analyze the texts in the order they were first published to chart the development in incest narratives from male-authored fiction to female-authored memoir and to argue that they compel us to confront the traumatic nature of social oppression, especially that which is endemic to the structure of the patriarchal family and of American racism and classism. This progression shows how female victims of incest, like Dylan Farrow, went from being silent to being silenced.

This study should interest those in the literary and medical communities. One of the clinical field's biggest challenges is developing a politically responsible approach to trauma that accounts for women's experiences, which is further complicated by the fact that the scientific community is in disagreement over what trauma is. In May 2013, the *DSM-5* was published, with significant changes made to the definition of PTSD. No longer classified as an anxiety disorder, it is now included in a new chapter on trauma- and stress-related disorders. The diagnostic criteria for a traumatic event are better outlined, and sexual assault is specifically included. Additionally, two subtypes of PTSD are now identified—in children younger than six years of age and with prominent dissociative symptoms. And yet, for all the *DSM-5* did to further our understanding of PTSD, it failed to recognize CPTSD, leaving many incest victims misdiagnosed and therefore mistreated. The advances and limitations in the psychological community speak to the timeliness of this project.[50]

A strength of the CPTSD construct is that it takes into consideration the context, which the literary writers of this study so expressively showcase in their works. As Gillian Straker notes in "Continuous Traumatic Stress: Personal Reflections 25 Years On," "the issue of mental health, diagnosis, and access to treatment, has always been, and always will be, a political issue."[51] "The question remains of how one does justice to stress and distress in individuals, and makes this legible both to mental health professionals and society at large, while retaining a focus on the contexts that generate these difficulties and dictate their treatment."[52] In highlighting that prolonged traumatic stress has different effects than more circumscribed exposure to trauma, Herman calls our attention to how the notion of trauma itself is linked to political concerns. Complex trauma was conceptualized with not only a mental health agenda in mind but also a political and social one. Herman maintains that in addition to treating the individual, we need to change the context. We now know that PTSD is diagnosed more frequently in women than in men and is most commonly related to multiple instances of interpersonal violence including those reaching back to childhood experiences of sexual and physical abuse, as is often the case with father–daughter incest. We also know that the probability that PTSD will result from rape and incest is much higher than that from exposure to natural disasters. Although we may need better conceptual coherence and empirical support for the CPTSD construct to be officially recognized, its victims are suffering every day from the conspiracy of silence by the invalidation of this diagnosis in the *DSM*.[53]

The question of why voicelessness and father–daughter incest go together is the central question raised in this book. Speech is paradoxically both a main feature that defines trauma when it is absent and that can be a solution to the problem of traumatic pathology. As Herman puts it, "When the victim is already devalued (a woman, a child), she may find that the most traumatic events of her life take place outside the realm of socially validated reality. Her experience becomes unspeakable."[54] Because the voice of patriarchy, even in our avowedly post-patriarchal culture, remains an immense force in power structures, everyone wants to be connected with the powerful father and avoid connection with the sacrificed daughter. As Kathleen Rowe Karlyn notes in her 2011 study, "young women desire to maintain connections with the existing (still largely male) power structure."[55] Karlyn echoes Jane Gallop, who suggested that patriarchy lures girls into a femininity based on overvaluing and idealizing men and devaluing women, including themselves. This burden of speaking against the father—as read through popular culture and through literature—is the cause of voicelessness for survivors of father–daughter incest, which may explain why Dylan waited so long to speak out. In her work on narrative poetics, Susan Snaider Lanser notes that voice, although elusive in literary-critical terms, is not only a pivotal category, established as a key structural component of narrative, but also one of political implications within feminist theory: "Few words are as resonant to contemporary feminists as 'voice.'"[56] Voice signifies a personal element that defies textuality and that tells the "truth" about embodied, lived experience. The term has become a trope of identity and power, a quest for discursive authority to be heard, respected, and believed. "It has not been voice in general so much as public voice that women have been denied," Lanser adds.[57] As the Allen–Farrow case illustrates, we live in a culture that censors, devalues, or outright disbelieves the female voice.

The six texts of this study allow us to see the links between sexual abuse and sexism, which show that event trauma can play a prominent role in drawing attention to more insidious forms of trauma leading up to the incest. For example, incest narratives reveal that the females were conditioned into victimhood long before the rape occurred, as Dylan endured having to suck on Allen's thumb and lie in bed with him wearing only his underwear before that August day in 1992. Part of my book's agenda involves examining how these works portray the experiences of the female gender to give voice to complex trauma. To that end, it questions what kind of society continues to produce, yet deny, fathers who rape their own daughters. Unsurprisingly the perpetrators of father–daughter incest rarely seek help, the exception being when they are court ordered to talk to the medical community; therefore, little data exists on fathers who commit these acts. Some of the works in this study suggest why fathers would resort to such behavior. Arguing that both women and men are harmed by patriarchy, feminist author and social activist bell hooks points out in *The Will to Change: Men, Masculinity, and Love* that we should not dismiss the scarring effects patriarchy has on men in teaching them to be emotionally unavailable and that patriarchy is particularly dehumanizing for males without class or race privilege.

It took us a long time to realize that, despite what anthropologist Claude Lévi-Strauss argued, incest isn't the taboo (for it happens too often); talking about it is. Herman reminds us that many decades would pass before we "recognize[d] that the most common post-traumatic disorders are not those of men in war but of women in civilian life."[58] Dylan told her story, and I write this book, at an uncertain time for feminism, painfully evident in the claim that there's nothing feminist about believing the daughter victim. After almost forty years of feminist work on incest, we now live during a time when the topic of incest is so common that some have questioned if it's the "only story of women's distress that could be heard."[59] It has found its way into tabloids, talk shows, teen films, soap operas, and police dramas. As feminist therapist Janice Haaken observes, incest "became the name of the many problems that 'had no name,' in Betty Friedan's 1963 phrase."[60]

Although feminism was never a monolithic movement, its first two waves made significant contributions to our understanding of incest as a criminal, political problem; the Third Wave or post-feminist environment we now live in is much more ambiguous on its stances regarding incest. Between 1880 and 1930, during feminism's First Wave, which culminated in women winning the vote, "suffrage movements concerned about the well-being of children campaigned to make incest illegal, leading to the first laws criminalizing incest and establishing the age of consent."[61] After First-Wave feminism swept by, studies of incest usually emphasized one of three points: its infrequency, its benign or even beneficial effects, or its links to class and racial pathologies. Second-Wave feminism helped women take control of their bodies and reproductive rights. It put rape, domestic violence, and incest on the map as political, social problems instead of just obscure, individual ones. As an organizing issue for the feminist movement, the focus "on rape and domestic violence shifted the subject of incest from a psychologized framework into the politicized context of power and socialization within the family. As a result, large numbers of women in the 1980s, including many celebrities, made public their histories of incest. These women denied the culture's insistence that incest didn't happen among outwardly 'normal' families and that when it did the father was not responsible."[62] The emphasis on incest was a part of a larger effort to draw attention to the status of women and to change it. The first to call incest the "secret trauma," Diana Russell cites 1978 as a turning point in the discussion, when sexual abuse was socially discovered as a public problem and a more victim-oriented perspective was taken. The victim and perpetrator categories were recast. Rather than sexually precocious, complicit, or even inviting of the sexual abuse, the young girls' category was reconstructed as innocent victims; rather than mentally disordered, which implied not as responsible and thereby culpable, the offender category was revised as normal men who choose to do harm. And the characteristics of the sexual contact itself were defined as inherently traumatic.

In 1978 the first feminist analyses of incest were published in book form: Sandra Butler's *Conspiracy of Silence: The Trauma of Incest,* Susan Forward and Craig Buck's *Betrayal of Innocence: Incest and Its Devastation,* Karin Meiselman's *Incest: A Psychological Study of Cause and Effects with Treatment Recommendations,* and Louise Armstrong's *Kiss Daddy Goodnight.* The first of its kind, Armstrong's book is a collection of conversations and letters from incest victims interwoven with her own account of incest and feminist commentary. The book "received considerable attention and was widely read and discussed. According to Armstrong, her subsequent engagement with the media made her something of an icon, the 'World's First Walking, Talking Incest Victim.'"[63] But as Armstrong notes in her 1994 *Rocking the Cradle of Sexual Politics: What Happened When Women Said Incest,* breaking the silence did not lead to change. Instead it served to neutralize the topic and had an antipolitical effect. Furthermore, Armstrong remained skeptical of psychology's role in reconceiving incest from individual therapy to social criticism and argued that it instead encouraged women to adapt to unjust social structures.

In the range of the cultural discourses that is called post-feminism and in the quasi-political movement known as Third Wave, incest has been overlooked, re-repressed in what Susan Faludi has called a "backlash" in her 1991 book with that title. Whereas date rape and sexual harassment used to unite the feminists of Second Wave, the "media feminists" (Christina Hoff Sommers, Camille Paglia, and Katie Roiphe, for example) made a name for themselves by questioning the rape crisis. This preoccupation with sexual violence against females has given feminism a bad rap, they claim. It makes her passive, in need of protection. While embracing femininity and consuming goods, the post-feminists have espoused a vocabulary of independence, choice, empowerment, and sexual freedom. These "feminists" "tak[e] pole-dancing exercise classes, [listen] to Katy Perry, [and get] Brazilian bikini waxes as markers of their newfound liberation."[64] They often take the gains of Second Wave for granted or are hostile to them. A product of poststructuralist, postmodernist, and multicultural theories, post-feminism questions the stable, unitary political subject. Likewise, the Third Wave feminists reject ideas of essential categories of *woman*, making it nearly impossible to speak about "women's issues." So most don't: their agenda is to further issues of human rights, globalization, and new media technologies to evoke social justice for all. Some have even focused their energy on remedying the crisis in masculinity, something that continues to confuse me because, despite the vulnerable victories of the women's movement, it seems like the only casualties were the bras that didn't even get burned.

In Vivien Labaton and Dawn Lundy Martin's *The Fire This Time,* a seminal work that helped define Third Wave, they "write that the 'core issues' of feminism like reproductive rights and domestic violence are still important, but worry that if feminists become too 'distracted' by these issues, they will forget the work on other social justice concerns."[65] As Carisa Showden questions, if reproductive rights and violence against women and girls are a "distraction" from more important feminist issues, then how is this still feminist? Moreover, these "feminists" claim that the victimization rhetoric is the primary obstacle preventing women from fully taking control of their lives. Some go so far as to argue that "sexual regulation is as harmful and demeaning to women as pornography, or more so."[66] Simply put, they criticize this brand of feminism as "victim-feminism," a product of a larger "victim culture," which carries even more of a sting because it is coming from women who claim feminist affiliations. They have a real aversion to seeing themselves as victims.

What they fail to see, however, is that their empowerment is illusory because they are not able to control how their actions are read. Millions of American girls are socialized into victim roles in a culture that allows and supports violence. Incest, which is on the continuum of violence against women, is a paradigmatic expression of patriarchy with its male-aggressive, female-passive patterns. Contrary to what theorists long claimed about the incest taboo (with the act representing a regression from civilization), the writers of this study show how father–daughter incest reflects and maintains the status quo: the order of patriarchy. Perhaps an exaggeration, it is not a departure from patriarchal family norms but its inevitable by-product. Bottom line, which I, too, had difficulty coming to terms with at first: the construction of femininity in a patriarchal society, such as the one in which we live, is itself traumatizing. Even Camille Paglia admits so much when she states, "Feminism keeps saying the sexes are the same. It keeps telling women they can do anything, go anywhere, say anything, wear anything. No, they can't. Women will always be in sexual danger."[67]

The six works in this study give voice to the complex trauma of father–daughter incest. They were chosen not only for their aesthetic value but also because of their political significance. In other words, they are beautifully written and consciously political. In my first chapter, I argue that Fitzgerald's *Tender Is the Night* ambivalently exposes the gendered politics of psychological trauma, particularly the conspiracy of silence perpetuated by a psychiatric culture that revictimizes the female victim of incest. Chapter 2 examines how Ralph Ellison's *Invisible Man* uses a story of paternal incest to work through the trauma of racism, challenging stereotypes of black masculinity. I argue that Ellison's second chapter, the "Trueblood episode," also subtly critiques patriarchal phallocentrism by hinting at a protofeminist message that suggests father–daughter incest is a normal function of patriarchy, not a breakdown in the social order. Referencing Ellison's depiction of father–daughter incest, Morrison's *The Bluest Eye* marks a watershed in the inscription of incest narratives as it is written mostly from the perspective of a "could-be" victim of incest. In my third chapter, I explore how Morrison includes the perspective of the father while foregrounding the experience of the daughter, exposing child abuse as an extensive social and political problem ultimately supported by imperialist ideals.

Enabled by Morrison, Dorothy Allison's semiautobiographical *Bastard Out of Carolina* is narrated by a young "white trash" girl who shares her story of sexual violation in defiance of that culture's patriarchal structure, the topic of chapter 4. Conforming to certain class stereotypes of father–daughter incest, *Bastard* escaped the hostile backlash provoked by Kathryn Harrison's memoir, *The Kiss*, discussed in chapter 5. *The Kiss*'s critical reception suggests that, even while allowing some discussion of incest, mainstream culture continued to collude in its silencing within the context of white middle-class. The study concludes by reading Stacey Lannert's 2011 memoir titled *Redemption*, which recounts how she killed her incestuous father and was given a harsher sentence than Charles

Manson. This chapter explores the current legal climate in which female victims continue to be subjected to complex trauma.

The works by Lannert, Harrison, Allison, Morrison, Ellison, and Fitzgerald provide more insight into the issues raised by the Allen–Farrow case, not the least of which is the role of the mother. As Armstrong maintains, "if there was one thing everyone would verbally have agreed to about incest, it was that it was up to a mother to protect her child from her husband's sexual assault."[68] Whereas Mia Farrow tried to protect her daughter, the actions of the mothers in this study are more ambiguous. In addition to exploring the mother's role, these chapters examine the conspiracy of silence surrounding father–daughter incest, how easily the victim is blamed, and yet how urgent it is to share her story publicly and in her own words—essentially, to give voice to the complexly traumatic experiences.

Chapter 1 turns to one of the earliest American modernist novels to include father–daughter incest. Before we dive into a reading of how Fitzgerald negotiated textual space to capture the daughter's voice in *Tender Is the Night*, we journey back to 1896, his birth year, the year Freud *almost* became the spokesman on behalf of incest's childhood victims.

NOTES

1. Dylan Farrow, "An Open Letter from Dylan Farrow," *New York Times*, February 1, 2014.
2. Woody Allen, "Woody Allen Speaks Out," *New York Times*, February 9, 2014.
3. Maureen Orth, "Mia Farrow and Eight of Her Children Speak Out," *Vanity Fair*, October 2, 2013.
4. Tom Leonard, "Tinsel Town Torn Apart Over 'Child Abuser' Woody Allen," *Daily Mail*, February 8, 2014.
5. JoAnn Wypijewski, "Woody, Dylan & Doubt," *The Nation*, March 10, 2014.
6. Laurie Penny, "The Woody Allen Case Reminds Us that It's the Accuser Who Invariably Ends up on Trial," *New Statesman*, February 7–13, 2014.
7. Louise Armstrong, *Rocking the Cradle of Sexual Politics: What Happened When Women Said Incest* (Reading, MA: Addison-Wesley Publishing, 1994), 189.
8. Leonard, "Tinsel Town."
9. Penny, "The Woody Allen Case."
10. Robert B. Weide, "The Woody Allen Allegations: Not So Fast," *The Daily Beast*, January 27, 2014.
11. Leonard, "Tinsel Town."
12. Elizabeth Marshall, "The Daughter's Disenchantment: Incest as Pedagogy in Fairy Tales and Kathryn Harrison's *The Kiss*," *College English* 66, no. 4 (2004): 403; Nancy L. Fischer, "Oedipus Wrecked? The Moral Boundaries of Incest," *Gender and Society* 17, no. 1 (2003): 96.
13. Judith Lewis Herman and Lisa Hirschman, *Father–Daughter Incest* (Cambridge: Harvard University Press, 1981), 70.
14. Lewis, Herman, and Hirschman, *Father–Daughter Incest*, 70.
15. Lewis, Herman, and Hirschman, *Father–Daughter Incest*, 70.
16. Joan D. Atwood, "When Love Hurts: Preadolescent Girls' Reports of Incest," *The American Journal of Family Therapy* 35 (2007): 306.
17. Fischer, "Oedipus Wrecked?" 96.

18. Fischer, "Oedipus Wrecked?" 97.
19. Atwood, "When Love Hurts," 307.
20. Penny, "The Woody Allen Case."
21. Judith Lewis Herman, *Trauma and Recovery* (New York: Basic, 1992), 7.
22. Susan Pease Banitt, "Why Dylan Farrow's Disclosure Matter," suepeasebanitt.com, February 4, 2014.
23. Jessica Valenti, "Choosing Comfort Over Truth: What It Means to Defend Woody Allen," *The Nation*, February 3, 2014.
24. Penny, "The Woody Allen Case."
25. Eliana Dockterman, "Dylan Farrow on Woody Allen Allegations Backlash." *Time.com*, February 18, 2014.
26. Maureen Orth, "Mia's Story," *Vanity Fair*, November 1992.
27. Matthew J. Friedman, Patricia A. Resick, Richard A. Bryant, and Chris R. Brewin, "Considering PTSD for *DSM-5*," *Depression and Anxiety* 28 (2011): 750–51.
28. In her 2012 study titled *The Nature of Trauma in American Novels*, Michelle Balaev cites Elaine Scarry's *The Body in Pain: The Making and Unmaking of the World* (1985) and Ronald Granofsky's *The Trauma Novel: Contemporary Symbolic Depiction of Collective Disaster* (1995) as precursors to literary criticism on trauma. She also acknowledges Kali Tal's *Worlds of Hurt: Reading the Literatures of Trauma* (1996) as a seminal text for literary trauma theory.
29. Michelle Balaev, *The Nature of Trauma in American Novels* (Evanston: Northwestern University Press, 2012), xiii. Throughout her study, Balaev problematizes what she considers a "narrow definition of trauma culled from only one among many psychological theories," stressing that "psychological research has produced a multifaceted and at times contentious body of work on the subject over the centuries" (3).
30. Describing what defense mechanisms operate during or immediately after a traumatic event is difficult. Some maintain that *dissociation* results (a process happening outside awareness), whereas others contend that the phenomenon called *repression* occurs, which is characterized as a willful banishing from consciousness, a conscious attempt to expel material from awareness. Both concepts date back to the studies of hysteria at the end of the nineteenth century. Doubly confusing is that different writers, including Freud, have used the terms differently and sometimes interchangeably. This debate reared its ugly head during the notorious "memory wars" of the 1990s, in which the central issue was whether or not it is possible to remember dissociated memories of sexual abuse.
31. Joshua Pederson, "Speak, Trauma: Toward a Revised Understanding of Literary Trauma Theory," *Narrative* 22, no. 3 (2014): 333.
32. Pederson, "Speak, Trauma," 334.
33. Pederson, "Speak, Trauma," 342.
34. Balaev, *The Nature of Trauma*, 10.
35. Balaev, *The Nature of TraumaI*, 19.
36. As noted previously in this introduction, "false-memory syndrome" is "a syndrome that purports to describe the process by which patients come to believe in the truth of false memories, that is, in incest memories that are fabricated rather than recovered within a therapeutic session" (Doane and Hodges, 7). The False Memory Syndrome Foundation (FMSF) was founded in 1992. A non-profit organization funded by membership dues and contributions from families and friends, FMSF was started by Pamela and Peter Freyd after their daughter accused them (wrongly they felt) of childhood sexual abuse. Advocating for parents who believed they had been falsely accused of abusing their children, FMSF's initial group was composed of academics and professionals; researchers in the fields of memory and clinical practice were sought out to form its advisory board. The goal of the organization spread from advocacy to attempting to address issues of memory. Describing itself as a scientific organization, FMSF engages in partisan political and social activity. In focusing on problems of memory, some of their activities have excused criminal behavior and reversed gains made by feminists and victims in acknowledging incest. Although

some reports of incest are the product of therapist-induced false memories, and denial on the part of alleged perpetrators is to be expected, the "witch hunt" is fraught with politics. Also, as Elizabeth Wilson notes, "the incidence of incest is far, far greater than the incidence of false allegations." Wilson, "Not in This House: Incest, Denial, and Doubt in the White Middle Class Family," *Yale Journal of Criticism* 8, no. 1 (1995): 37. Rosaria Champagne calls attention to the FMSF's "rampant antifeminism and misogyny" (167). For a discussion that casts further doubt on the foundation's mission and that challenges the idea of "false memories," see Brown University's "Recovered Memory Project," which collects and disseminates information relevant to the debate surrounding the question, "Can traumatic events be forgotten . . . and then remembered later in life?"

37. Anne Whitehead, *Trauma Fiction* (Edinburgh: Edinburgh University Press, 2004), 4.

38. Ruth Leys, *Trauma: A Genealogy* (Chicago: University of Chicago Press, 2000), 232.

39. Richard J. McNally, *Remembering Trauma* (Cambridge: Belknap, 2003), 88.

40. Joseph E. Davis, *Accounts of Innocence: Sexual Abuse, Trauma, and the Self* (Chicago: University of Chicago Press, 2005), 116.

41. Janis Sanchez-Hucles and Patrick Hudgins, "Trauma across Diverse Settings," in *Encyclopedia of Women and Gender: Sex Similarities and Differences and the Impact of Society on Gender*, L-Z, vol. 2, ed. Judith Worell (San Diego: Academic, 2001), 1151–52.

42. Although Herman is credited with developing the phrase Complex PTSD, many other clinicians suggested this concept independently. For example, a 1987 South African article was published on "continuous traumatic stress," followed in 1989 by Martín-Baró's article about the effects of political violence on the mental health of Salvadorian people. Gillian Straker, "Continuous Traumatic Stress: Personal Reflections 25 Years On," *Peace and Conflict: Journal of Peace Psychology* 19, no. 2 (2013): 210. L. C. Kolb discusses the "heterogeneity" of PTSD in 1989, maintaining, "PTSD is to psychiatry as syphilis was to medicine. At one time or another PTSD may appear to mimic every personality disorder." Qtd. in Judith Herman, "Complex PTSD: A Syndrome in Survivors of Prolonged and Repeated Trauma," *Journal of Traumatic Stress* 5, no. 3 (1992): 378. In addition to Kolb, W. G. Niederland, who worked with Holocaust survivors, stated that for the survivor, "the concept of traumatic neurosis does not appear sufficient to cover the multitude and severity of clinical manifestations." Ibid. Working with Southeast Asian refugees, Habenicht Kroll and colleagues acknowledged the need for an "expanded concept of PTSD that takes into account the observations [of the effects of] severe, prolonged, and/or massive psychological and physical traumata." Ibid., 378–79. M. Horowitz suggests the concept of a "post-traumatic character disorder," and D. P. Brown and E. Fromm speak of "complicated PTSD." Ibid., 379. Maria Root and Laura Brown use the phrase "insidious trauma." In her 1983 "The Persistent Negative Effects of Incest," D. Gelinas classifies survivors of childhood abuse as having severe post-traumatic syndrome. Other names for CPTSD have included "identity trauma" (Kira, 2001), "ongoing traumatic stress response" (OTSR; Diamond et al., 2010), and "collective or historical trauma" (Gone, 2007). Straker, "Continuous Traumatic Stress," 211.

43. Herman, "Complex PTSD," 378.

44. Herman, "Complex PTSD," 378.

45. Herman, "Complex PTSD," 379.

46. Herman, "Complex PTSD," 379.

47. Herman, "Complex PTSD," 385.

48. Judith Herman, "CPTSD is a Distinct Entity: Comment on Resick et al. (2012)," *Journal of Traumatic Stress* 25 (2012): 256.

49. Herman, *Trauma and Recovery*, 122.

50. Herman and others have taken Patricia Resick and colleagues to task for their article "A Critical Evaluation of the Complex PTSD Literature: Implications for *DSM-5*," in which they contend that CPTSD does not warrant inclusion in the *DSM-5*. Judith

Herman, "CPTSD is a Distinct Entity: Comment on Resick et al. (2012)," *Journal of Traumatic Stress* 25 (2012). Overall, Herman finds Resick et al.'s comments remarkably dismissive. She questions, among other things, their proposed research methods: "The authors arbitrarily set a standard for inclusion that requires a very high level of research development, and then predictably, demonstrate that their chosen standard has not been met." Ibid. Furthermore, she is doubtful that the research called for will be likely without official recognition of CPTSD as a distinct category. Although in their response to Herman's comments, Resick et al. claim that "Herman's (2012) assertion that a diagnosis must appear in the *DSM* before research will be funded is no longer as accurate as it may once have been," it seems unlikely that one would spend the time, energy, and money researching a category that officially does not exist. Patricia A. Resick, Erika J. Wolf, Shannon Wiltsey Stirman, Stephanie Y. Wells, Michael K. Suvak, Karen S. Mitchell, Matthew W. King, and Michelle J. Bovin, "Advocacy Through Science: Reply to Comments on Resick et al. (2012)," *Journal of Traumatic Stress* 25 (2012): 261. The editor of the *Journal of Traumatic Stress,* Daniel S. Weiss, notes that if the *DSM-III* had required for PTSD what Resick et al. recommend for CPTSD for inclusion in the *DSM-5,* then PTSD would not have been officially recognized—at least not in 1980. Daniel S. Weiss, "Introduction to the Special Feature on Complex PTSD," *Journal of Traumatic Stress* 25 (2012): 239.

51. Straker, "Continuous Traumatic Stress," 215.

52. Straker, "Continuous Traumatic Stress," 216.

53. Although the *DSM-5* did not recognize CPTSD, the *International Classification of Diseases, ICD-11*th revision, plans to. In 2018, the Work Group of the World Health Organization will publish *ICD-11.* Although the development of *ICD-11* and *DSM-5* was seen as an opportunity to harmonize the two major classification systems for mental disorders, the proposed changes will make the differences between *DSM-5* and *ICD-11* far greater than those between *DSM-IV* and *ICD-10.* Like *DSM-5,* PTSD will be a separate category rather than included with anxiety disorders as in the past. But the similarities end there. In addition to the addition of CPTSD, the criteria in *ICD-11* for PTSD will be reduced to just 6 items: two re-experiencing (nightmares and flashbacks), two avoidance (of thoughts and feelings, of people, places, and activities), and two hyperarousal (increased startle and hypervigilance). J. I. Bisson, "What Happened to Harmonization of the PTSD Diagnosis? The Divergence of *ICD-11* and *DSM-5,*" *Epidemiology and Psychiatric Sciences* 22, no. 3 (2013): 205–07. Whereas the *ICD* and not the *DSM* is the official classification system in the United States, the *DSM* was widely used internationally to diagnose PTSD, most likely because it was the only way to diagnose it between 1980 and 1992. PTSD did not become an *ICD* diagnosis until the 1992 *ICD-10.* Because of divergent perspectives and attitudes represented in these two classification systems, it will, as Friedman notes, be interesting to compare the *ICD-11*'s Complex PTSD with the *DSM-5*'s dissociative subtype. Friedman, "Finalizing PTSD in *DSM-5*: Getting Here From There and Where to Go Next," *Journal of Traumatic Stress* 26 (2013): 555.

54. Herman, *Trauma and Recovery,* 8.

55. Kathleen Rowe Karlyn, *Unruly Girls, Unrepentant Mothers: Redefining Feminism on Screen* (Austin: University of Texas Press, 2011), 28–29.

56. Susan Snaider Lanser, *Fictions of Authority: Women Writers and Narrative Voice* (Ithaca: Cornell University Press, 1992), 3.

57. Lanser, *Fictions of* Authority, 8.

58. Herman, *Trauma and Recovery,* 28.

59. Janice Doane and Devon Hodges, *Telling Incest: Narratives of Dangerous Remembering from Stein to Sapphire* (Ann Arbor: University of Michigan Press, 2001), 7.

60. Haaken, quoted in Wypijewski, "Woody, Dylan & Doubt."

61. Karlyn, *Unruly Girls,* 58.

62. Karlyn, *Unruly Girls,* 58.

63. Davis, *Accounts of Innocence,* 244.

64. Jess Butler, "For White Girls Only? Postfeminism and the Politics of Inclusion," *Feminist Formations* 25, no.1 (2013): 42.
65. Carisa R. Showden, "What's Political about the New Feminisms?" *Frontiers: A Journal of Women Studies* 30, no. 2 (2009): 186.
66. Showden, "What's Political about the New Feminisms?" 172.
67. Camille Paglia, *Sex, Art, and American Culture* (New York: Vintage, 1992), 50.
68. Armstrong, *Rocking the Cradle*, 123.

ONE

"Flinching at the Word *Father*"

Trauma Politics in Fitzgerald's Tender Is the Night

On the evening of May 2, 1896, at a meeting of the Society for Psychiatry and Neurology in Vienna, Sigmund Freud delivered a paper on eighteen case studies titled "The Aetiology of Hysteria." It was the culmination of years of listening to female patients' accounts of sexual assault, abuse, and incest. During his talk, Freud announced that hysteria, which was thought to be a nervous disorder linked to the female sexual and reproductive organs, the womb, no longer had ties to physiology but was rather a product of one's upbringing. Social, not biological, factors caused neurosis, he contended. Freud went on to boldly assert that hysteria derived from a traumatic event in childhood of a sexual nature. In his words: "at the bottom of every case of hysteria will be found one or more experiences of premature sexual experience, belonging to the first years of childhood."[1] In other words, he admitted that it was highly likely that most of his female patients had been victims of father–daughter incest as little girls and that, by implication, as he later stated, "in every case the father, not excluding my own, had to be blamed as a pervert."[2]

Instead of receiving applause, as he'd anticipated, Freud met stark silence from his distinguished peers, whose response threatened to ostracize him from their patriarchal pantheon. Unsurprisingly, he never again publicly promoted his seduction theory and by the following year he shifted from a trauma etiology of hysteria to an Oedipal model of psychic ontogeny, exclaiming, "I was at last obliged to recognize that these scenes of seduction had never taken place, and that they were only phantasies which my patients had made up or which I myself had perhaps forced on them, I was for some time completely at a loss."[3] In other words, Freud now claimed that his female patients had merely fantasized that father–daughter incest occurred. This clever move allowed him to contend that the traumatic sexual event does not have to be real; it can be a product of one's imagination. Doing so eliminated the allegation that sexual abuse was so rampant in the Victorian world. It served to vindicate fathers and implicate daughters.[4]

Despite his theoretical shift that ultimately defended the system and not its victims, Freud was among the first to explore the terrain of psychological trauma and to suggest that our conscious rationalizations fall short of explaining our behavior. He was also among the earliest men of science to bear witness to women's stories of sexual abuse and to discover that childhood sexual exploitation often lay at the root of psychological trauma. Contributing to our understanding of how trauma works, Freud stated that the psyche repeats what it is unable to assimilate or understand. It does so as a way of remembering when the actual memory has become inaccessible. Such repetition is the victim's attempt to claim his or her survival. He used the term "working through" to describe the process of mitigating the effects of trauma's compulsive repetitions by generating counterforces, thus enabling a more viable articulation and cognition. Above all, Freud glimpsed the horror of father–daughter incest and understood that it is not uncommon and is far too often traumatic. The Viennese doctor came dangerously close to admitting that studying the psychology of a female victim pointed to larger social and political problems—the literal wounding effects of patriarchy.

Retracting his first theory of hysteria and severing the link between sexual abuse and trauma, Freud fostered a tradition of denying women's realities and discrediting accounts of incest as Oedipal fantasies. The theory of psychological trauma, evolving out of medical, philosophical, and social history, has, as Herman states in *Trauma and Recovery,* a "forgotten history," which she takes for the title of her first chapter—and a willful forgetfulness at that. After the late nineteenth century witnessed Freud and the age of hysteria in which the dominant psychological theory rested, not on the reality of women's lives, but the mythical story of Oedipus Rex, the catastrophe of World War I revitalized discussions of psychological trauma when the public was forced to deal with soldiers who began to act oddly like hysterical Victorian women.[5] At first their symptoms were thought to be physical in origin—lesions of the brain. The British psychologist Charles Myers even attributed them to the effects of exploding shells, hence the term "shell shock." Though the name remained in use, it was becoming obvious that these soldiers were experiencing psychological, and not physical, trauma. Despite this new understanding, these warnings "were generally ignored."[6]

Intrigued by Freudian ideas and the psychiatric profession, F. Scott Fitzgerald wrote his fourth and what would be his last completed novel, *Tender Is the Night,* during this uncertain time for psychological trauma. He develops in literary terms what Freud first introduced in his psychoanalytic theory. In his book, Fitzgerald pays conscious attention to father–daughter incest, and, like a young Freud, he does so to the chagrin of his contemporaries. In fact, in his letter to Fitzgerald, friend and fellow artist John Peale Bishop ends an otherwise complimentary note on *Tender Is the Night* by expressing what he sees as the unconvincing part of the novel—the theme of father–daughter incest: "The one point in the book which stuck for me was the incest. I couldn't quite believe it. Nor do I think it was necessary. But it's done, and is being forgotten."[7] Critic Milton Hindus outdoes Bishop's assertion and "ignores the novel's stated facts, and goes so far as to assume that Nicole was never raped by Daddy, that it was all in her mind, and that Dick was a sexually stupid psychiatrist foolish enough to believe her."[8] Like Bishop and Hindus, many early critics wanted to ignore the paternal incest and argue that Fitzgerald employs it merely as a metaphor for the decline of Western civilization, a reading first forged by Robert Stanton in his 1958 "'Daddy's Girl': Symbol and Theme in *Tender Is the Night*." The question remains, however, why did Fitzgerald not just use the wastelandic imagery of the postwar landscape to capture the ruins? Why does he cast Nicole Diver, his lead female character, as a recovering victim of father–daughter incest?[9]

Besides being confused by the paternal incest, some early critics had a difficult time with the entire book. They found the long-awaited, post-*Gatsby* work to be second best. Even though Fitzgerald started working on *Tender* immediately after *Gatsby*, it took him almost ten years to finish, not appearing in complete form until April 12, 1934.[10] Initially criticized as "an anachronistic hang-over from the twenties," "a curious footnote to the jazz age," and a sprawling, imperfect, utterly personal novel that took too many drafts and too many years, *Tender* briefly made it to the bestseller list and garnered some sensitive reviews, but it was clear that its initial reception did not compensate for the anguish Fitzgerald endured while writing it.[11] It was not until the 1950s, what Milton R. Stern calls "the Fitzgerald revival," that sustained scholarly attention was given to the book.[12] Fitzgerald's ambivalent treatment of Nicole and other female characters became topics of discussion; some articles compared Scott's *Tender* to his wife Zelda's *Save Me the Waltz*, which was seen as a biographical companion piece. In addition to exploring Fitzgerald's contributions to our understanding of modernism, criticism over the last sixty years has examined the novel's intersecting concerns with gender, sexuality, race, and nationality. Although there has been a deepening appreciation of *Tender* as a perceptive novel about history, its psychological elements continue to be contested.

This chapter enlarges the critical discussion of gender and psychological politics in the novel by focusing attention on the incest theme and its relation to trauma. Even though Fitzgerald's sympathies lie with his male protagonist, Dick Diver, and that *Tender* is primarily Dick's story, his characterization of Nicole as a recovering victim of father–daughter incest reveals sexual domestic abuse, in a white, wealthy family, no less, as a topic worthy of critical attention. Building on William Blazek's argument in "'Some Fault in the Plan': Fitzgerald's Critique of Psychiatry in *Tender Is the Night*" (2007), in which he maintains that Fitzgerald exposes the limits of psychiatry as practiced during his day, I argue that in doing so, Fitzgerald also uncovers the gender politics of psychological trauma. I contend that in addition to reading *Tender Is the Night* as a critique of the profession of psychiatry for its impotence at healing what the narrator calls "the broken universe of the war's ending," Fitzgerald reveals the politics surrounding psychiatry, particularly, if not at times ambivalently, the complex trauma perpetuated by a profession that purports to heal.[13] He hints that the institution of psychiatry was heavily implicated in women's subordination.

During the time that Fitzgerald was composing the novel, incest was thought to be an extremely rare occurrence—one case in a million.[14] Freud's Oedipus complex was in full swing. A new science of psychiatry was emerging and a younger generation of trained practitioners was experimenting with new therapies, including hypnosis, psychoanalysis, ergo-therapy, and electric-shock treatment. One of the most influential concepts was *reeducation*, which is mentioned in the novel, and which confirms Louise Armstrong's fear that the medical community conditioned women to adapt to a sexist society. Endorsed by Abram Kardiner, who not coincidentally studied with Freud, it held that the goal of therapy was not necessarily to recover traumatic memories from amnesia but rather to achieve "a fundamental alteration in the patient's conscious adaptation to the outer world."[15] Or, as Judith Fetterley puts it in "Who Killed Dick Diver? The Sexual Politics of *Tender Is the Night*," *reeducation* means "that Nicole must understand that what happened to her has no political significance, no bearing on the relation between men and women."[16] And that to get better, as Fetterley explains, she must learn to rely on men again.[17] In the midst of uncertainty about the causes and cures of psychological trauma, Fitzgerald, unlike the older Freud, takes women at their word by creating a female character who suffers from complex post-traumatic stress disorder, or the "plenty of consequences" that ensue as a direct result of father–daughter incest.[18]

The book started out as a novel of matricide based on a sensational account of a tabloid murder in San Francisco in which a sixteen-year-old girl named Dorothy Ellingson shot and killed her mother because she was not allowed to attend a wild flapper party, but it slowly morphed into a story of psychological illness, given credence by Zelda's psychiatric condition.[19] Instead of using incest as a topos of cultural decline, Fitzgerald's employment of incest and the psychological trauma that accompanies it are portrayed realistically. Profoundly autobiographical, *Tender* would not have emerged as the book it has had it not been for Zelda's breakdown on April 23, 1930, "and her subsequent unsuccessful attempts to regain her health."[20] In fact, because of Zelda's deterioration and extensive hospitalization and treatment, Fitzgerald abandoned all work on the novel from 1929 to 1931.[21] Richard Lehan points out, "Fitzgerald did not have to rely upon sophisticated clichés to write *Tender Is the Night*: by the thirties he knew firsthand—and all too well—the meaning of sickness, physical decline, and disappointment."[22]

In an effort to help his wife, Fitzgerald read widely and deeply the literature of psychiatry and engaged the leading therapists in Europe to treat Zelda as he sent her to the best and most expensive institutions available.[23] James L. W. West III explains that he "was familiar with the theories of Sigmund Freud, Carl Jung, Emil Kraepelin, Eugen Bleuler, and Alfred Adler; he had corresponded with Oscar Forel and Adolf Meyer, two of Zelda's doctors, displaying in his letters a good comprehension of the treatments she was receiving."[24] Bleuler and Forel were two of the eminent physicians who treated Zelda at Les Rives de Prangins Clinic on Lake Geneva in Switzerland during her institutionalization from 1930 to 1931. Dr. Oscar Forel was the son of the world-renowned Swiss psychiatrist Auguste Forel, and Dr. Bleuler was the world's leading authority on schizophrenia, which he named. Zelda was later treated by the distinguished Dr. Meyer at Phipps Clinic of Johns Hopkins University Hospital in Baltimore. Fitzgerald became knowledgeable enough to follow Zelda's treatment, discuss it with her doctors, draw some of his own psychiatric conclusions, and even incorporate his learnings in his novel.

For his efforts, *Tender* garnered praise for its contribution to the mental health field. For example, a year after its publication, a reviewer for the *Journal of Nervous and Mental Disease* wrote that for "the psychiatrist and psychoanalyst the book is of special value as a probing story of some of the major dynamic interlockings in marriage . . . conditioned by a set of economic and psychobiological situations."[25] It went on to call the novel "an achievement which no student of the psychobiological sources of human behavior, and of its particular social correlates extant today, can afford not to read."[26] Likewise, the clinical psychiatrist David I. Gottlieb said that the novel is "a worthwhile book from a psychological and psychiatric point of view . . . because it can serve to teach psychiatrists, psychologists, social workers and many other mental health practitioners something about human nature and something about personalities that cannot be found any other way!"[27]

And yet, Fitzgerald's faith in the field of mental health was shaky, at best. A four-page letter from 1936 that surfaced many decades later voices his distrust of the profession. To a Joan Tyson of Caldwell, New Jersey, Fitzgerald instructs her to go to the nearest library and fetch a copy of *Tender*, "which has plenty of psychiatry in it."[28] He writes, "My wife lost her mind six years ago—a family thing . . . and I had consultations and plenty of them with Bleuler and the younger Forel + Jung and eventually with Adolph Myer [sic]."[29] Despite entrusting his wife to the care of psychiatrists, Fitzgerald goes on to add that he himself would never go to one: "I would never consider trusting myself to what passes for psychology-psychiatry in this country. How could someone not up to your *ankles* in intelligence + character help you. By some miracle? some act of God?"[30] In addition to this letter, Fitzgerald's criticism of the profession is indeed apparent in *Tender Is the Night*.

Although Fitzgerald did not set out to write a scientific treatise or what he called a "doctor's story," in his notes he warned himself to be "careful not to reveal basic ignorance of psychiatric and medical training."[31] And there is no mistaking that Zelda's mental illness was crucial to the reconceptualization of *Tender Is the Night*. The 1930 breakdown of Zelda, whom Nicole is modeled after, led Fitzgerald to revise his original thinking for the novel, as the outline for his new plans indicates:

> The heroine was born in 1901. She is beautiful on the order of Marlene Dietrich or better still the Norah Gregor-Kiki Allen girl with those peculiar eyes. She is American with a streak of some foreign blood. At fifteen she was raped by her own father under peculiar circumstances—work out. She collapses, goes to the clinic and there at sixteen meets the young doctor hero who is ten years older. Only her transference to him saves her—when it is not working she reverts to homicidal mania and tries to kill men. She is an innocent, widely read but with no experience and no orientation except what he supplies her. Portrait of Zelda—that is, a part of Zelda.[32]

This paragraph, along with Fitzgerald's other sketches, demonstrates that his wife's illness was the precipitating factor to the novel's new direction. It also indicates that Nicole's transference to Dick is what saves her. According to Freud, transference is defined as "the projection or displacement upon the analyst of unconscious feelings and wishes originally directed toward important individuals, such as parents, in the patient's childhood."[33] Similarly, countertransference occurs when a clinical practitioner projects or displaces his feelings and wishes onto the patient. Like Zelda, Nicole is diagnosed with schizophrenia, although she seems more hysteric than schizophrenic. Fitzgerald quoted directly from Bleuler's diagnosis of Zelda's case[34] and "went so far as to graph on a sheet of paper the parallel psychiatric 'histories' of Nicole and Zelda."[35] Just how much Fitzgerald made Nicole a "portrait of Zelda," "a part of Zelda," is up for debate. Although the effects of Zelda's illness were all too real and familiar to both Zelda and Fitzgerald, the cause of Nicole's disintegration, the incest factor, is, according to Matthew Bruccoli and others, pure invention.[36] However, Fitzgerald's moving depiction and understanding of Nicole's illness may make one question if Zelda was in fact a victim of father–daughter incest and that is why Fitzgerald wrote so authentically about it.

Although scholars have long discussed the role Zelda's illness played in her husband's artistry, few have explored the cause of her sickness. As Jeffrey Berman puts it, "We have a great deal of information about the factual details surrounding Zelda's breakdowns and psychiatric institutionalizations, although we know little about the inner causes of her madness."[37] In a letter to Fitzgerald, dated mid-April 1934, around the time the final installment of *Tender* was released in *Scribner's Magazine* and the work was published in novel form, Zelda tells him "to revert to the money-triangle as you can't possibly use the incest."[38] Zelda doesn't go on to explain why he can't use the incest. In Nancy Milford's biography, the first and most authoritative biography of Zelda, she mentions that two of Zelda's short stories (not surviving in manuscript) include the topic of incest, but that "Zelda was not raped by her father."[39] In *Exiles from Paradise,* Sara Mayfield concurs a bit more emphatically: "Zelda was certainly never raped by her father."[40] Linda Wagner-Martin argues that it was irresponsible for Fitzgerald to use father–daughter incest, "the most horrific plotline he could imagine" as the source of Nicole's psychosis.[41] She explains, "Zelda's friends were irate"; it was inevitable for readers to assume that all parts of Nicole's background were based on Zelda's life.[42] For example, in addition to Zelda's diagnosis, Fitzgerald used her letters and other factual accounts; the scene at Agiri Fair in which Nicole purposefully almost wrecks the car and nearly kills her family is based on fact. With the incest plot line, Fitzgerald "permanently defamed"[43] Zelda's father, Judge Sayre, whom Zelda strangely referred to as "Old Dick" to her friends, a shortened version of his middle name, Dickinson.[44]

We do know that after Zelda read the book, she relapsed.[45] In *Zelda Fitzgerald: Her Voice in Paradise,* Sally Cline reports on Zelda's response after reading *Tender*: "Zelda, in bed at Phipps, admitted she was 'a little upset about it [*Tender*],' then said bitterly: 'What made me mad was he made the girl so awful and kept on reiterating how she had ruined his life and I couldn't help identifying myself with her because she had so many of my experiences.'"[46]

Cline explains that Zelda began to cry and said, "It was a chronological distortion. . . . I don't think it's true—I don't think it's really what happened."[47] And yet, as Cline mentions, Zelda never comes out and refers "directly to the effect on her of the fictionalized father–daughter rape, for which there is *no* biographical evidence, merely a series of rumours."[48] Cline elaborates on the rumors in one of her endnotes, which reads:

> Virginia Durr said that in later years Minnie Sayre confided to her that the Judge came to her bedroom and she locked him out. Some researchers have taken this as evidence that he might have turned to one of his daughters if he was refused sexual relations by his wife. This, together with Fitzgerald's creation of a heroine based partly on Zelda who is raped by her father, accounts for a flurry of incest rumours. But this

> author found no definite supporting evidence for this allegation and many interviewees in Montgomery refuted the idea.[49]

Sarah Beebe Fryer casts doubt on these opinions in her 1988 book *Fitzgerald's New Women: Harbingers of Change,* in which she writes "It seems improbable that any scholar, however thorough, would have definitive knowledge on so personal a point [as incest]."[50] However, as she correctly adds, "given the nature of the incest taboo, the cloak of secrecy that generally surrounds cases of incest, the fact that incest memories are often repressed, and the widespread tendency—even among mental health care professionals—to dismiss reports of incestuous abuse as 'fantasies,' it seems somewhat naïve for so educated a group of biographers to suggest—with apparent conviction—that any woman, particularly a woman with a deeply troubled psyche like Zelda Fitzgerald's—could not possibly have been an incest victim."[51] Although we might never know the contributing factors to Zelda's illness, we should not rule out father–daughter incest.

THE LIMITS OF PSYCHIATRY

Deploying and depleting his resources on the novel that would cost him almost a decade of literary labor, Fitzgerald enlists as his male protagonist an inept psychiatrist, who in Book 1 is not even practicing and did not get to fight in the war. Moreover, he is unable to diagnose his own psychological ailments and is himself arguably suffering from what the novel terms "*Non*-combatant's shell-shock" (emphasis added).[52] Although quite sympathetic to Dick's personal and professional battles, the novel offers a subtle critique of the field of psychiatry as Fitzgerald questions what leads these white, middle- to upper-class men into the profession. He suggests that in this field of predominantly male practitioners and female patients, the power dynamics that keeps females subservient to males remained intact and that the occupation may have been used as a means for these men to recover some of the masculinity they felt they had lost during the World War.

In the case of Dick, his motivations for becoming a doctor of the mentally ill are far from noble. No stranger to being attracted to beautiful young women, and, like many psychiatrists of his day, Dick breaches the doctor–patient contract on more than one occasion.[53] In the exposition provided in Book 2, Dick admits to Dr. Franz Gregorovius, resident pathologist at Dohmler's clinic on the Zürichsee and later business partners with Dick at the clinic of Braun on the Zugersee, that he had a "bent" for going into the field of psychiatry—"there was a girl at St. Hilda's in Oxford that went to the same lectures."[54] We also read that once practicing, Dick was accused "in no uncertain terms of having seduced" the daughter of one of his patients.[55] He admits that he kissed her, "In an idle, almost indulgent way," even though he was not interested in pursuing the affair any further.[56] Similarly, Dick takes a special interest in the woman at Braun suffering from "nervous eczema"; he is the only doctor who could "do anything with her."[57] Before leaving her on one of his rounds, he stoops and kisses her forehead. After her death, when we learn that she most likely suffered from neuro-syphilis, Dick can't get over his loss for "the scabbed anonymous woman-artist he had come to love."[58] Furthermore, in sleeping with and later marrying Nicole Warren, the young girl from Chicago, against the advice of Doctor Dohmler, Dick assumes the role of doctor–husband, forever blurring the distinction between his professional and personal lives. The novel suggests that some physicians became emotionally involved with their own patients. As Blazek maintains, neither psychiatry nor any science is "as purely rational as it purports to be."[59] Fitzgerald certainly exposes the emotional, at times irrational, dimensions of the field and shows that detached, scientific superiority is a myth.

In addition to undermining psychiatry's claims to reason, Fitzgerald exposes it to be a self-serving, money-making occupation that maintains the differential power relations between male doctors and female patients and the haves and the have-nots. In "Fitzgerald's Portrait of a Psychiatrist," A. H. Steinberg claims that the patients at Dohmler's clinic are "more the victims of self-indulgence than of disease."[60] Franz glimpses the truth of this and capitalizes on it. For example, Franz asks Dick if the war changed him as it changed the rest. Dick responds, "I didn't see any of the war."[61] "That doesn't matter—," counters Franz, "we have some shell-shocks who merely heard an air raid from the distance. We have a few who merely read newspapers."[62] Dick dismisses this as nonsense and Franz admits that it may be, but he also explains to Dick that theirs is "a rich person's clinic."[63] Through this dialogue Fitzgerald casts doubt on the ethics guiding the field of psychiatry. It seems that attention goes not to those who need help the most, but to the highest bidder. The Warren family knows this. In fact, Nicole's sister, Baby, contemplates buying Nicole a doctor, reasoning, "what could be better in her condition than if she fell in love with some good doctor."[64] Moreover, the Warren money enables Dick and Franz to buy the old clinic of Braun on the Zugersee for $220,000, which Baby thinks is a small price to pay for having peace of mind about her sister. Franz approaches Dick for this venture not because Dick is a highly skilled physician, but because Franz needs money and knows that the Warren family has it. He exclaims to Dick, and to an eavesdropping Baby, "There we have it! Money!" "I have little money."[65] However, as he is quick to add, "the clinic is a gold mine."[66] Put simply, the Warren money has succeeded in buying a doctor–husband for Nicole and a money-making clinic for Dick. It is no wonder why Dick, who agrees to the purchase, feels forever indebted to the Warrens, who he—not incorrectly—thinks own him. He seems to understand that his professional life is at the mercy of borrowed time and money.

Fitzgerald further displays the chinks in Dick's armor and thereby the field of psychiatry by suggesting that his ego plays into Dick's reasons for pursuing this profession. Just as Rosemary Hoyt, the superficial version of Nicole, first sees Dick on the Mediterranean beach in Book 1 as the pinnacle of perfection, readers are (re)introduced to a promising, youthful Doctor Diver at the start of Book 2. His résumé is impressive: he has graduated from Yale, won a Rhodes Scholarship, studied at Oxford, took a medical degree from Johns Hopkins, and traveled to Vienna and Switzerland, when Zurich was the Jungian fortress, no less. At this point in his budding career, Dick wishes to be the greatest psychologist that ever lived.[67] However, Fitzgerald undermines Dick's ambitions in a number of ways. We read that at the beginning of 1917, not coincidentally the same year that the United States became involved in World War I, Dick burned almost a hundred of his textbooks to heat his rooms because he couldn't find coal.[68] Moreover, he has doubts about his calling. Despite Franz's reassuring words that fate selected Dick for the profession before he was born, he can't seem to shake the fact that "The weakness of this profession is its attraction for the man a little crippled and broken."[69]

Indeed, throughout the book Fitzgerald drops subtle hints that these doctors are themselves a little battered and wounded. For example, Franz's rival, Gisler, is said to be a manic depressive and is unable to manage his own clinic, which is really run by his wife and her lover.[70] Similarly, during one of his rounds, Dick ministers to a "collapsed psychiatrist."[71] Of course, by the novel's end, the most damaged doctor is Dick, exiled to small-town New York, with "a big stack of papers on his desk that were known to be an important treatise on some medical subject, almost in process of completion."[72] Although Dick seems to be practicing again, the narrator tells us that "his career was biding its time."[73] Fitzgerald points out the irony in that some psychiatrists who treat others for mental illness are not immune to breakdowns themselves.

Perhaps one of the reasons that Dick wants to be the best psychologist that ever lived is to compensate for his lack of masculinity in a world that Fitzgerald presents as becoming increasingly feminized, as illustrated through his subtle comments on war and economically independent female characters. For Dick's generation, masculinity is demonstrated through military force. Tellingly, Dick isn't conscripted and therefore never fires a weapon. For example, we read that he was "too much of a capital investment to be shot off in a gun," that "the war didn't touch him at all," and that "Doctor Diver had seen around the edges of the war" (these examples all occur on the same page). Dick shows the most respect in the scene where they visit the site of the Battle of the Somme, one of the bloodiest military operations ever recorded; however, he most likely puts on a grave face to show off for Rosemary, reducing the deadly battlefield to a highly explosive "love battle."[74] Dick, who was poised for war after taking his degree from Johns Hopkins, is dissatisfied by his work in France, which proves to be "executive rather than practical."[75] In other words, he was disillusioned by the war because he did *not* fight on the frontlines.[76]

Fitzgerald has Dick compensate for his lack of battle experience in what prove to be unsatisfactory ways. Instead of helping the men in battle, the "blinded or one-legged men," Fitzgerald has Dick do paperwork.[77] In place of fighting, Dick spends the war writing a short textbook, one of his many forthcoming pseudo-scholarly meditations. Even Franz comments on the lack of merit in Dick's books, saying "Soon you will be writing little books called 'Deep Thoughts for the Layman,' so simplified that they are positively guaranteed not to cause thinking."[78] Furthermore, Fitzgerald describes the prewar Dick in phallic terms that may be read as mocking his masculinity. The narrator explains that in his last year at New Haven someone referred to Dick as "lucky Dick" to which Dick adds, "Lucky Dick, you big stiff."[79] In keeping with this theme, Dick is often seen carrying a big stick. Similarly, his name is a not-so-sly wink to the male genitals, perhaps modeled after Zelda's nickname for her father. But Dick's big break at redeeming his masculinity comes in the form of a "scarcely saved waif of disaster bringing him the essence of a continent"—Nicole Diver, victim of father–daughter incest.[80]

THE GENDER POLITICS OF TRAUMA

Just as Fitzgerald reveals through Dick that many white, middle- to upper-class men become psychiatrists to compensate for feeling emasculated, he suggests through the character of Nicole that psychiatry is often used as a tool of patriarchal control, a part of the misogynistic medical establishment. Nicole is twice victimized—first by incest and then by psychiatric malpractice. Not coincidentally, all of Nicole's doctors are men. We learn that she was put in Dr. Dohmler's clinic largely on account of a generalized fear of men and the threat they appear to pose to her. In this patriarchal microcosm, Nicole is silent and silenced, with one of the first disclosures about her being that "she knew few words and believed in none, and in the world she was rather silent."[81] Her voice is absent from the scene in which the story of incest is told, also not coincidentally, through a daisy-chain of men—first reluctantly from alcoholic Devereux Warren to Doctor Dohmler, then from Dohmler to Franz, and finally from Franz to Dick. Not surprisingly, Warren hints that Nicole is complicit or even that she initiates; he explains that she would come to his bed every morning after her mother died and sometimes sing to him.[82] The story of the incest is buried in the middle of the book, the original act is elided, Warren's motives are conspicuously absent, and Nicole does not get to author her story. However, Fitzgerald's rendition is not an apology for the father's actions because he does not justify the reasons for Warren's behavior. The "plenty of consequences" of the paternal incest seem to be Fitzgerald's main concern in *Tender Is the Night*.[83]

Despite the gaps and omissions in the incest narrative, Devereux Warren's actions cast a dark shadow on the entire novel. In fact, what makes most readers turn the pages of Book 1 is an attempt to find out what causes Nicole's mysterious bathroom breakdowns. Fitzgerald builds up suspense in Book 1 and most of the plot hinges on—or rather is unhinged by—the father–daughter incest. In other words, the movement of the novel revolves around Nicole's traumatic repetitions and follows the integration of her personality and how it impacts the disintegration of Dick's. Fitzgerald, who was deeply concerned with form and technical mastery, had doubts about the organization of *Tender* after reading critics' responses. Before formally introducing Dick, the 1934 edition opens from the perspective of the young girl, Rosemary, the Hollywood starlet, who, in many respects sets the stage for the real daddy's girl to enter.

Many are familiar with Fitzgerald's original enthusiasm about the groundbreaking style of his 1934 novel when he stated that he found the new form for which James Joyce, Gertrude Stein, and Joseph Conrad had been looking.[84] Many are also familiar with his later assertion that the book's "great fault is that the *true* beginning—the young psychiatrist in Switzerland—is tucked away in the middle of the book."[85] His change of mind is not unlike the actions of Freud. Both men at first realized the severity of incest, but when they were criticized for their disclosures, they retreated (Freud in a much more drastic way than Fitzgerald). Fitzgerald's latter comment suggests that Dick is the real focus of interest, with Nicole and her problems as functions of a dilemma that remain in essence that of the gifted-but-flawed male (anti-)hero. In case there are any doubts about whose story Fitzgerald meant for this to be, we should remember that the penultimate title was *Richard Diver, A Romance*. Early negative reviews about the distorted chronology of the novel and the concealed Dick troubled Fitzgerald so much that Malcolm Cowley published the posthumous, "author's final version" in 1951 at which time the original Book 2 was moved to Book 1.

Yet, the 1934 novel's disjointed structure works to reveal Nicole's psychological trauma. The nonlinear narrative and the shifts in point of view illustrate how the form of the book follows its function, with the function showing that the parts are not well integrated. The pieces do not form a coherent whole, but then neither do the characters, most of whom are dissipated by the novel's end. Fitzgerald's innovative, experimental style embodies, as Mary Burton notes, the psychotherapeutic situation where first the present is offered, then the past explored, and finally the present again analyzed.[86] It works well to open from the perspective of Rosemary, whom we at first think will be the star attraction, because we later see that Rosemary's point of view dances on the shimmering surface and provides a superficial take on what soon gets probed and exposed—the dark depths of the Divers. Appropriately, through the naïve perspective of Rosemary, Dick and Nicole are seen as "all complete."[87] Not until Book 2, when he is introduced in medias res, is Dick revealed to be a composite figure and shown as inept. The plot's unpredictability and random transfer embody the purposeful incoherence of *Tender*, a book marked by senseless violence and psychological instability. The structural distortion of linear time is one of the main clues that we are dealing with trauma and its circular nature in which Devereux Warren's words, "There isn't any beginning," said in confidence to Dohmler when first telling the story of incest, are more true than he realizes.[88]

In the midst of Dick's story, the narration takes a sudden turn and includes sections from Nicole's perspective, granting her complexity and humanity and rendering her mental illness with unparalleled clarity and precision for its day. However progressive it may seem that Fitzgerald grants his female victim voice in 1934—a huge feat given the political and social climate—Fitzgerald accomplishes this largely by betraying his wife's privacy by reproducing her letters written to him while she was institutionalized. Milford explains how Fitzgerald "mercilessly exposed Zelda in his characterization of Nicole Diver. He drew upon Zelda's most terrible and private letters to him, written in the anguish of the early months of her illness in Switzerland, snipped and pieced them together in Book II with very little regard for Zelda's reaction or for the precarious balance of her sanity."[89] As Milford states, Fitzgerald's actions had to have hurt her deeply. Disappointingly, to add credibility to his novel, such a talented fiction writer felt the need to borrow from his wife at her most vulnerable. Nevertheless, through Nicole's letters to Dick, her seventeen-paragraph monologue, and emerging perspective in Book 3, Fitzgerald exposes the complexity of Nicole's trauma and shows how she is a victim of a collusive system of male power masquerading as a profession of healing. In these impressionistic passages Fitzgerald reveals the patriarchal forces acting on Nicole that make it difficult, if not impossible, for her to transition from victim to survivor.

Strategically placed immediately before the story of incest are nine letters that Nicole wrote to Dick while she was a patient at Dohmler's clinic. If one divorces the biographical traces from these letters, they offer a sensitive and perceptive rendering of Nicole's inner condition and indicate that she was in better mental health during Dick's absence from the clinic than she was during most of their marriage. Giving Nicole voice—albeit an incoherent voice at times—shows Fitzgerald's efforts at capturing her trauma. We know that Nicole sends Dick about fifty letters over the course of eight months and that he answers all of them. The fact that Nicole sends Dick fifty letters after meeting him only once indicates that she has transferred her paternal fixation to Dick; the fact that he answers all of them implies that Dick experiences a countertransference to Nicole. Curiously, none of Dick's responses are reproduced, only Nicole's letters, which make frequent reference to war and link the broader cultural trauma to Nicole's personal trauma. These pre-armistice and pre-marriage letters to Dick indicate a dire pathological condition, but they also suggest that Nicole may have more understanding of her illness than the doctors of the hospital are willing to admit, and, moreover, that in keeping the truth from Nicole, they are guilty of revictimizing her.

In two of the letters, Nicole mentions her father. She writes, "Unless they will let me write my father, whom I loved dearly."[90] The past tense suggests that Nicole no longer loves her father, and the definition of love is unclear here. In another letter, Nicole tells Dick that she has written her father to come and take her away. The narrator notes a change between letters seven and eight: "And then suddenly the change."[91] However, I detect a significant shift in the tone and level of self-awareness in letter four, when Nicole expresses anger with the silence surrounding her sickness. In this letter Nicole voices her frustration with being kept in the dark about her trauma. She writes, "Here I am in what appears to be a semi-insane-asylum, all because nobody saw fit to tell me the truth about anything. If I had only known what was going on like I know now I could have stood it I guess for I am pretty strong, but those who should have, did not see fit to enlighten me."[92] She not only rightly blames the institution of psychiatry for failing to inform her about her illness, but also demonstrates her ability to process information and her likely awareness that she is a victim of father–daughter incest ("like I know now"). Nicole is aware that her pain comes from not just her father's rape but from the silence and lies that cover up his actions, of which Dick is guilty. In this letter, Nicole comes across as capable of handling the truth. As Jacqueline Tavernier-Courbin puts it: "Nicole is a far stronger and more complex character than she is usually given credit for. She is inherently strong and a natural survivor who sank into neuroticism as a result of one ugly incident and the *conspiracy of silence* surrounding it on the part of both her family and her doctors" (emphasis added).[93] Nicole seems to be aware that the "conspiracy of silence" prevents her from working through her trauma.

In one of the last reproduced letters, written after drifting in and out of mental stability, Nicole affirms that she is "slowly coming back to life."[94] She mentions that the "war is over and I scarcely knew there was a war,"[95] which could indicate that the doctors, including Dick, who did not see "fit to tell [her] the truth about anything," made her too wrapped up in her own personal troubles, wearing the domino she refers to at the close of Book 1, to realize what is going on in the outside world.[96] The significance of Nicole's letters is that they are marked by an increasing self-knowledge. Moreover, they hint at the potential failure of psychiatry—that many patients are never cured. Nicole knows that she has not recovered and may never be cured—hence, she qualifies "coming back to life" with the word "slowly." Nicole knows all too well that her continuing trauma will prevent her from living a normal life in the near future. The final sentences of her last letter read: "I wish someone were in love with me like boys were ages ago before I was sick. I suppose it will be years, though, before I could think of anything like that."[97] Interestingly, Fitzgerald has Nicole, the mental patient, understand that she is no candidate for love and marriage any time soon whereas Dick, the psychiatrist, the one who should know better, admits that the "the question of marrying her has passed through my mind."[98] Furthermore, we learn at the novel's end that Dick crossed an even larger boundary by engaging in premarital sex with Nicole while she was one of his patients; after Nicole sleeps with Tommy, the narrator says that Nicole "scarcely recalled how she had felt when she and Dick had possessed each other in secret places around the corners of the world, during the month before they were married."[99]

Suggested in these letters, and pronounced later in the novel, is the fine line between therapist and rapist. After hearing the story of incest, Dick sighs and tells Franz that all he said in his letters back to Nicole was "Be a good girl and mind the doctors" and "Try to forget the past."[100] Dick's short statements capture the politics of the system. Psychiatry is shown to be a corrupt institution that infantilizes women, referring to them as girls and teaching them to submit to white male power. Also during this exchange with Dick, Franz tells him Nicole struggled with feeling complicit in what happened with her father. Tellingly, when she was in the company of girls at the boarding school, she had no feelings of complicity. The implication is that when she is at the hospital surrounded by male doctors and reading the "little Freud" the doctors give her, she feels somewhat responsible.[101] Nicole seems well enough to know that the doctors are revictimizing her by failing to disclose the information surrounding her illness. In other words, the therapy of reeducation is shown to be a form of brainwashing, fraught with gender politics. Strikingly, Fitzgerald has Dick admit so much toward the end of Book 2. The book that opened with such promise for him ends with an emasculated Dick who is mistaken for a man accused of raping and killing a five-year-old child and who cries, "I want to explain to these people how I raped a five-year-old girl. Maybe I did—."[102] Although Dick may have Rosemary in mind when he makes this speech, for he and Rosemary had just consummated their affair, it seems likely that he is also thinking of Nicole and comes close here to admitting that she was failed by not just the medical community, but also by her husband's silence.

The more important question than what causes Nicole to crack—because we know it is father–daughter incest—is what or who puts her back together. Against all odds, she seemingly recovers from the incest.[103] In addition to the nine letters that Nicole writes to Dick, we hear her voice again in the exact middle, the heart, of the novel, and in this section we gain insight into Nicole's illness *and* wellness. Udo Natterman argues that in this retrospective part of the narrative given through Nicole's eyes, the entire novel is captured. This section of the book is the only time, aside from the letters, that the point of view changes from third person to first person. In this passage, which Zelda liked "immensely," we gain access into the patient's mind and receive her voice unfiltered.[104] Natterman argues that this passage supports reading *Tender* as a book with many characteristics of a psychological novel, commenting on the strategic placement of the scene:

> Though this segment of 17 paragraphs and some 1,500 words makes up only about one percent of the entire novel, it is nevertheless significant. It is placed in the exact middle of the novel; it constitutes the longest passage directly dealing with Nicole's mental state; it is presented prominently as stream-of-consciousness; and it covers almost six years of the novel's time in only four pages of the book.[105]

In this section, Nicole's "insecurity, her dependence on Dick, her fear of being alone and being pregnant, as well as the terrors of her breakup are described with great subtlety."[106] The major events, later elaborated in the novel, are mentioned in this passage, which suggests that the book is concerned with trauma's compulsive repetitions, the idea that repressed elements reappear in symptoms, often as symptomatic actions. In other words, Fitzgerald recognizes the cyclical, elusive, belated effects of trauma.

Nicole's section, "from Woolloomooloo Bay to Biskra" hits on, among other things, the highlights of the marriage of Dick and Nicole and provides insight into why a divorce is imminent.[107] The passage, which seems to come out of the blue, is found in the middle of Chapter 10 of Book 2. It opens with the line, "How do you do, lawyer," in which Nicole is negotiating with her lawyer and sister how much money she is allowed.[108] From the beginning of Nicole's monologue, money is clearly shown to be a point of contention between Nicole and Dick, as is evident when Nicole says, "No, Dick refuses to have anything whatever to do with [the money]" and again "there's more Warren money than Diver money."[109] Then immediately, Nicole is off on another (equally troubling) topic—love. Nicole tells Dick that she thinks "it's wonderful to be just like everybody else," a subtle nod to the question posed by Franz during their discussion of war and the vicarious shell-shock of those who only read about war in the newspapers at which time Dick tells him he wants to be extraordinary (the greatest psychologist that ever lived).[110] In contrast, Nicole just wants to be normal.

Moreover, Nicole notes that the seeds for Dick's destruction have already been planted, independent of her "lovely grassless garden."[111] She says, "Dick is tired of singing it, so go on alone, Dick," which suggests that she realizes Dick is dissipating.[112] Nicole alludes to her breakdown following the birth of her daughter, Topsy. Most likely, Nicole is distraught over the birth of her daughter because she fears, with good reason, that Topsy may be a victim of incest, like her mother.[113] Nicole's thwarted ambitions to be more than a mother are evident in this passage in which she expresses a desire to translate English novels into French and study medicine like Dick. She repeats Dick's words that "work is everything," and "a man knows things and when he stops knowing things he's like anybody else."[114] The passage closes by hinting at her affair with Tommy and Dick's affair with Rosemary, bringing the reader full circle; the section ends with Nicole on the "pleasant shore of the French Riviera," translating a recipe for chicken à la Maryland, which is exactly how Book 1 opens.[115]

Embedded in Nicole's monologue are references to feeling well, indicating that she is on the mend. She states that when she gets well, she wants "to be a fine person like you, Dick."[116] Just prior to this assertion, Nicole writes, "I am tired of knowing nothing and being reminded of it all the time."[117] Clearly, this message was proclaimed in her letters to Dick. The rich juxtaposition indicates that once the conspiracy of silence is broken, Nicole can recover. She also mentions being "well the first time" with Dick; however, she tells this not to Dick, but to Tommy Barban.[118] Nicole thinks that through an affair with Tommy she will be restored to health, if only for a short time. Just prior to ending her passage, Fitzgerald writes that for Nicole "Everything is all right" aside from the presence of Rosemary, whom, lest we forget, played the starring role in "Daddy's Girl."[119]

One of the most significant parts of Nicole's stream-of-consciousness section occurs when she states that "Talk is men."[120] Nicole reasons that when she talks she embodies one of the men in her life—Dick, her son, Dohmler, and Tommy. Nicole's words support what the narrator discloses in Book 1: "she knew few words and believed in none."[121] Like most victims of father–daughter incest, Nicole finds language too far removed from the traumatic event to represent it in words: she is skeptical of words. Additionally, as a woman, Nicole realizes that the female voice is not validated or legitimatized as the male's.

FITZGERALD'S AMBIVALENCE

For all that Fitzgerald does to give Nicole voice throughout *Tender* and for his foresight in exposing the patriarchal forces acting against Nicole's recovery, he undermines his progressive views about the position of women in society and never fully escapes patriarchy's trappings. Fitzgerald's deep ambivalence about his female characters indicates that he feared the consequences an egalitarian society would have on men. We read in Book 1 that Nicole was "happy to exist in a man's world" and that she "preserved [her] individuality through men and not by opposition to them."[122] Those places in the text rendered from Nicole's perspective, however, suggest otherwise. One of Dick's—and perhaps Fitzgerald's—worst fears is that Nicole (Zelda) is doing what Franz's wife, Kaethe, thinks—cherishing her illness as an instrument of power.[123] Nicole does seem to be in better health than Dick wants to admit. At the end, she is in a position not only to deal with the truth but also to challenge Dick to civil battle. Fitzgerald reveals early in the novel that Dick is preparing for war with Nicole: "Though he thought she was the most attractive human creature he had ever seen, though he got from her everything he needed, he scented battle from afar, and subconsciously he had been hardening and arming himself, hour by hour."[124] However, it becomes increasingly clear that Nicole has been mobilizing as well. In the final book, she challenges Dick's authority when, to his dismay, she does not believe that the girl he was accused of kissing was just a delusion. In a poignant response, she shouts, "It's always a delusion when I see what you don't want me to see."[125] She holds Dick partly responsible for withholding information about her illness. Nicole's biggest challenge is posed toward the end of the book when Dick attempts to censor a song with the word *father* in it, and Nicole exclaims, "Oh, play it! Am I going through the rest of life flinching at the word 'father'?"[126] It seems probable that if Dick and the other doctors had it their way, yes, Nicole would recoil in fear every time she hears the word *father*. This would keep her forever under their patriarchal power, in need of their protection.

But arguably, Fitzgerald's conflicted views on women's social standing are most apparent in the passage with the "nervous eczema" woman.[127] Unlike Nicole, this woman makes no such claims about being content living in a man's world. She is "unsatisfactorily catalogued as nervous eczema," thus, defined not by name but by illness.[128] She is said to be Dick's "most interesting case."[129] The little history he knows of the thirty-year-old woman is that she was an American painter in Paris. She used to be beautiful but "now she was a living agonizing sore."[130] Dick claims her as his patient and in a conversation between them, the nameless woman reveals that she thinks she is suffering because she had "challenged men to battle."[131] She notes that she is "a symbol of something."[132] Unlike Nicole, whose incest is shown to be literal, this woman's illness is employed figuratively. Dick's patient, who is really dying from a sexually transmitted disease, is the symbol of a generation of women who dared to step out of their prescribed gender roles and define themselves not in subordination to men but in opposition to them. On the one hand, creating such a sexually liberated character speaks to Fitzgerald's progressive thinking. On the other hand, he kills her off. Against Dick's wishes, she succumbs to final defeat in Book 3.

Whereas the woman with "nervous eczema" is written out of the narrative, Nicole continues the fight, seemingly emerging as victor at Dick's expense by the novel's end, unlike Zelda, whose treatments had done little to restore her to health. In Book 3, Dick's point of view fades into the background as Nicole's becomes more prominent. In this section she finds her voice and shows that she is capable of not flinching at the word *father*, a turning point that suggests Nicole is strong enough to work through her trauma, independent of Dick. In uttering these words, she turns the linguistic key and begins to unravel trauma's hold on her. Contrary to Freud's idea of "working through," which suggests something much more ambiguous and uncertain than a "cure," Nicole wishes to be "cured"—"and in a new way."[133] The remainder of the book, however, implies that her trauma is a vicious cycle where she gets passed from one man to another. Instead of being "reeducated," Nicole thinks her cure will come through a love affair. Her "cure," however, turns out to be a mere repetition of transference. Fitzgerald writes:

> "Why, I'm almost complete," she thought. "I'm practically standing alone, without [Dick]." And like a happy child, wanting the completion as soon as possible, and knowing vaguely that Dick had planned for her to have it, she lay on her bed as soon as she got home and wrote Tommy Barban in Nice a short provocative letter.[134]

Nicole's feigned sense of empowerment, along with the statement that "For the first time in ten years she was under the sway of a personality other than her husband's. Everything Tommy said to her became part of her forever," lend credence to what the narrator calls Nicole's "nascent transference to another man."[135] From the damning portrait Fitzgerald provides of Tommy, a career soldier, a barbaric character whose main goal in life is war, it is difficult to see Nicole's idea of being "cured" via an affair with Tommy as a healthy resolution. Moreover, Fitzgerald undermines the idea that Nicole is restored to health by having her marry Tommy. Fitzgerald provides a realistic depiction of trauma in that one is never completely restored to health. But in having Nicole marry a man picked for her by Dick, Fitzgerald denies his female character independence and agency, and by having Nicole marry Tommy, of all men, the suggestion is that we are entering the Age of Barban, the age of the hypermasculine, an age that Fitzgerald does not seem to endorse, yet one in which Fitzgerald makes Nicole complicit.[136]

The collapse of civilization into barbarism is realized by the novel's end. Whereas Tommy gets the last words in the novel, the final focus is on Dick's demise, which some have blamed on Nicole's metaphoric parricide.[137] Fitzgerald closes *Tender* ambiguously, with a wandering Dick whose whereabouts are unclear, much as they had been for Devereux Warren. Just as Nicole's "cure" is undermined by her relationship with Tommy, Dick's "liberty" is questioned by his lack of substantial relationships.[138] After it becomes clear to Dick that Nicole is in love with Tommy, the narrator states, "Then he leaned his head forward on the parapet. The case was finished. Doctor Diver was at liberty."[139] He leaves Europe for America, journeying from Geneva, Switzerland, to the less sophisticated small town of Geneva, New York. We know that he is "much admired by the ladies" and is dabbling in psychiatry as a general practitioner, a far cry from the greatest psychologist.[140] The reader hears vague facts about Dick, such as he was entangled in an affair with a girl who worked in a grocery store and involved in a lawsuit about some medical question. Unlike the wartime letters to which Dick always responded, he now no longer answers Nicole's letters, which suggests his attempt to entirely close the case, but Dick's lack of communication offers no real indication that he is freed in the process.

If the ending of *Tender* feels unresolved, perhaps it is because Fitzgerald, who wrote much of himself into the character of Dick and much of Zelda into the character of Nicole, felt uncertain about their future.[141] Divorcing fact from fiction became increasingly difficult for Fitzgerald during the writing of *Tender*. The material that he uses in his novel encourages comparisons to his and Zelda's lives. As Scott Donaldson says, Book 3 "is painful to read, one of the saddest stories ever written, similar to and more moving than the account Fitzgerald would write a year later of his own crack-up."[142] Fitzgerald has said that "the man who started *Tender Is the Night* was not the one who finished it."[143] Suffice it to say, Zelda's mental breakdowns and attacks of dissociation make the book what it is—a study of psychological illness resulting from traumatic experience.

Whereas Fitzgerald is never quite clear regarding what causes Dick's mental troubles, he leaves no doubt about what causes Nicole's. War imagery serves as a backdrop to the plot, but incest takes center stage. If Zelda was indeed a victim of incest, Fitzgerald may have known that psychological trauma caused by war was a serious, validated, seemingly unquestioned condition whereas trauma caused by father–daughter incest was not. By making it clear that Nicole is a victim of paternal incest whereas Dick is a confused case of non-combatant's shell-shock, Fitzgerald exposes the gender politics of psychological trauma and challenges contemporary assumptions that held war trauma legitimate, whereas domestic sexual abuse was seen as questionable at best. Giving paternal incest critical attention, Fitzgerald demonstrates political consciousness and moral conviction.

"A strange thing is that in retrospect his *Tender Is the Night* gets better and better," commented Ernest Hemingway to editor Maxwell Perkins.[144] Stern adds that it took almost two decades after Fitzgerald's death for critics to realize how much "better and better" it became.[145] And it has taken even longer for us to appreciate Fitzgerald's foresight regarding the consequences of father–daughter incest. The novel is more than a clinical study of deterioration as it illuminates the politics surrounding psychological trauma. Fitzgerald's most insightful contributions to our understanding of it are that women in civilian life are subjected to trauma far more often than previously thought and that father–daughter incest crosses class and race lines, occurring in privileged, white families such as the ducal Warrens as much as in poor or black families, as we'll see in the following chapters. Fitzgerald anticipates a great deal of what won't be acknowledged until more than a half of a century later, that traumatic incest and the silence surrounding it severely impact too many families and make the real taboo not so much the act itself, as it is the disclosing of the family secret. Unlike Freud, who, Herman notes, "glimpsed this truth and retreated in horror," Fitzgerald bares the horror, if at times ambivalently, in his insightful novel in which he suggests that trauma is both social and personal and those experiences are often gendered.[146] He recognizes as early as 1934 that women's subordinate positions were often maintained by the hidden manipulations of the medical community. Fitzgerald hints at the need for psychiatric reform for diagnoses and treatments that would take into account the complexity of gendered experiences. In this light, it seems that the father–daughter incest is a necessary, indeed monumental, part of the novel, that, despite what John Peale Bishop said, should not be forgotten.

NOTES

1. Sigmund Freud, "The Aetiology of Hysteria," in *Collected Paper*, vol. 1, trans. Joan Riviere (London: Hogarth, 1950), 198.
2. Sigmund Freud, *The Standard Edition of the Complete Psychological Works of Sigmund Freud*, vol. 1, trans. James Strachey (London: Hogarth, 1957), 259.
3. Sigmund Freud, "An Autobiographical Study," in *The Standard Edition of the Complete Psychological Works of Sigmund Freud*, vol. 20, trans. James Strachey (London: Hogarth, 1959), 34.
4. In *Remembering Trauma*, Richard McNally argues that Freud's patients were *not* victims of father–daughter incest. Instead, the early Freud foisted his seduction theory onto these patients. He charges Freud with being the first false-memory planter but not guilty of an incest cover-up as believed by Jeffrey Masson, former project director of the Sigmund Freud Archives, along with Florence Rush and Judith Herman. Richard J. McNally, *Remembering Trauma* (Cambridge: Belknap, 2003).
5. In *Trauma: A Genealogy*, Ruth Leys traces trauma theory's roots further back than Freud. She argues that our modern understanding of trauma began in the 1860s with the work of the British physician John Erichsen. He attributed the distress of railway-accident victims to shock or concussion of the spine. Ruth Leys, *Trauma: A Genealogy* (Chicago: University of Chicago Press, 2000), 3.
6. Judith Lewis Herman, *Trauma and Recovery* (New York: Basic, 1992), 26.
7. Matthew J. Bruccoli and Margaret M. Duggan, eds., *Correspondence of F. Scott Fitzgerald* (New York: Random, 1980), 339.
8. Quoted in Milton R. Stern, introduction to *Critical Essays on F. Scott Fitzgerald's* Tender Is the Night, ed. Milton R. Stern (Boston: G. K. Hall, 1986), 19.
9. Ruth Prigozy also takes up this question. Her interpretation differs from mine in that she argues that Fitzgerald employs the incest to expose the exploitative myth of

female innocence that was so cherished in popular culture, particularly in cinema. Ruth Prigozy, "From Griffith's Girls to Daddy's Girl: The Masks of Innocence in *Tender Is the Night*," *Twentieth Century Literature* 26, no. 2 (1980): 189–221.

10. The book was serialized in four monthly installments in *Scribner's Magazine* from January to April 1934.

11. Bruccoli, *Composition of* Tender Is the Night, 3; A. H. Steinberg, "Fitzgerald's Portrait of a Psychiatrist," in Tender Is the Night: *Essays in Criticism*, ed. Marvin J. LaHood (Bloomington: Indiana University Press, 1969), 143.

12. Stern, *Critical Essays on F. Scott Fitzgerald*, 10.

13. F. Scott Fitzgerald, *Tender Is the Night* (1934; New York: Scribner's, 1982), 245.

14. Elizabeth Wilson, "Not in This House: Incest, Denial, and Doubt in the White Middle Class Family," *Yale Journal of Criticism* 8, no. 1 (1995): 35.

15. Leys, *Trauma: A Genealogy*, 194.

16. Judith Fetterley, "Who Killed Dick Diver? The Sexual Politics of *Tender Is the Night*," *Mosaic* 17, no. 1 (1984): 124.

17. Ibid.

18. Fitzgerald, *Tender Is the Night*, 129.

19. Interestingly, Zelda's brother, Anthony "Tony" Dickinson Sayre, Jr., had nightmares of matricide, killing himself shortly after (on August 27, 1933). Sally Cline, *Zelda Fitzgerald: Her Voice in Paradise* (New York: Arcade, 2002), 335.

20. Scott Donaldson, "Short History of *Tender Is the Night*," in *Writing the American Classics*, ed. James Barbour and Tom Quirk (Chapel Hill: University of North Carolina Press, 1990), 186.

21. James L. W. West III, "The Internal Chronology of *Tender Is the Night*," *The Papers of the Bibliographical Society of America* 104, no. 4 (2010): 528.

22. Richard D. Lehan, "Tender Is the Night," in Tender Is the Night: *Essays in Criticism*, ed. Marvin J. LaHood (Bloomington: Indiana University Press, 1969), 76.

23. James L. W. West III, "F. Scott Fitzgerald and American Psychiatry: A New Letter," *American Imago* 68, no. 1 (2011): 63 and 60.

24. Ibid., 63.

25. Quoted in William Blazek, "'Some Fault in the Plan': Fitzgerald's Critique of Psychiatry in *Tender Is the Night*," in *Twenty-First-Century Readings of* Tender Is the Night, ed. William Blazek and Laura Rattray (Liverpool: Liverpool University Press, 2007), 67.

26. Quoted in Kendall Taylor, *Sometimes Madness Is Wisdom: Zelda and Scott Fitzgerald: A Marriage* (New York: Ballantine, 2001), 284.

27. Quoted in Pamela A. Boker, "Beloved Illness: Transference Love as Romantic Pathology in F. Scott Fitzgerald's *Tender Is the Night*," *Literature and Medicine* 11, no. 2 (1992): 295.

28. Quoted in West, "F. Scott Fitzgerald and American Psychiatry," 62.

29. Ibid.

30. Ibid.

31. Quoted in Udo Natterman, "Nicole Diver's Monologue: A Close Examination of a Key Segment," *Massachusetts Studies in English* 10, no. 4 (1986): 222; quoted in Sarah Beebe Fryer, *Fitzgerald's New Women: Harbingers of Change* (Ann Arbor: UMI Research Press, 1988), 74.

32. Quoted in Bruccoli, *The Composition of* Tender Is the Night, 80.

33. Fryer, *Fitzgerald's New Women*, 79.

34. Nancy Milford, *Zelda: A Biography* (New York: Harper, 1970), 285.

35. Scribner, Charles, III. Introduction to *Tender Is the Night*, xi.

36. Bruccoli, *The Composition of* Tender Is the Night, 82.

37. Jeffrey Berman, *The Talking Cure: Literary Representations of Psychoanalysis* (New York: New York University Press, 1985), 61.

38. Quoted in *Dear Scott, Dearest Zelda: The Love Letters of F. Scott and Zelda Fitzgerald*, ed. Jackson R. Bryer and Cathy W. Barks (New York: St. Martin's, 2002), 189.

39. Milford, *Zelda*, 194 and 219.

40. Sara Mayfield, *Exiles from Paradise: Zelda and Scott Fitzgerald* (New York: Delacorte, 1971), 212.
41. Linda Wagner-Martin, *Zelda Sayre Fitzgerald: An American Woman's Life* (New York: Palgrave, 2004), 177.
42. Ibid.
43. Ibid., 178.
44. Cline, *Zelda Fitzgerald*, 20.
45. Taylor, *Sometimes Madness Is Wisdom*, 284.
46. Cline, *Zelda Fitzgerald*, 338–39.
47. Ibid., 339.
48. Ibid.
49. Ibid., 451.
50. Fryer, *Fitzgerald's New Women*, 72.
51. Ibid.
52. Fitzgerald, *Tender Is the Night*, 80.
53. Affairs between male doctors and female patients seemed to have been an accepted part of the culture of early psychoanalysis and its politics. Freud's biographer Ernest Jones was implicated in sexual affairs with his patients and little girls. Florence Rush, "The Freudian Coverup," Featured Reprint, *Feminism & Psychology* 6, no. 2 (1996): 261–76. Freud's close associate and Hungarian psychoanalyst, Sándor Ferenczi, was "known to be intimate with his patients and his wife's daughter," which was "tolerated by Freud and his circle." Ibid., 275. Even Carl Jung was said to have breached professional ethics by pursuing a relationship with—although not one of his patients—one of his students, Sabina Spielrein. Boker, "Beloved Illness," 306–07. It is not clear if Fitzgerald was aware of Jung's relationship, but as stated, he read Jung and on at least one occasion considered asking him to be Zelda's doctor. Milford, *Zelda*, 179.
54. Fitzgerald, *Tender Is the Night*, 138.
55. Ibid., 187.
56. Ibid.
57. Ibid., 183.
58. Ibid., 242.
59. Blazek, "Some Fault in the Plan," 72.
60. Steinberg, "Fitzgerald's Portrait of a Psychiatrist," 140.
61. Fitzgerald, *Tender Is the Night*, 119.
62. Ibid.
63. Ibid.
64. Ibid., 152.
65. Ibid., 175.
66. Ibid.
67. Ibid., 132.
68. Ibid., 116.
69. Ibid., 137. For a discussion of Dick's disillusionment with psychiatry *before* he meets Nicole, see James Ellis, "Fitzgerald's Fragmented Hero: Dick Diver," in Tender Is the Night: *Essays in Criticism*, ed. Marvin J. LaHood (Bloomington: Indiana University Press), 1969.
70. Fitzgerald, *Tender Is the Night*, 132.
71. Ibid., 186.
72. Ibid., 315.
73. Ibid.
74. Ibid., 57.
75. Ibid., 117–18.
76. Perhaps Dick's condition is not so rare. "Major Marvin F. Grieber found that non-combatants within the military suffered the highest level of psychological breakdown because the pacific nature of their jobs brought them little satisfaction." Quoted

in Tiffany Joseph, "'Non-Combatant's Shell-Shock': Trauma and Gender in F. Scott Fitzgerald's *Tender Is the Night*," *NWSA Journal* 15, no. 3 (2003): 70.

77. Fitzgerald, *Tender Is the Night*, 115.
78. Ibid., 138.
79. Ibid., 116.
80. Ibid., 136.
81. Ibid., 26.
82. Ibid., 129.
83. Ibid.
84. Donaldson, "Short History," 177.
85. Quoted in Malcolm Cowley, "Introduction to the Revised Edition," in *Critical Essays on F. Scott Fitzgerald's* Tender Is the Night, ed. Milton R. Stern (Boston: G. K. Hall, 1986), 104.
86. Mary E. Burton, "The Counter-Transference of Dr. Diver," *ELH* 38, no. 3 (1971): 468.
87. Fitzgerald, *Tender Is the Night*, 19.
88. Ibid., 126.
89. Milford, *Zelda*, 284.
90. Fitzgerald, *Tender Is the Night*, 122.
91. Ibid., 124.
92. Ibid., 123.
93. Jacqueline Tavernier-Courbin, "The Influence of France on Nicole Diver's Recovery in *Tender Is the Night*," in *French Connections: Hemingway and Fitzgerald Abroad*, ed. J. Gerald Kennedy and Jackson R. Bryer (New York: St. Martin's, 1998), 216.
94. Fitzgerald, *Tender Is the Night*, 124.
95. Ibid.
96. Ibid., 123.
97. Ibid., 124.
98. Ibid., 140.
99. Ibid., 300.
100. Ibid., 130, 142.
101. Ibid., 131.
102. Ibid., 235.
103. In "The Influence of France," Jacqueline Tavernier-Courbin argues that "Nicole recovers in spite of the psychiatrists rather than because of them," and attributes her recovery to the less-repressed atmosphere of France (216–17).
104. Milford, *Zelda*, 287.
105. Natterman, "Nicole Diver's Monologue," 213.
106. Ibid., 222.
107. Fitzgerald, *Tender Is the Night*, 160.
108. Ibid., 159.
109. Ibid.
110. Ibid.
111. Ibid., 25.
112. Ibid., 160.
113. At least twice in the text, Dick thinks questionably about his daughter: "At first he thought nothing. [Rosemary] was young and magnetic, but so was Topsy" (207), and "What do I care whether Topsy 'adores' me or not? I'm not bringing her up to be my wife" (257).
114. Fitzgerald, *Tender Is the Night*, 161, 162.
115. Ibid., 3.
116. Ibid., 161.
117. Ibid.
118. Ibid., 162.
119. Ibid.
120. Ibid.

121. Ibid., 26.
122. Ibid., 53.
123. Ibid., 239.
124. Ibid., 100.
125. Ibid., 190.
126. Ibid.
127. Donaldson argues that the character most closely modeled on Zelda is not Nicole but the nameless woman-artist tortured by eczema. "Short History," 186. Milford confirms that Zelda did indeed suffer a bout of severe eczema in mid-June 1930. *Zelda,* 169.
128. Fitzgerald, *Tender Is the Night,* 183.
129. Ibid.
130. Ibid.
131. Ibid., 184.
132. Ibid., 185.
133. Ibid., 289.
134. Ibid.
135. Ibid., 293, 301.
136. In an early part of the novel, we read that "Tommy is one of those men that Dick's passed along to Nicole," establishing from the beginning Dick's control of the situation, which undermines Nicole's attempts to come into her own by the novel's ending. Fitzgerald, *Tender Is the Night,* 43.
137. See Susann Cokal, "Caught in the Wrong Story: Psychoanalysis and Narrative Structure in *Tender Is the Night,*" *Texas Studies in Literature and Language* 47, no. 1 (2005): 90–91.
138. Fitzgerald, *Tender Is the Night,* 302.
139. Ibid.
140. Ibid., 314–15.
141. He also modeled Tommy on the French aviator Edouard Jozan, with whom Zelda most likely had an affair, and Rosemary on Lois Moran, the movie star with whom he had an affair.
142. Scott Donaldson, "The Seduction of Dr. Diver," *The Hopkins Review* 8, no. 1 (2015): 21.
143. Donaldson, "Short History," 177.
144. Quoted in Bruccoli, *The Composition of* Tender Is the Night, 9.
145. Stern, *Critical Essays,* 2.
146. Herman, *Trauma and Recovery,* 28.

TWO

"Naw You Ain't No Man"

Ellison's Invisible Man *and the Woman Question Revisited*

Much like Nicole Diver's bold questioning if she is to go through life cringing at the word *father*, Kate Trueblood of Ralph Ellison's *Invisible Man* poses a challenge to the patriarchal forces that threaten to silence her and her daughter, Matty Lou. In the second chapter of Ellison's novel, often referred to as the Trueblood episode, Ellison hands over narration to Jim Trueblood, a poor sharecropper who stuns his audience with an incredible tale of father–daughter incest. Toward the end of his story, Trueblood mentions that the first words his wife Kate says to him are, "How come you don't go on 'way and leave us?"[1] His response is, "I caint leave you. . . . I'm a man and man don't leave his family."[2] Kate's response, which bears a closer look, is "Naw you ain't no man. No man'd do what you did."[3] Trueblood, however, assures her that he's "still a man."[4]

The argument made by theorist bell hooks in "Reconstructing Black Masculinity" might help us make sense of Trueblood's response. She explains that black men have embraced traditional, white notions of manhood or patriarchal phallocentrism—ideals that privilege the masculine and maintain that masculinity is the central source of power and authority—to devastating effects.[5] Instead of challenging a white-supremacist, sexist system that has denied them a satisfying manhood, hooks explains, they have reinscribed it. And instead of lashing out at white male domination, they have often turned on women, using rape and incest as reactions against their inability to be "real men" as defined by the dominant culture.[6]

Ellison's *Invisible Man* offers an introspective literary exploration of black male identity, in which we follow an unnamed narrator who comes of age before the Civil Rights movement and who is rendered invisible by the impositions of a racially rigged society. It charts his slow-growing awareness of how society schemes to, in the words of his grandfather, "Keep This Nigger Boy Running."[7] In this *Bildungsroman*, Invisible Man journeys from a "naïve Southern schoolboy to urban outlaw living in an underground lair" in Harlem.[8] During his journey to self-knowledge, he meets many characters who shape his perspectives. One character he encounters early in his adventures is Trueblood, a man who insists on staying with his family even after he allegedly committed father–daughter incest. Critics agree that Ellison is not writing a case for incest; however, what precisely he is doing in the second chapter of his epic novel and the importance of feminine values in his work have not been so obvious.

In her 2007 article, "Jim Trueblood and His Critic-Readers: Ralph Ellison's Rhetoric of Dramatic Irony and Tall Humor in the Mid-Century American Literary Public Sphere," Gillian Johns provides a rereading of the Trueblood episode to argue that Ellison's work should not be read as an accommodationist piece to appease the novel's implied white readers but rather as a novel that discreetly undermines "assumptions about the inferiority of black cultural values, knowledge, and authority."[9] One of Johns's most insightful observations is that Trueblood's story is a tall tale (not to mention a dirty joke), and thus, the actions that Trueblood describes with vivid details never happened. When viewed in this light, it becomes clear that Ellison is using this graphic story of father–daughter incest to challenge stereotypes about black male sexual desire and to exploit listeners' naïve biases. Moreover, Ellison employs paternal incest metaphorically to reverse the social raping of black men in an effort to make readers confront the trauma of racism that lies at the heart of American society.

As I argue in this chapter, despite his valiant efforts to work through the trauma of racism, Ellison fails to bear witness to the trauma of father–daughter incest. However, a careful rereading of Trueblood's incestuous dreamwork indicates something that feminists would much later articulate—that the real social taboo is not incest. Father–daughter incest, as Ellison suggests, is a normal function of patriarchy, not a breakdown in the social order. This chapter examines Ellison's masculinist treatment of his female characters through a close reading of the Trueblood episode, specifically of Kate's response, because it questions to what extent Trueblood's narrative reinforces male domination and reinscribes patriarchal phallocentrism. Although Trueblood's tale neglects to illustrate the complex trauma that plagues many incest victims, perhaps Ellison's views on women have been too harshly criticized.

Unlike Fitzgerald's *Tender Is the Night*, *Invisible Man* is not autobiographical, although it does draw on Ellison's lived experiences and historical context. The book was seven years in the making, written during Ellison's thirties, and the only novel he published during his lifetime. Released on the eve of the Civil Rights movement, African Americans still reeling from the 1896 Supreme Court decision in *Plessy v. Ferguson*, the novel was immediately praised for its aesthetic and philosophical qualities and recognized as a landmark post-WWII novel central to American and later African American literary history.[10] Ellison was applauded for reaching "the literary summit on the first try."[11] In "'Something Warmly, Infuriatingly Feminine': Gender, Sexuality, and the Work of Ralph Ellison," James Smethurst notes the book's acclaim as an American novel: "*Invisible Man* . . . became not merely a popular and important novel, but also a key *American* text that became virtually inescapable on any syllabus in a modern American novel survey class long before the widespread existence of courses, seminars, programs, and departments in African-American studies."[12] By 1953 it became a bestseller and won the National Book Award. This is no small feat for a book published before *Brown v. Board of Education* in 1954, which repudiated the "separate but equal" doctrine upheld in *Plessy v. Ferguson*, thus heralding the end of segregation and marking the advent of the Civil Rights movement. It was written during a time when "the threat of vigilante justice in the form of lynching was a constant presence in the lives of black men, particularly in the South."[13] Three years after its publication saw "arguably the most notorious lynching of a black man"; the teenager from Chicago, Emmett Till, was murdered while visiting his relatives in Mississippi.[14] His crime: whistling at a white woman.

Invisible Man's personal diaspora reflects the larger historical narrative of black migration in the first half of the twentieth century. The moment in history that produced *Invisible Man* witnessed the effects of the black Great Migration to the northern cities and its subsequent "ghettoization." As Shanna Greene Benjamin states in "There's Something about Mary: Female Wisdom and the Folk Presence in Ralph Ellison's *Invisible Man*," many African Americans journeyed north, anticipating "a milk-and-honey reality replete with abundant industrial work and limited racial backlash—a welcome alternative to their meager sharecropping existence in the South."[15] What they sought, however, was not what they found. In the North, they experienced urban slum conditions, pervasive black unemployment, and although perhaps subtler, dehumanizing racism.

Against this historical backdrop of the threats of lynching and the disillusions of the black migration, *Invisible Man* testifies to six decades of racial segregation and the cultural displacement of African Americans. As a whole, it bears witness to the trajectory of blacks in America, who journeyed from slavery and abolitionism through the Civil War and Reconstruction to its collapse. They saw the rise of Jim Crow laws in the 1890s and the mass diaspora to northern cities in what also turned out to be a disappointment. Although, as Ellison's biographer Arnold Rampersad observes, it is impossible to date the events in the novel precisely—because the Depression is not identified, allusions are made to World War I but not to World War II, and other historical events are left out altogether—Ellison was undoubtedly affected by the historical trends and crisis, including the Cold War political climate of the late 1940s and early 1950s.[16] Ellison never actually joined the Communist party and he presents the quasi-Communist party in his novel as flawed and ineffectual, but he acknowledges in his novel what at first attracted many blacks to Marxist ideology. The party provided an institutional space and language in which issues and concerns of the disempowered could be articulated, debated, and sometimes successfully addressed. It held the promise of equality. Unsurprisingly, many black artists and early originators of Second-Wave feminism, such as Richard Wright and Betty Friedan, had backgrounds in the communist Left.[17]

Invisible Man's engagement with the politics of racism and gender, however, sparked, and continues to elicit, impassioned debate. Some early reviewers claimed that because it did not fit in the vein of Richard Wright's naturalistic, "protest literature," it wasn't political enough.[18] During the tumultuous 1960s era when the militant black power movement emerged, a new generation of black youth asserted that the theme of invisibility did not apply, and the novel's apparent embrace of existential freedom was too abstract. The first book-length, single-author study of Ellison and his oeuvre was not published until almost thirty years after *Invisible Man*'s initial publication: Robert O'Meally's *The Craft of Ralph Ellison* in 1980 contains as its central chapter a close reading of *Invisible Man*. By the 1990s, critics began to explore the ideological struggles at work in the novel as bold claims were made for its literary historical significance and political sensibilities. With the rise of poststructuralist theoretical approaches, the novel was praised for "opening up new technical and thematic possibilities for black fiction writers."[19]

The first decade of the twenty-first century saw the publication of two biographies of Ellison: Lawrence Jackson's *Ralph Ellison: Emergence of Genius* (2002), which follows his subject from birth in 1913 through the publication of *Invisible Man* in 1952, and Arnold Rampersad's *Ralph Ellison: A Biography* (2007), which documents its subject through his life to his death in 1994, a life that spanned most of the twentieth century. The appearance of several posthumously published writings in recent years, most notably *Juneteenth* in 1999 and *Three Days Before the Shooting: The Unfinished Second Novel* in 2010 encouraged renewed interest in Ellison and his works, spawning more literary outpourings on *Invisible Man* that revisit a multitude of topics including Ellison's use of folk materials, the novel's modernist qualities, integration poetics, and as I address in this chapter, gender dynamics. These discussions will likely continue well into this century.

Amid the enormous existing body of critical work on *Invisible Man,* critics have noted the importance of the Trueblood episode, but only a few commented at length on the chapter. Selma Fraiberg explored Ellison's use of incest first in her 1961 "Two Modern Incest Heroes." As her title suggests, she praises Trueblood for rising above the Oedipus myth and casting off the pretense of innocence by acknowledging his unconscious motives. She concludes, "it is the myth that destroys."[20] Later that same decade, Peter Hays revisited the theme of incest in Ellison's novel, arguing that the Trueblood scene should be read as a satire: "Ellison is satirizing the prejudices of all who believe that any black, true-to-his-blood, regularly commits bestial acts like incest."[21] Hays maintains that Ellison employs incest as a metaphor for interpersonal and interracial relations in the novel. In his 1984 "To Move Without Moving: An Analysis of Creativity and Commerce in Ralph Ellison's Trueblood Episode," Houston Baker added his voice to the discussion to contend that Trueblood's narrative enables him to transcend the stereotypes that whites have imposed on him. He emerges as a creative and commercial man, capitalizing on his story of incest. Trueblood, claims Baker, successfully challenges the castrating effects of white philanthropy.

By the end of the 1980s, as feminist scholars began to object to Ellison's depictions of female characters in *Invisible Man,* Hortense Spillers published "'The Permanent Obliquity of an In(pha)llibly Straight': In the Time of the Daughters and the Fathers." She criticized Ellison's portrayal of Trueblood's wife and daughter as silenced characters, concluding her essay by claiming that the incest taboo prevails for good reason. The publication of Toni Morrison's *The Bluest Eye* and other incest narratives reinvigorated discussion of the Trueblood episode as critics such as Michael Awkward, Janice Doane, and Devon Hodges argued that Morrison consciously revises Ellison's chapter to foreground the daughter's experience of incest.

Understandably, few critics devote entire essays to the incest: *Invisible Man* is not centrally about father–daughter incest. In fact, the portrayal of incest is confined to the second chapter of the novel, a mere thirty-five pages in a book just shy of six hundred. The novel is not Trueblood's story but is essentially the tale of a nameless black man who journeys from the rural south to New York City, seeking personal identity. Aside from the prologue and epilogue, the entire story is told in flashback, with the reader learning about the many memorable, yet traumatic, events Invisible Man experiences.

In the first chapter, Ellison unearths that the most potent sex taboo is not father–daughter incest but rather black men sexually desiring white women. The novel opens with a description of the "battle royal," a humiliating event where the narrator, who has just graduated from high school, is made to perform for the white men before he can deliver his graduation speech, a speech that emphasizes black humility as the means to progress. At first he and the other black graduates are led into a hotel ballroom, where a naked blonde woman is paraded before their eyes, causing at least one to faint and another to have an erection. The black men are trapped in a paradoxical position, simultaneously told to look and to not look. We should not forget that Ellison wrote this during a time when a black man's gaze on a white woman in the segregated South could warrant death by lynching. Our narrator admits to having mixed emotions about white womanhood: desire, fear, terror, even identification with his fellow victim. He is torn between wanting to spit on her and stroke her thighs, to caress and destroy her, to love and murder her. After the woman is literally tossed from the room, the black men are then made to box blindfolded and tricked into picking up from an electrified rug what is later revealed to be fake money.[22]

Evident in this passage is white male homosociality, which is characterized by Southern racist discourse and anxiety about black male sexuality. In this scene, the white men bond together, establishing strong masculine networks primarily through exchanging the white woman, proving their heterosexuality, and as we see in this scene and throughout the novel, exhibiting their abhorrence of black men. Ellison illustrates how this phenomenon is a white male prerogative that does not apply to the black male community whose solidarity is foreclosed. The oppressive white male society splits Invisible Man from his community, which is essential for maintaining the inequitable power dynamics as it thwarts an effective cohesive struggle against the oppressor. Prevented from bonding with other black males, the black "boys" of the battle royal are made to perform for entertainment purposes. In the first chapter, Ellison sets the tone for the rest of the book in which black men are denied not just masculinity but humanity and pitted against each other for the enjoyment of white men.

Although Invisible Man is given a scholarship for the black college upon delivering his speech at the end of the battle royal, his undergraduate years are cut short. He gets expelled from college (most likely modeled after Tuskegee Institute, Ellison's college) as a result of the Trueblood events. He then ventures to New York with what he assumes are letters of recommendation from the president of his college but turn out to be anything but. After teaming up with the quasi-Communist organization, "the Brotherhood," which Invisible Man thinks will provide a venue for evoking social change and gaining equal rights for black men, he becomes disillusioned by the group using him as an ideological marionette and their failure to honor individuality. And so, by the novel's end, we find Invisible Man in a secluded hole in a Harlem basement contemplating his personal and social responsibility.

Charting the novel's plot might indicate that the Trueblood chapter is a convenient device that furthers the storyline, for Invisible Man gets expelled from the university because, instead of showing one of the white college founders, Mr. Norton, evidence of racial progress, Invisible Man showed him what the school president considers the unsavory elements of town—the shack of Trueblood, who so willingly shares his incest story. The episode is brief and Trueblood and his family are barely referred to in the rest of the novel. But Ellison could have chosen any number of reasons to have his narrator expelled from college. He chose a story of father–daughter incest told from the perspective of a poor black farmer to a white, wealthy, seemingly cultured Mr. Norton and to Invisible Man, who is chauffeuring Norton for the day.

The novel as a whole can be read as a *Bildungsroman* that dramatizes Invisible Man's neo-mythic journey and transformation from innocence to experience/hipster-ism. The Trueblood episode and the battle royal scene mark initiating events that signify Invisible Man's "loss of virginity" and true beginning of being educated in the ways of a racist, patriarchal society that bonds together in fear of black male sexuality. Invisible Man's journey begins in earnest after he leaves the college founded and controlled by white men. For most of the novel, he grapples with reconciling the conflicting messages dealt to him by the Nortons and the Truebloods of society. This chapter first examines how the Trueblood episode complicates traditional white assumptions of black masculinity. The second part discusses how female experience is a part of Ellison's vision.

REREADING TRUEBLOOD'S TALE

In chapter 2, with painstaking deliberation, Ellison subtly defies the stereotypes that equate black masculinity with incestuous bestiality. He accomplishes this by suggesting that Trueblood may be a trickster figure, who weaves a tall tale satirizing white philanthropy's hypocrisy to successfully shift power relations between white and black men. This chapter is a dizzying hall of mirrors in which the reader never quite knows if Trueblood committed the incest. Often read as a literal story of father–daughter incest, the truthfulness of Trueblood's tale is questioned by Johns, who points out good reasons to doubt its validity and to read it as a rhetorically sophisticated game where master storyteller Trueblood outsmarts his captive audience. As Invisible Man is made to entertain an audience of white men in the previous chapter during the battle royal, Trueblood also performs for the white man, in his case with a humorous, albeit crude, story of incest. Knowing that direct acts of aggression against whites are socially prohibited, he fashions a story that conforms to stereotypes of black male desire. Much like the narrator does with his speech in the first chapter, so too does Trueblood tell the white men what they want to hear.

Even before Invisible Man and Norton hear Trueblood's tale, Ellison drops subtle hints to suggest the story's fabrication. We are first told that Trueblood's reputation prior to the incest is one of hard worker and caring father.[23] Moreover, we learn that Trueblood has a knack for storytelling: he was known as "one who told the old stories with a sense of humor and a magic that made them come alive."[24] When Trueblood is asked by Norton to talk with him, he complies "without surprise" and begins his tale as if rehearsed—"as though he had told the story many, many times."[25] And, of course, one cannot gloss over Trueblood's wink as he glances from Invisible Man to Norton in the midst of his story: "Trueblood seemed to smile at me behind his eyes as he looked from the white man to me and continued."[26]

Such details do not account for daughter Matty Lou's pregnancy or the axe wound inflicted by wife Kate upon discovering the incest; however, it seems plausible that Matty Lou was impregnated by the young boy who, Trueblood notes, has been "startin' to hang 'round her" and that the axe wound is a self-inflicted injury, a rather small price to pay when compared to the money the white folks give him after hearing his story.[27] Moreover, we are told that when Invisible Man and Norton pull up to Trueblood's house, "both women moved with the weary, full-fronted motions of far-gone pregnancy," which suggests that both Kate and Matty Lou are in their final trimester.[28] And yet, the axe wound that Trueblood claims he received the night of the incident has "flies and fine white gnats" swarming around it, indicating that the wound is still open.[29] Interestingly, Trueblood makes the gnats white in color, perhaps symbolizing the white, rich men who prey on black men's fresh wounds. Did Kate really harm him so badly that months after its infliction, his injury is still gaping? It doesn't seem likely. When all is said and done, Trueblood instructs Invisible Man and Norton to listen to his children singing "London Bridge Is Falling Down," which leads Invisible Man to think, "Something was going on which I didn't get."[30] Even our naïve narrator, who seemingly accepts the present power structures unquestioningly, suspects foul play by this point.

The incongruities are not just confined to Trueblood's tale. The story leading up to the story of incest is rife with contrasts that upset assumptions about "civilized" white patriarchal society, whose compulsion for trueblooded racial purity and desire for one's daughter are exposed. Skillfully, Ellison juxtaposes Trueblood's story with Norton's incestuous lust for his now-deceased daughter. In his initial description of Norton, Ellison writes, "A Bostonian, smoker of cigars, teller of polite Negro stories, shrewd banker, skilled scientist, director, philanthropist, forty years a bearer of the white man's burden, and for sixty a symbol of the Great Traditions."[31] One can't help wondering about the content of the "polite

Negro stories" that Norton circulates. Mostly likely named after the famous Harvard educator, Charles Norton Eliot, Norton serves as a national symbol of racial paternalism, a puritan of sorts. As Invisible Man drives him around for the afternoon, Norton shares a story about his daughter, his own true blood. The white college benefactor explains to Invisible Man that his destiny is somehow connected with the destiny of black people. As Norton tries to make clear what he means by their shared fate, he indulges in detailed description of his daughter who died while abroad with her father, a loss that consumes an aging Norton. Describing his daughter, Norton tells Invisible Man:

> She was a being more rare, more beautiful, purer, more perfect and more delicate than the wildest dream of a poet. I could never believe her to be my own flesh and blood. Her beauty was a well-spring of purest water-of-life, and to look upon her was to drink and drink and drink again. . . . She was rare, a perfect creation, a work of purest art. A delicate flower that bloomed in the liquid light of the moon. A nature not of this world, a personality like that of some biblical maiden, gracious and queenly. I found it difficult to believe her my own.[32]

As heartfelt—and provocative—as Norton's evocation of his daughter might sound, his words take on new meaning in the context of Trueblood's story. Commenting on Norton's peculiar relationship with his daughter, Robert Stepto affirms: "Appropriately enough, her image is not a photograph on the wall or a totem on the lawn, but a cameo of sorts which her father reverently carries on his person, as close to his waist as to his heart."[33] Curiously, this grieving father has yet to forgive himself for his daughter's death, or for his "fatal attraction," to her. Ostensibly moved by Norton's tale of his daughter, Invisible Man "half-consciously" veers off the beaten path and ends up at Trueblood's shack.[34] Ellison hints that Invisible Man drives Norton here intentionally, as he subtly points out the irony of the black college: although the school outwardly promotes the goal of advancing the African American community, it did not extend its mission into its surrounding impoverished areas. With thoughts of his daughter on his mind and her photograph pressed to his person, Norton meets Trueblood, whose wife and daughter are both pregnant, allegedly by Trueblood. Upon seeing what he perceives as a monstrous demonstration of surfacing unbridled sexual urges, Norton is envious that Trueblood committed such an inconceivable act and is baffled that he is "unharmed": "'You did and are unharmed!' he shouted, his blue eyes blazing into the black face with *something like envy* and indignation" (emphasis added).[35]

The white patriarch's envy is hard to overlook in trying to make sense of the Trueblood episode in the grand scheme of *Invisible Man*'s epic design. Mary Rohrberger correctly observes, "Norton's interest in Trueblood's story is characterized by an urgency explainable only by the assumption that he must have shared a powerful attraction to his own daughter, now dead."[36] Hays is even more direct in his reading of the Norton/Trueblood pairing: "The word 'envy' above gives us a clue, if we need one: Trueblood has done what Norton had wanted to do."[37] Indeed, to vicariously experience the incest, Norton "almost [runs] across the road" to Trueblood's lawn to greedily absorb the lurid tale.[38] When questioned how he has "looked upon chaos" and has not been destroyed, Trueblood responds, "I'm all right, suh. . . . My eyes is all right too."[39] Trueblood's intriguing reply suggests that, unlike so many of the characters in the novel who are plagued by social blindness, Trueblood can see just fine, which is a stark contrast to Norton, who fails to see that he himself, the white patriarch, is deeply implicated in the story of father–daughter incest.

Trueblood seems well aware of how he is seen by society. His black male selfhood is defined as the image of the brute with unchecked animalistic sexuality, which, in *We Real Cool: Black Men and Masculinity*, bell hooks describes as "untamed, uncivilized, unthinking, and unfeeling."[40] Hooks explains that in a "white-supremacist capitalist patriarchy," the black man is thought to have inferior intelligence and morality.[41] As such, he is believed predisposed to commit father–daughter incest. Invisible Man notes how easily Trueblood matches the assumptions that breed institutional inter- and intraracism: "We were embarrassed by the earthy harmonies [the country quartet of the black-belt people] sang, but since the [white] visitors were awed we dared not laugh at the crude, high, plaintively animal sounds Jim Trueblood made as he led the quartet."[42] He is said to have earthy qualities and to emit animal noises. In sum, Ellison constructs him as embodying the stereotype of unrestrained, primitive sexuality whose innate tendency is to rape. For most of the chapter, Trueblood as raconteur presents himself in an unrefined, presocial state, almost bragging about how he violated the incest taboo.

Ellison further complicates the stereotypical image of the oversexed black male by having the incest result from a convoluted, coded, yet highly-suggestive dream that indicates that the real social taboo is not entry into one's daughter—but entry into a white woman's bedroom, a synecdoche for usurping white men's power, in a Jim Crow world, no less.[43] Here, Ellison shows awareness that father–daughter incest—despite the prevalence of the incest taboo—is really a normal function of a white supremacist patriarchy, in which rape is a means to maintain male power. Trueblood claims that the incest arises not from some conscious desire on his part but rather from a miscellaneous dream in which it becomes increasingly clear that Trueblood desires his daughter neither as much as Norton longed for his own nor as much as Trueblood himself desires the white man's power. To conform to Norton's and other white men's expectations, Trueblood fills his story with sensual detail that evokes stereotypes of black male promiscuity. The story of how Trueblood "done *fouled*!" (to use Kate's words) begins with the best of intentions as Trueblood is innocently enough sleeping three abed with himself and wife on either ends and daughter Matty Lou in the middle, all in an effort to keep warm.[44]

As Trueblood "drop[s] into the dream," he provides not-so-subtle clues to suggest that his entry into his daughter is analogous to entry into the white woman's bedroom as he entwines the dream and the act.[45] Trueblood says, "all around me I can smell woman, can smell it gittin' stronger all the time."[46] Immediately realizing his mistake of being in a white woman's bedroom, he tries to escape, but to no avail. In fact, the dream turns into something of a nightmare when Trueblood realizes that there is "one of them tall grandfather clocks" that strikes the time.[47] He attempts to flee when out of the clock steps a white lady who's "got on a nightgown of soft white silky stuff and nothin' else."[48] Too afraid to "touch her 'cause she's white," Trueblood throws her on the bed in a moment of frenzy.[49] The white man who then enters the dream dismisses Trueblood's dilemma with the statement, "They just nigguhs, leave 'em do it."[50] Trueblood enters the door of the grandfather clock, a symbol of patriarchal, civilized time/history, and runs off.

After sharing his dream with Norton and Invisible Man, Trueblood next launches into details about the nightmare he claims to be unwittingly engaged in with his daughter, which completes Ellison's satire of black male barbarism. As Spillers puts it, "If the preceding sequence might be termed a narrative replay, then what follows equals a full-dress opening night."[51] Upon waking, Trueblood realizes that he is coupled in carnal knowledge of Matty Lou, who is repeatedly crying out "Daddy."[52] Trying to get himself out of a "tight spot," "to move *without* movin'," to "walk out" after "flyin'" in, Trueblood states that he struggles with conflicted emotions, with which Norton easily empathizes.[53]

Not only does this chapter suggest that seizing power from white men is more socially prohibited than having sex with one's daughter, it also reveals Trueblood's knowledge of the internal African American class tensions and ensuing intraracism that whites expect. Trueblood feigns uncertainty of his guilt: "I thinks and thinks, until I thinks my brain go'n bust, 'bout how I'm guilty and how I ain't guilty."[54] He casts the black community as surely thinking that he is culpable. Upon learning of the incest, Kate, we're told, starts "talkin' the unknown tongue, like a wild woman."[55] She goes after Trueblood with a double-barrel shotgun, an iron, and finally an axe, reasoning that it is better to "spill [blood] than to foul."[56] Neither Kate nor Matty Lou speak to Trueblood. Likewise, the black preacher doesn't believe that Trueblood is sorry and he "tells [him] to git out of his house, that [he's] the most wicked man he's ever seen and that [he] better go confess [his] sin and make [his] peace with God."[57] And, the "biggity school folks up on the hill" try to run him out of the county for being a disgrace to their community.[58] Even Invisible Man, who admits to being "torn between humiliation and fascination" is upset by Trueblood's ability to talk so freely about incest in the presence of a respectable white man.[59] Invisible Man thinks that despite the college's attempts to lift up Trueblood and the other "black-belt people," Trueblood "did everything it seemed to pull us down."[60] In the midst of his story, Invisible Man fears that Norton will find him guilty by implication: "How can he tell this to white men, I thought, when he knows they'll say that all Negroes do such things?"[61] At this point in his journey, Invisible Man does not understand why Trueblood would fashion a story of sexual violation.

In addition to exposing white men's incestuous desire, the Trueblood episode challenges white male domination as it shows power shifting, if only temporarily, from the white upper class to the black lower class, or what Ellison calls in his epilogue, "the lower frequencies."[62] Contrasted with the way Trueblood is ostracized by the black community and disowned by his own family, he is rewarded by the white folks, which he claims he can't make sense of although the reader knows that he understands it quite well, even capitalizes on it. Trueblood notes that the white men "wanted to hear about the gal lots of times and they gimme somethin' to eat and drink and some tobacco."[63] Claiming to be scared of the white authorities at first, he then relaxes when he sees that "lotta folks is curious and goes outta they way to help."[64] Instead of being outraged or perturbed, the whites want to keep the sharecropper among them, arguably for less than noble reasons. By helping Trueblood, the white community can maintain the hierarchal social structure and sublimate their desires. It is a way for them to assuage their own feelings of guilt, whether stemming from incestuous desires or from racism, and to reward Trueblood for showcasing the stereotypical traits of black masculinity as violent and bestial.

Trueblood's story seemingly confirms the culturally dominant beliefs in the immorality of those racially othered, and thereby helps to justify the white community's own prejudices in a way they can cleverly disguise as charity. He tells Norton and Invisible Man that he is better now than ever before: "Why, I guess there ain't a colored man in the county who ever got to take so much of the white folkses' time as I did. . . . But best of all, suh, I got more work now than I ever did have before."[65] In addition to more jobs, Trueblood receives many handouts: "he and his family acquire new clothes and shoes, abundant food and work, long-needed eyeglasses, and even the means to reshingle their cabin."[66]

Instead of being chased out of the county, the white community give Trueblood more help "than they ever give any other colored man, no matter how good a nigguh he was."[67] Even, perhaps especially, Norton follows suit. When first hearing about the pregnancy ("They say that her father did it"), Norton questions how Trueblood is faring and says, "Perhaps I could help."[68] At the end of the tale, a traumatized Norton, who has turned a whiter shade of pale, reaches into his wallet, not coincidentally pulling out the picture of his daughter, and hands Trueblood a hundred-dollar bill, the exact amount that the "school folks" were going to give him to leave the county and settle elsewhere.[69] Also not accidentally, as Norton hands Trueblood the money, his children sing "London Bridge Is Falling Down," appropriately signifying the decline of Western civilization. Furthermore, in contrast to Invisible Man, who strives to do everything right, Trueblood "admits" to doing everything wrong and is rewarded. At the beginning of the chapter, Invisible Man had high hopes that Norton will give him "a large tip, or a suit, or a scholarship next year."[70] At the end of the chapter, a defeated Invisible Man curses Trueblood: "I saw Jim Trueblood wave as I threw the car into gear. 'You bastard,' I said under my breath. 'You no-good bastard! *You* get a hundred-dollar bill!'"[71] As it turns out, Invisible Man gains nothing and seemingly loses everything that day. Because of the day's events, he is stripped of his scholarship and expelled from the university, receiving letters that ensure he won't meet with success any time soon.

INVISIBLE WOMEN

It can be argued that Ellison misleads inexperienced or not-yet-initiated readers into believing that the incest results in prosperity for Trueblood. We learn at the beginning of his tale that Trueblood, Kate, and Matty Lou sleep in one bed because of utter poverty: it is so cold and they are too poor to afford coal. Racial discrimination becomes apparent when Trueblood explains, "I tried to git help but wouldn't nobody help us and I couldn't find no work or nothing."[72] The implication is that no one wanted to hire a black man. However, even though he gains financial wealth through the telling of his tale, his narrative is a commodity in which he, much like Invisible Man and the other black men of the battle royal, is made to perform stereotypes of male blackness and entertain the white men. Moreover, Trueblood's "wealth" is dependent on the white people's charity, further solidifying the hierarchal structure that keeps blacks subservient to whites. Indeed, the white men provide for Trueblood's family in a way he never could; thus, he is shown to be less of a man in a society that prides itself on having its male members fulfill the roles of provider and protector. His storytelling becomes an almost ritualized repetition of trauma that further indebts him to the white community. And yet, Trueblood's cleverly contrived narrative poses a challenge to the assumption that all African American men are happily promiscuous, incestuous, or absent fathers. Despite these challenges to stereotypes of black masculinity, however, what do Trueblood's narrative and Invisible Man's story tell us about femininity?

A troubling part of the tale is that in working through the trauma of racism, Ellison has Trueblood invent a story of father–daughter incest that overlooks the traumatic potential for the daughter. Playing with stereotypes of black masculinity and having Trueblood contrive a tall tale of familial sex, Ellison's character exploits the complex trauma of father–daughter incest. Writing at a time when ideas were deeply rooted in racist and misogynistic social structures, Ellison notes that to counteract feelings of emasculation and impotence brought on by a white male supremacist society that bonds together over racism, one of Trueblood's only alternatives is to demonstrate his potency through his seductive tale about how he impregnated his daughter and has not just one but two women with child.

Trauma theorists Cathy Caruth, Judith Herman, and Suzette Henke, among others, have argued that there is therapeutic potential to narrating one's story of trauma; this is not the case with Trueblood's female characters, as feminist critics have noted. Trueblood's tale provides him a voice, but the story he articulates is one in which his daughter and wife are objectified and retraumatized. Ellison denies Matty Lou and Kate self-representation by having them remain under Trueblood's narrative control. Ellison's treatment of women in general, and Matty Lou in particular, have understandably been criticized as a male-centric narrative that represses and silences the black female voice.

In a novel long criticized for its stereotyping of women, *Invisible Man* lacks fully realized female characters. As Adam Bradley's 2010 study of the expurgated drafts of *Invisible Man* make clear, Ellison originally planned for women to have a larger role. He envisioned *Invisible Man* to be a love story of sorts in which his protagonist, as difficult as it is to imagine, had a wife.[73] He was married to Louise, a white member of the Brotherhood. Some drafts show that it is his relationship with Louise that allows him to eventually see the humanity of white people. Other drafts indicate that the narrator is never quite sure whether he marries her because she is white or because he actually loves her. He forced her to tan her skin to look like a mulatto, only to betray her. The marriage fails because he "is so divided against himself that he cannot accept her."[74] Another love interest, a young black woman named Cleo, was also deleted from the final version.[75]

Similarly, the *Invisible Man* drafts, made available to the public in 1998, reveal that the Mary Rambo section underwent more revision than any other and is the sole portion of the drafts to be published as a narrative unto itself. Mary, who nurses Invisible Man back to health in the published novel and who plays somewhat the mammy role, goes on to have her own story from what was excised from the novel.[76] Why Ellison cut these passages from the final novel is anyone's guess. As Bradley maintains, the eliminated material restricts the role of love and sex in the novel and unifies the book so that the focus is on the protagonist's individual identity.[77] Thus, the Invisible Man we encounter in the published piece is wifeless and girlfriendless.

On more than one occasion the narrator is confronted with vulnerable females, but, instead of forging a connection between his journey to self-actualization and women's attempts for equality, he disregards black females as inconsequential mammy figures (Mary) and uses white women as sex objects (Sybil, the battle royal's naked woman). Most of the female characters are trapped in clichés and not fully rendered. Sprinkled throughout the published book are statements that indicate the complicated place of women in *Invisible Man*'s world, as Ellison's tone shifts between sympathy and disgust. Invisible Man is told that the "most easily accessible symbol of freedom" is "a woman, of course," a statement supported in Trueblood's tale.[78] The prospect of just dancing with a white girl is seen as a dream come true during a time when black men could be murdered for merely looking at white women the wrong way. Even Ras the Exhorter realizes how powerful is the exchange of white women, evident when he asks Invisible Man what made him join the Brotherhood, reasoning that the organization must have promised him their women.[79]

Arguably the most apparent illustration of Ellison's conflicted view of feminine values lies in his depiction of the Woman Question. After being told that he is no longer to work in Harlem, Invisible Man is informed by the Brotherhood that he is to lecture downtown on the Woman Question. Upon learning about his new assignment, Invisible Man is outraged: "I stood there, hearing the rapping of [Brother Jack's] gavel echoing in my ears, thinking the *woman question* and searching their faces for signs of amusement, listening to their voices as they filed out into the hall for the slightest sound of suppressed laughter, stood there fighting the sense that I had just been made the butt of an outrageous joke."[80] Ellison has Invisible Man finally reason that he should be honored to speak on such a taboo topic for a black man; however, he comes to this realization only after he thought it was an amusing joke, at best, or severe punishment, at worst. And, not surprisingly, the Woman Question is quickly dropped and left unanswered when Invisible Man is called back to Harlem; the implication is that there is more important work to do than lecture on women's issues. Neither Invisible Man nor Ellison seems to have much interest in fully exploring female concerns.

In one of the earliest essays to examine the representation of women in the novel, Carol Sylvander argues that it is peculiar for a work so consumed with the narrator's humanity to rely on familiar female types and stereotypes in a relatively straightforward manner. Likewise Catherine Saunders wonders "why Ellison's understanding of the mechanisms of invisibility stopped short of his recognizing men's projection of their own desires and fears onto women."[81] Summarizing feminist responses to *Invisible Man* in her article on Ellison's invisible women, Claudia Tate writes:

> Questions about the female characters in Ralph Ellison's *Invisible Man* seem to elicit two types of response: The initial one is, "What women?" since women clearly occupy peripheral roles in the novel. And then after Mary Rambo and the other female characters—that is, the old slave woman, the magnificent blonde, the rich sophisticate Emma, the anonymous seductress, and finally the prophetic and pathetic Sybil—are recalled, the second response is something like, "Oh, those stereotypes."[82]

Female characters are few and far between, and those included in the novel are overwhelmingly stereotypes without much apparent self-reflection, as noted by Rohrberger and Spillers. Taking Ellison to task for his depiction of women, they argue that these "women are one-dimensional figures playing roles in a drama written by men."[83]

Commenting specifically on the female characters in the Trueblood chapter, Spillers states:

> For all intents and purposes, the wife/mother Kate and the daughter/surrogate lover Matty Lou are deprived of speech, of tongue, since what they said and did and when are reported/translated through the medium of Trueblood. These silent figures, like materialized vectors in a field of force, are curiously silent.[84]

Unlike *Tender Is the Night*, in which Nicole Diver's voice and thoughts are included, in *Invisible Man*, Matty Lou's feelings are never shared with the reader. Because the entire tale of incest is told by Trueblood (and the rest of the novel told by Invisible Man), Matty Lou is deprived of speech, and the reader receives a limited account of the incest, never knowing the extent of her trauma, whether stemming from racism, familial abuse, or both.

To counter the charges leveled at Ellison for his complicated depiction of women, Tate contends that the gender politics are more vexed than has been allowed—and she made this argument in the early 1970s when, as Bradley says, the "drafts of *Invisible Man* still remained locked away in Ellison's personal files."[85] She states that Ellison starts with female stereotypes but then transcends them to dramatize their humanity. Tate argues that Invisible Man's encounters with these women teach him lessons about himself and the world. Following Tate's line of thinking, I suggest that part of Ellison's agenda in the Trueblood chapter can be viewed as proto-feminist in that Ellison hints at something that would not be fully articulated and acknowledged until the Second-Wave feminist movement, that violence, particularly in the sphere of the domestic, is central to maintaining the patriarchal order. In the late 1970s, feminists, such as Susan Brownmiller and Susan Griffin, questioned the existence of an incest taboo and noticed that the practice is not so much universally prohibited as selectively regulated. Paternal incest began to be seen as a paradigm of female victimization, with sexual access to the female as basic to patriarchal right. Violence against females was viewed as inherent in a patriarchal society, and rape and incest were acknowledged as ways to keep women in a state of fear by threatening their safety, limiting their mobility, and denigrating their self-worth.

In the second chapter of *Invisible Man*, Trueblood, who is smarter than Norton or even Invisible Man would be willing to admit, seems to understand that although incest is *said* to be an act of transgression, it is also a secretly sanctioned way to gain access to patriarchal phallocentrism. Discussing the black man's limited, if not outright denied, access to the patriarchal role, hooks argues in "Reconstructing Black Masculinity" that rape by black men should be viewed as a political action in which they act out their feelings of powerlessness in an attempt to gain entry into patriarchal culture.[86] Although many have read the second chapter as an illustration of Trueblood's allegiance to patriarchal ideals, this argument becomes problematic when we factor in that Trueblood most likely made up the entire story.

When thinking that Trueblood fashions his story, we might revisit the parts in which he casts Matty Lou as seductress and argue that he does so not necessarily to displace guilt and blame the vulnerable female, but to expose the hypocrisy of the civilized white men, most of whom want to attribute incest to the abnormal, poor, or racially othered. Trueblood seems to know that the prevalent thinking of that time held that girls were complicit in, if not encouraging, the incest: they were acting on their natural fantasies, as even the leading psychiatric textbooks maintained. In addition to conforming to expectations of black masculinity, as we have already seen, Trueblood closely adheres to the dominant story about incest. He understands that in these stories, the female must carry some, if not all, of the blame. Upon waking from his vivid dream, Trueblood says that he suddenly realizes he is on top of Matty Lou, who is repeatedly crying out "Daddy."[87] At this point in his narrative, Trueblood notes that Matty Lou has just recently become sexually active. He then questions, "maybe sometimes a man can look at a little ole pigtail gal and see him a whore—you'all know that?"[88] Careful readers should note this is directed at Norton, who, if not already sympathizing with Trueblood, now becomes an ally. Further commenting on Matty Lou's complicity, Trueblood interprets her sleepy mumbles to be what "a woman says when she wants to tease and please a man."[89] When trying to end the incest, Trueblood states that he is not the only one struggling with conflicted emotions.[90] According to Trueblood, "Matty Lou can't hold out no longer and gits to movin' herself."[91] Matty Lou, just like the white woman in his dream, grabs hold of him, and, as Trueblood says, "She didn't want me to go then—and to tell the honest-to-God truth I found out that I didn't want to go neither."[92] Cleverly, Trueblood exploits Norton's guilt for desiring his own daughter by portraying himself as the perverse father whose lowly rank in society allows him to do, or claim to have done, what Norton and other white men wished they could.

Similarly, the casting of wife Kate may be initially viewed as not much better than her daughter, but a careful reading shows her to be very important, perhaps even Ellison's mouthpiece. When Invisible Man and Norton pull up to the Trueblood cabin, a very pregnant Matty Lou and Kate are performing a typical female job—washing clothes. They set the stage nicely for Trueblood, who "airs the dirty laundry." As the women scurry off upon Invisible Man's and Norton's arrival, the implication is that these women are meant to be seen and not heard, a standard practice/role of the female in patriarchy. Emphasis is placed on their pregnant bodies, not on their voices, and one might think that Ellison is celebrating the poor farmer by making him the most fertile father in the entire novel and further subordinating the females by burdening them with the heavy motions of "far-gone pregnancy."[93]

However, Kate's actions and words bear another look for they reveal that she has the potential to be the moral center of the chapter and moreover, to pose the biggest challenge to patriarchal phallocentrism. As I quote in this chapter's title, Kate's response to her husband is significant. Upon discovering the incest, Trueblood tells us that she tries to do what she can to punish her husband and protect her daughter, even literally taking action into her own hands. For instance, she charges at Trueblood with weapons, finally harming him with an axe. Realizing what Trueblood did to their daughter and what she in turn did to Trueblood, Kate prays "Lawd, have mercy!"[94] Kate calls on God to help her family through the ordeal. Trueblood too claims to seek God for help, consulting the preacher for guidance, although we've seen how that ends. Having Kate and the black preacher react so vehemently indicates that black American folk values are more intolerant to incest than white middle- to upper-class values. When thinking that Trueblood ran off for good, Kate surrounds her daughter with "a heap of women" and even calls Aunt Cloe to perform an abortion on Matty Lou's baby, reasoning that this is the most humane outcome.[95] To conform to traditional expectations of patriarchal narratives, Trueblood claims to have come back to his home and assumed his rightful spot as head of the family: Trueblood says that he "made up [his] mind that [he] was goin' back home and face Kate; yeah, and face Matty Lou too."[96] Upon coming home, Kate confronts Trueblood, asking why he didn't just leave them alone. Despite Kate's protests, Trueblood insists that he is a man and "man don't leave his family."[97]

I find Kate's next words to be a rare moment in the chapter and even the entire book when Ellison exposes the dangers of adhering to patriarchal ideals. Kate cries, "Naw you ain't no man. No man'd do what you did."[98] With these few words, Kate challenges a system that has too often validated one's manhood by victimizing women. Because Trueblood includes this in his rendition to Norton, it can be read that Kate's words, filtered through Trueblood, question Norton's manhood by implicating a seemingly civilized white man who sexually longs for his own daughter. Cleverly, Trueblood gets away with such questioning because he gives these lines to Kate, a woman. Toward the end of his story, Trueblood explains that he runs off the heap of women and threatens to kill Cloe if she even touches a finger on any of "my womenfolks."[99] Not surprisingly, Trueblood makes it seem like Kate's only alternative, like her daughter's, is to retreat in silence. And yet, it sounds like Trueblood, who successfully externalizes stereotypes of black masculinity to challenge its social constructions, recognizes that these typecasts may be just as damaging to black females as stereotypes have been to black males.

As Trueblood tells his story of incest to a white man, Ellison tells his story of racism to a white audience. Said best by Toni Morrison, Ellison wrote for the "white gaze."[100] Morrison questions, "invisible to whom?"[101] Not to her. As the novel comes full circle, Ellison leaves his white readers to ponder white society's pervasive social blindness, which he juxtaposes with Invisible Man's newfound vision. In the final chapter Invisible Man has an epiphany in which he makes a connection between himself and Trueblood. Caught in a situation eerily similar to the one described by Trueblood in the second chapter, he says, "It was a state neither of dreaming nor of waking, but somewhere in between, in which I was caught like Trueblood's jaybird that yellow jackets had paralyzed in every part but his eyes."[102] In the second chapter, Trueblood first used the jaybird metaphor to explain to Invisible Man and Norton that he felt "frozen" once Kate discovered the incest: "I was just like a jaybird that the yellow jackets done stung 'til he's paralyzed—but still alive in his eyes and he's watchin' 'em sting his body to death."[103] At the very end of the novel as the narrator reflects on his journey, he realizes that he is not that different from Trueblood: they are both immobilized yet clearly see their situation and can place it in a larger context.

Recognizing his alliance with Trueblood, Invisible Man discovers his distance from Norton, and thereby from the patriarchy he represents. In the epilogue, the brief reunion between Invisible Man and Norton marks a turning point in Invisible Man's maturation in which Norton's persistent delusions contrast with his emerging perceptions. In the novel's concluding pages, Invisible Man runs into a disoriented Norton on a New York City subway. The "thinner," "wrinkled" Norton asks Invisible Man for directions to Centre Street.[104] Invisible Man, however, is struck by Norton's lack of recognition for a man whom he claimed as his destiny. Upon questioning, "But don't you really know who I am?" Invisible Man is disheartened to learn he neither recognizes him nor remembers claiming him as his future.[105] Furthermore, Norton is not in the least bit ashamed. At the end of their exchange, Invisible Man tells Norton that "if you don't know *where* you are, you probably don't know *who* you are."[106] "In the public space of the New York train," Johns writes, "the Invisible Man is at home with moral and social ambiguity, as well as verbal play, while Norton holds fast to the comparatively mechanical social privilege to which he is accustomed."[107] Invisible Man has a better understanding that Trueblood is one of the invisible men who use the power of the spoken word to combat the trauma he experiences because of the color of his skin.

At the end of his overview of *Invisible Man*'s critical reception, Robert Butler states, "Certainly much more needs to be said about Ellison's envisioning of female experience and how feminine values are an important part of his vision."[108] Undeniably seeing beyond the stereotypes of black masculinity, affirming black manhood, lies at the heart of Ellison's novel. *Invisible Man* is primarily concerned with how white society has failed to see the complexity (a word Ellison loved) of black male identity, nullifying and rendering it invisible. But we should also look closely to see why Ellison depicts his female characters as occupying subservient roles in patriarchal culture. Succeeding in challenging assumptions of black masculinity, the novel also contests white men's interests and privileges, especially those concerning the victimization of females. Just as Ellison uses Trueblood's lowly sharecropper position to disguise a subversive story directed at white men, he may also be strategically using Kate's lower rank to challenge the ideals of patriarchal phallocentrism.

NOTES

1. Ralph Ellison, *Invisible Man* (1952; New York: Vintage, 1995), 66.
2. Ibid.
3. Ibid.
4. Ibid.
5. bell hooks, "Reconstructing Black Masculinity," in *The Masculine Masquerade: Masculinity and Representation*, ed. Andrew Perchuk and Helaine Posner (Cambridge: MIT Press, 1995), 77.
6. Ibid., 76.
7. Ellison, *Invisible Man*, 33.
8. Jean-Christophe Cloutier, "The Comic Book World of Ralph Ellison's *Invisible Man*," *Novel: A Forum on Fiction* 43, no. 2 (2010): 296.
9. Gillian Johns, "Jim Trueblood and His Critic-Readers: Ralph Ellison's Rhetoric of Dramatic Irony and Tall Humor in the Mid-Century American Literary Public Sphere," *Texas Studies in Literature and Language* 49, no. 3 (2007): 231.
10. *Invisible Man* was published as a whole in 1952; however, copyright dates show the initial publication date as 1947, 1948. The discrepancy is explained by the fact that Ellison published fifteen pages of what would become *Invisible Man* in *Horizon*, Britain's highbrow art and literature journal, in 1947. In January 1948, John Hersey's *48 Magazine of the Year* included the novel's first chapter, "Battle Royal," as a short story.
11. Quoted in Adam Bradley, *Ralph Ellison in Progress: From* Invisible Man *to* Three Days Before the Shooting . . . (New Haven: Yale University Press, 2010), 14.

12. James Smethurst, "'Something Warmly, Infuriatingly Feminine': Gender, Sexuality, and the Work of Ralph Ellison," in *A Historical Guide to Ralph Ellison*, ed. Steven C. Tracey, 115–42 (Oxford: Oxford University Press, 2004), 138.
13. Shelley Jarenski, "Invisibility Embraced: The Abject as a Site of Agency in Ellison's *Invisible Man*," *MELUS* 35, no. 4 (2010): 92.
14. Ibid., 92–93.
15. Shanna Greene Benjamin, "There's Something about Mary: Female Wisdom and the Folk Presence in Ralph Ellison's *Invisible Man*," *Meridians* 12, no. 1 (2014): 125.
16. Arnold Rampersad, *Ralph Ellison: A Biography* (New York: Knopf, 2007), 225.
17. Smethurst, "Something Warmly, Infuriatingly Feminine," 133.
18. Michael D. Hill and Lena M. Hill, *Ralph Ellison's* Invisible Man*: A Reference Guide* (Westport: Greenwood, 2008), 136.
19. Robert J. Butler, introduction to *The Critical Response to Ralph Ellison*, ed. Robert J. Butler (Westport: Greenwood, 2000), xxxiii.
20. Selma Fraiberg, "Two Modern Incest Heroes," *Partisan Review* 28 (1961): 661.
21. Peter L. Hays, "The Incest Theme in *Invisible Man*," *Western Humanities Review* 23 (1969): 335.
22. Ellison, *Invisible Man*, 26.
23. Ibid., 46.
24. Ibid.
25. Ibid., 51, 54.
26. Ibid., 61.
27. Ibid., 54.
28. Ibid., 47.
29. Ibid., 54.
30. Ibid., 68.
31. Ibid., 37.
32. Ibid., 42.
33. Robert B. Stepto, "Literacy and Hibernation: Ralph Ellison's *Invisible Man*," in *Speaking for You: The Vision of Ralph Ellison*, ed. Kimberly Benston (Washington, D.C.: Howard University Press, 1987), 374.
34. Ellison, *Invisible Man*, 46.
35. Ibid., 51.
36. Mary Rohrberger, "'Ball the jack': Surreality, Sexuality, and the Role of Women in *Invisible Man*," in *Approaches to Teaching Ellison's* Invisible Man, ed. Susan Resneck Parr and Pancho Savery (New York: MLA, 1989), 127.
37. Hays, "The Incest Theme," 336.
38. Ellison, *Invisible Man*, 50.
39. Ibid., 51.
40. bell hooks, *We Real Cool: Black Men and Masculinity* (New York: Routledge, 2004), xii.
41. Ibid.
42. Ellison, *Invisible Man*, 47. Intraracism describes the phenomenon in which a racialized group internalizes white supremacy, and, in turn, self-loathing, and redirects the gaze and judgment at members of its own community. Those individuals at the lighter end of the spectrum are considered more attractive, and therefore privileged, whereas dark skin is stigmatized. Ellison addresses the stratified color line in a 1964 interview in which he reiterates the "old saying amongst Negroes: If you're black, stay back; if you're brown, stick around; if you're white, you're right" ("The Influence" 864). For one of the earliest critical uses of the word *intraracism*, see Wallace Thurman, "Harlem Facets," in *The Collected Writings of Wallace Thurman: A Harlem Renaissance Reader*, ed. Amritjit Singh and Daniel M. Scott III (1927; New Brunswick: Rutgers University Press, 2003). For a more recent article that explores intraracism and African American artistic expression, see Faedra Chatard Carpenter, "Addressing 'The Complex'-ities of Skin Color: Intra-Racism and the Plays of Hurston, Kennedy, and Orlandersmith," *Theatre Topics* 19, no. 1 (2009): 15–27.

43. As Baker sees it, "From Freud's point of view, Trueblood's dream and subsequent incest seem to represent a historical regression," revealing "man in what might be called his presocial and unaccommodated state." Houston A. Baker, "To Move Without Moving: An Analysis of Creativity and Commerce in Ralph Ellison's Trueblood Episode," in *The Critical Response to Ralph Ellison*, ed. Robert J. Butler (Westport: Greenwood, 2000), 78. In case we missed the Freudian undertones in the Trueblood chapter, Ellison plants a reminder later in the novel in which "An open book, something called *Totem and Taboo*," was resting on the desk of the homosexual Emerson Jr. (180). But as John Hersey quotes Ellison as saying in another context, "none of the Freudian explanations seem adequate" to fully explain what he is doing in the Trueblood chapter. John Hersey, "'A Completion of Personality': A Talk with Ralph Ellison," in *Speaking for You: The Vision of Ralph Ellison* (Washington, D. C.: Howard University Press, 1987), 291.
44. Ellison, *Invisible Man*, 62.
45. Ibid., 57.
46. Ibid.
47. Ibid.
48. Ibid., 57–58.
49. Ibid., 58.
50. Ibid.
51. Hortense Spillers, "The Permanent Obliquity of an In(pha)llibly Straight': In the Time of the Daughters and the Fathers," in *Changing Our Own Words: Essays on Criticism, Theory, and Writing by Black* Women, ed. Cheryl A. Wall (New Brunswick: Rutgers University Press, 1989), 135.
52. Ellison, *Invisible Man*, 59.
53. Ibid.
54. Ibid., 66.
55. Ibid., 61.
56. Ibid., 62.
57. Ibid., 66.
58. Ibid., 52.
59. Ibid., 68.
60. Ibid., 47.
61. Ibid., 58.
62. Ibid., 581.
63. Ibid., 53.
64. Ibid., 52.
65. Ibid., 53.
66. Baker, "To Move Without Moving," 80–81.
67. Ellison, *Invisible Man*, 67.
68. Ibid., 49, 52.
69. Ibid., 52.
70. Ibid., 38.
71. Ibid., 69.
72. Ibid., 53.
73. Bradley, *Ralph Ellison in Progress*, 145.
74. Ibid., 146.
75. Ibid., 148.
76. Ibid., 195.
77. Ibid., 147.
78. Ellison, *Invisible Man*, 153.
79. Ibid., 372.
80. Ibid., 407.
81. Catherine E. Saunders, "Makers or Bearers of Meaning? Sex and the Struggle for Self-Definition in Ralph Ellison's *Invisible Man*," *Critical Matrix* 5, no. 1 (1989): n.p.

82. Claudia Tate, "Notes on the Invisible Women in Ralph Ellison's *Invisible Man,*" in *Speaking for You: The Vision of Ralph Ellison*, ed. Kimberly Benston (Washington, D.C.: Howard University Press, 1987), 163.
83. Rohrberger, "Ball the jack," 130.
84. Spillers, "The Permanent Obliquity," 132.
85. Bradley, *Ralph Ellison in Progress*, 149.
86. hooks, "Reconstructing Black Masculinity," 76.
87. Ellison, *Invisible Man*, 59.
88. Ibid.
89. Ibid., 56.
90. Ibid., 60.
91. Ibid.
92. Ibid.
93. Ibid., 47.
94. Ibid., 65.
95. Ibid., 66.
96. Ibid.
97. Ibid.
98. Ibid.
99. Ibid., 67.
100. Pam Houston, "Pam Houston Talks with Toni Morrison," in *Toni Morrison: Conversations*, ed. Carolyn Denard (Jackson: University Press of Mississippi, 2008), 253.
101. Ibid.
102. Ellison, *Invisible Man*, 568.
103. Ibid., 63.
104. Ibid., 577.
105. Ibid., 578.
106. Ibid.
107. Johns, "Jim Trueblood and His Critic-Readers," 250.
108. Butler, *The Critical Response*, xxxvii.\

THREE

Morrison Responds to the Psychological Community in *The Bluest Eye*

In a 1992 interview with Christopher Bigsby, Toni Morrison stated that she desired a female voice that was not present in Ellison's odyssey:

> The works of . . . Ralph Ellison . . . were not talking to me. There was some editorial address going on as though [he was] clarifying something for other men, or maybe white people. . . . I know now that what I was longing for was a female presence, not a female character but a female voice. There was an attitude and a gaze that I wanted to read through. So, since I wanted it so desperately, I created it.[1]

Like *Invisible Man*, Morrison's *The Bluest Eye* can be read as a search for an authentic identity in a white culture that exploits black existence.[2] And like Ellison, Morrison connects paternal incest to other forms of oppression, illustrating that incest is used to produce power instead of signal social collapse. However, departing from Ellison in significant ways, Morrison's novel makes visible not only black men, but young, poor, black girls who had never been granted center stage in literature—ever. Moreover, *The Bluest Eye* was the first novel to give full expression to a character suffering from complex trauma caused by father–daughter incest, captured in her own voice.

An early version of the novel employed third-person narration to tell the story of Pecola and the Breedlove family. Dissatisfied with its ability to engage the reader, Morrison revised the point of view to introduce the perspective of Claudia MacTeer, who grew up black and poor, a "could-be victim" of father–daughter incest herself.[3] Serving as main narrator of the fragmented account, Claudia reflects on the experiences of Pecola and bears witness to her friend's trauma through narrative. Diverging from the male literary tradition, Morrison has Claudia's perspective, divided between her nine-year-old and adult self, dominate the story.

In addition to being a pioneering work for narrating from the "could-be victim's" perspective, *The Bluest Eye* marks a turning point in father–daughter incest narratives. It was a novel of many firsts because it reoriented the treatment of incest from a symbolic level to a more realistic one to center on the daughter's experience. Crediting Morrison's bravery at openly addressing incest, along with racial self-loathing and intraracism, Adrienne Seward explains that the novel "dealt with a lot of no-no's," subjects "that weren't supposed to be discussed in the black community."[4] In the midst of a long-standing history of black women's sexual violation, Morrison criticized patterns of patriarchal dominance in the black community; its act of breaking the community's silence was thought by some to be even more taboo than the act of incest itself. Some viewed it as performing a disservice to the black community for exposing intraracial sexual and domestic violence. It still remains a controversial book; in August 2005, the Board of Education in Littleton, Colorado, banned *The Bluest Eye* from both its curriculum and library bookshelves after receiving "complaints about its explicit sex, including the rape of an 11-year-old girl by her father."[5]

Deeply invested in revealing the pain of incest, *The Bluest Eye* was ahead of its time and close to two decades passed before critics recognized the importance of the work, as Morrison points out in her 1993 afterword. Given the novel's initial lukewarm reception and the lack of attention placed on Pecola, she states that it took twenty-five years for society to acknowledge the oppression of young girls, particularly poor, black girls like Pecola.[6] Rejected by twelve publishers, one of whom claimed that the book lacked structure, it was out of print by 1974 after its initial publication with Holt, Rinehart and Winston. Although published in the midst of Second-Wave feminism "'when a growing, middle-class women's movement was just beginning to acknowledge the reality of its black and poor sisters,' an overview of the critical discourse of the time shows that from the readership the book received little, if any, understanding."[7] Morrison acknowledges its mixed reviews: "It got a really horrible review in *The New York Times Book Review* . . . and then got a very good daily review."[8] It was not a commercial success, earning Morrison only $3,000 and receiving less critical acclaim than most of her later works.[9] According to Nancy Peterson, it took five years for the first scholarly treatment of *The Bluest Eye* to even appear; however, Joan Bischoff's "The Novels of Toni Morrison: Studies in Thwarted Sensitivity" missed Morrison's essential concerns and seemed to confirm her fear that black female writers would not receive proper scholarly attention.[10]

There has been an impressive growth in Morrison scholarship in the last three decades as thousands of pages of criticism have been published that makes approaching the novel that launched her career a daunting task. According to Marc Conner, "no living American author has commanded more attention and critical production" between 1980 and 2000, and it is safe to say that Morrison, the first African American to receive the Nobel Prize, is the most lauded black female author of the twentieth century.[11] In addition to edited collections devoted exclusively to *The Bluest Eye,* there are numerous essays on Morrison in compilations, monographs, and literary journals. Critical discourse has focused on the significance of Pecola's name, the role of religion, magic realism, blues aesthetics, Morrison's intended audience, her influences, and whom she influenced. What is missing from the discussions of *The Bluest Eye* is how Morrison's novel can be read as a response to the psychological community.

This chapter explores the novel to gain a better understanding of the problems of telling, and of bearing witness to, incest during the 1960s and 1970s, when the act was thought to be rare and not inherently traumatic. It closely reads the incest scene to argue that the novel could be read as Morrison challenging the psychological community regarding their misled understanding of paternal incest. It argues that the novel does not lack structure, as one of the rejecting publishers said, but it is a carefully constructed narrative with aesthetic design that includes the male perspective while bringing the experience of the female to the fore. Although Morrison includes many pages detailing the trauma that men of color often experience, and in so doing extends sympathy to incestuous father figures, she remains in control of their sections, especially the Cholly chapter, which culminates in the incest scene. She never simply hands over narration but presents his thoughts through a third-person limited perspective, and one that is not Claudia's. In the Cholly chapter we are given his view but not his voice, as we gain understanding about how and why the incest happened. Morrison illustrates that psychic distress can be the consequence of not just one devastating event, but the result of long exposure to humiliation and abuse.[12] And she considers the effects these multiple violations have on Pecola, the community's scapegoat whose perspective is rendered in a first-person, dissociated narration, which offers an accurate depiction of someone suffering from CPTSD. It ends with a discussion of how Morrison's novel signifies on Ellison's work and the significant changes she made to include the feminine voice.

Although her book cannot be called autobiographical, Morrison, like Ellison, pulls "straight out of what autobiographical information [she] had," as she tells Robert Stepto.[13] The pulse of the novel first ran through her in 1962 and by 1965 began to take book form. The seeds grew out of a conversation she had with one of her elementary school friends, who told Morrison "she knew that God did not exist because her prayers for blue eyes had gone unanswered."[14] Troubled by the mental image of a beautiful black girl with blue eyes, the synecdoche for white beauty, Morrison wondered who told her she wasn't good enough without them. Aside from personal reasons for bringing the book to fruition, Morrison attributes its publication to social and political concerns: dissatisfied with the lack of young black female characters in published novels, she exclaimed that "nobody had taken a little black girl seriously in literature."[15]

In reading the works of black men, Morrison noted that "Things [were] going too fast in 1965," and she was afraid that these real girls were going to get skipped over.[16] *The Bluest Eye* is her attempt to capture the time before the 1960s revolution when "black is beautiful" became a rallying cry, and to remember why it became a necessary statement in the first place. Developing a minor scene in *Invisible Man* when the protagonist sees an advertisement in a Harlem store window for a product that promises a whiter complexion, Morrison reflects throughout her novel on the time when black was seen as ugly. She notes that some black women would go to devastating extremes to do what the dominant white society required—"get rid of the funkiness. The dreadful funkiness of passion, the funkiness of nature, the funkiness of the wide range of human emotions."[17] Morrison states that for women who subscribe to such ideas, the funkiness is embodied in a number of ways—a laugh too loud, a gesture too generous, a behind swaying too freely, and lips lined a little too fully.[18] The vigil for eruptions of funk had to be constant. Later Pecola, with her dirty torn dress, matted plaits, muddy shoes, soiled socks, and safety pin in place of where a hem should have been, is seen as embodying the dreaded funk and reprimanded for it—even by her own mother. She is indoctrinated at an early age into a society that discriminates, labeling some plants flowers and others weeds, as one of the novel's scenes makes painfully evident.

Two time periods are of interest when discussing *The Bluest Eye*: the 1960s to 1970s when the novel was written and published and the 1930s to 1940s when the novel is set. These decades were marked by overt racial tensions in the predominantly white United States. Like the protagonist of *Invisible Man, The Bluest Eye*'s denizens, specifically Pecola's parents, journeyed north during the Great Migration, coming from places like Mobile, Alabama; Aiken, South Carolina; Newport News, Virginia; Marietta, Georgia; and Baton Rouge, Louisiana, looking for a better life. However, even the northern town of Lorain, Ohio, where the Breedloves settle, is not immune to racial segregation, as pointed out in Claudia's passing comment about Lake Shore Park where no black people were allowed.[19] Job opportunities were not much better. The best that Pauline Breedlove could do was keep house for a white family.

During the 1930s and 1940s, when Pecola, Claudia, and Claudia's sister, Frieda, came of age, the culture valued neither blackness nor femininity. They grew up conditioned to see themselves as lesser beings, experiencing insidious forms of trauma that ultimately enabled incest and other forms of violence to occur. The Shirley Temple doll reigned as cultural icon queen. (It would take another twenty-five years for Barbie to make her debut.) Although Claudia resists embracing the white values, Pecola and even Frieda have a much harder time. They had conversations "about how cu-ute Shirley Temple was."[20] Perhaps it is no coincidence that the girls who buy into these standards of female beauty are the ones most susceptible to violation. In addition to Pecola and her father, Frieda is molested by the MacTeer's boarder, "Mr. Henry" Washington. Morrison also strategically opens her novel by having Claudia cite the autumn of 1941, just before the December 7, 1941, attack on Pearl Harbor. On the brink of the United States entering World War II, Morrison's setting recalls the Nazi genocide and calls attention to the irony that the United States failed to see its own eugenics movement and allegiance to racial purity and preference for blonde-haired, blue-eyed people while fighting Hitler and his henchmen.

Morrison exposes the damaging internalization of white standards and the black community's uncritical submission to the values of white beauty and their consequent complicity in racial self-loathing. This taboo topic was "terribly, terribly important" to Morrison who noticed its glaring absence in literature.[21] To undercut the power of white ideology and standards of beauty, Morrison opens with a subversive appropriation of William Elson and William Gray's nationally known Dick and Jane primer stories, which were widely used in elementary schools across the United States from the 1930s through the 1970s. Breaking up, running together, and deconstructing the primer's text on her novel's first page and in subsequent chapter headings, she reveals how these readers, while promoting literacy, disseminated racist, classist messages at the expense of black children, whose existence they effectively erased. The Breedloves and even the MacTeers serve as the antithesis to this idyllic image of home and family.

WORSE FOR THE EXPERIENCE

At the time Morrison crafted her first novel, the thinking regarding incest had not changed much since Fitzgerald's day; it was still thought to be an anomaly. As late as 1975, five years after *The Bluest Eye*'s publication, the authoritative psychiatric textbook (Freedman and Kaplan's *Comprehensive Textbook of Psychiatry*) stated that the act was extremely rare, affecting one out of 1.1 million people.[22] The leaders of psychiatry went on to note, "incestuous acts are, at least to some degree, collusive. In father–daughter incest, for example, the father is aided and abetted in his liaison by conscious or unconscious seduction by his daughter, and by his wife's collusion related to her hostility toward her daughter."[23] (They mention that sibling incest is "sometimes almost normal."[24]) And, they conclude, "incestuous relationships do not always seem to have a traumatic effect"; the consequences [of father–daughter incest] were thought to be "gratifying and pleasurable," as the act afforded "an opportunity to test in reality an infantile fantasy."[25] Moreover, they write, "It has even been suggested that the ego's capacity for sublimation is favored by the pleasure afforded by incest and that such incestuous activity diminishes the subject's chance of psychosis and allows a better adjustment to the external world."[26] They sum it up by saying that one study found "the vast majority of [these females] to be none the worse for the experience."[27]

During the incest scene, Morrison dramatizes the complex trauma suffered by the Breedloves as a family and refuses to isolate Cholly's sexual violation of Pecola from the larger context of racism and domestic imperialism. She does not divorce the single act of incest from the larger cycle of abuse. In so doing, she makes it difficult to blame any individual; her mission is not to indict people, but to bear witness to the victims of systemic violence. Morrison devotes a thirty-page chapter to providing Cholly's formative experiences and to witnessing how he is simultaneously victim and victimizer. Unlike the Trueblood tale that takes up the better part of one chapter, Morrison places incest at the center of her story. No dreams of white women's bedrooms decorated with tall grandfather clocks preface the incest passage in Morrison's work, as they do in Ellison's. Instead, the events leading up to the incident are far more nightmarish and hellish than Trueblood probably imagined. Likewise, no ready ears listen to Cholly narrate the event. In other words, *The Bluest Eye* contains no Norton longing to hear the story of how the black father impregnated his daughter, and no hundred-dollar bills are handed to Cholly at the tale's end. Instead of having Cholly emerge as wealthy and wise, or at least remorseful, after the experience, Morrison shows the forces that have led to his aggression and, arguably, his distorted expression of love. And yet, despite depicting father–daughter incest in all of its contradictions—including using what Morrison has called "feminized language," which describes what could be interpreted as an affectionate touch—Morrison shows that her characters are certainly the worse for the experience.

Before the reader even turns to the Cholly chapter, Morrison provides a couple of prefatory pages painting him with the stereotypical traits of the black man as irresponsible, abusive, and criminal, as Ellison had showcased through Trueblood, but then she departs by explaining how he got to be that way. He is at first defined as an incestuous father who impregnated his daughter, "had dropped his seeds in his own plot of black dirt."[28] In the beginning pages, the reader is introduced to "Dog Breedlove," who "had burned up his house, gone upside his wife's head, and everybody, as a result, was outdoors."[29] He makes Pecola and her brother welfare cases. Already established as poor, "a renting black," Cholly adds insult to injury by taking away the roof over his family's head, further showing how far the Breedloves are not only from the ideal

Dick and Jane storybook family, but also how outsided and othered they are from even their own black community who put Cholly in the ranks of animals—"an old dog, a snake, a ratty nigger."[30] Like Fitzgerald's Warren, he is no stranger to alcohol, described as drunk at least twice, including during the incest scene.

Tactically, through an omniscient narrator distinguished from Claudia, Morrison provides her reader with his dark history before she gives the account of Pecola's rape. The narrative positions readers to see the wounded and wounding Cholly and his unconscious effort to master the humiliation of his own sexuality. Making coherent the pieces of Cholly's traumatic past, as she claims only a musician could do, she shows him as lifelong victim.[31] From the beginning of his chapter, the reader knows that he never stood a chance to succeed in society, for his father left town before he was born and his mother abandoned him when he was a mere four days old. Knowing that his parents didn't want anything to do with him, it is no wonder that he doesn't know how to be a father to his own children, Pecola and Sammy: the latter, ironically named after Cholly's neglectful father, had run away at least twenty-seven times by the age of fourteen. When Cholly is that age, the one stable figure in his life, Aunt Jimmy, dies, leaving Cholly once again an orphan.[32] His efforts to reunite with his estranged father meet with disaster, as Samson Fuller dismisses his son in no uncertain terms: "Tell that bitch she get her money. Now, get the fuck outta my face!"[33] These words sting him, and the scene concludes with a soiled Cholly curled in the fetal position crying for his dead Aunt Jimmy. Morrison sums up his familial trauma: "Abandoned in a junk heap by his mother, rejected for a crap game by his father, there was nothing more to lose."[34]

By the time the reader gets to the end of Cholly's chapter, it is clear that the father–daughter incest completes the puzzle that is Cholly's traumatic life. The incest scene serves as a reminder of two other sexual experiences, his first time with Darlene and when he met his wife Pauline, both of which had a profound effect on Cholly's psyche. We're told that when a drunk Cholly stumbled home that spring Saturday afternoon, he was full of emotions, widely ranging from revulsion and rage to guilt and love. This scene calls to mind Cholly's initiating sexual experience, which helps to explain the hatred, helplessness, and anger. During Aunt Jimmy's funeral reception, a traumatic event in itself, Cholly has sex with Darlene. This experience is initially marked by curiosity and first-time innocence, as the narrator notes: "Their bodies began to make sense to him, and it was not as difficult as he had thought it would be."[35] However, the difficult part comes in due time. Cholly notices that two white hunters are standing over him, watching as they have sex. Like Trueblood, who entertains the white folks with his tale of incest, Cholly, the target of white discrimination, is made to perform at gunpoint for the racist raccoon hunters, whose "flashlight made a moon on his behind" as they instruct him to "Get on wid it," and to "make it good, nigger."[36]

Internalizing white supremacist constructions of masculinity all too quickly, Cholly directs feelings of hatred, not onto the white men, but onto the black girl, whom he then rapes. Morrison tells us why in a passage worth quoting at length:

> Never did he once consider directing his hatred toward the hunters. Such an emotion would have destroyed him. They were big, white, armed men. He was small, black, helpless. His subconscious knew what his conscious mind did not guess—that hating them would have consumed him, burned him up like a piece of soft coal, leaving only flakes of ash and a question mark of smoke. He was, in time, to discover that hatred of white men—but not now. Not in impotence but later, when the hatred could find sweet expression. For now, he hated the one who had created the situation, the one who bore witness to his failure, his impotence. The one whom he had not been able to protect, to spare, to cover from the round moon glow of the flashlight.[37]

Cholly, part of a subjugated group powerless to change the larger society, turns on his own. His "impotence," noted twice in this passage, suggests that he is emasculated in a society where femininity is equated with helplessness and is primed into thinking that venting his anger on weaker women like Darlene and later Pecola is acceptable.

Casting Pecola during the incest scene as bearing "witness to his failure, his impotence," the narrator shares some of Cholly's thoughts, which emerge as unanswerable questions, including "What could he do for her? and "What of his knowledge of the world and of life could be useful to her?"[38] What Morrison herself calls the "rape" of Cholly is important for seeing his thwarted sexual awakening as well as how his hatred for white men mistakenly finds expression as rape of black women.[39] Just as it is no wonder why he doesn't know how to be a good father—for he never had one himself—it is also understandable why he doesn't comprehend sex—for his first time ends in complete humiliation.

Furthermore, during the incest scene the narrator tells us that his daughter's act of leaning over the kitchen sink brings back fond memories of when Cholly met Pauline. Morrison writes, "it was Pauline, or rather marrying her, that did for him what the flashlight did not do."[40] In linking married life with the flashlight of the racist hunters, Morrison connects the fragments of Cholly's life, and suggests that marriage at first holds the potential for Cholly to reclaim some of his lost manhood and to right the wrongs he has suffered. As he sees his daughter washing a frying pan in the kitchen sink, shifting her weight to one foot to use the other to scratch the back of her calf, the gesture reminds him of Pauline's "timid, tucked-in" toe performing the same duty.[41] Confusing his wife and his daughter, Cholly sees a hunched-over figure in need of help. His feelings of anger and hatred mix with "softness," "tenderness," and "protectiveness," which complicates a reading of this scene as forceful rape.[42]

In her afterword, Morrison admits that her rendering of the incest scene is even more offensive because of Cholly's complicated emotions. She writes,

> It is interesting to me now that where I thought I would have the most difficulty subverting the language to a feminine mode, I had the least: connecting Cholly's "rape" by the white men to his own of his daughter. This most masculine act of aggression becomes feminized in my language, "passive," and, I think, more accurately repellant when deprived of the male "glamour of shame" rape is (or once was) routinely given.[43]

Morrison's account of incest is not described as a brutal act, unlike what we'll read in *Bastard Out of Carolina*. Rather, as he crawls on all fours toward his daughter, he catches her as she falls and proceeds with what first stems from a desire to protect and defend her.

It comes as no surprise that Cholly, who has learned that violence and intimacy go together, is confused by how to express love. The incest is not an eruption of some innate "funk" that many thought predisposes black men to rape, but is, rather, a reenactment of his childhood trauma with Darlene as well as a connection to the first time he met the woman who would go on to become his wife. "By the time you get [to the rape scene] it's almost irrelevant," Morrison comments, "because I want you to *look* at [Cholly] and see his love for his daughter and his powerlessness to help her pain. By that time, his embrace, the rape, is all the gift he has left."[44] One of the most difficult parts of the kitchen incest scene, and the entire novel, is that, like Ellison, Morrison hints that the father's actions are misguided manifestations of love. In recognizing how much his daughter resembles his wife, Cholly is filled with feelings of tenderness, which complicates the depiction of black masculinity as predatory in nature. The word *tender* or a form thereof litters the two-and-a-half-page scene along with a litany of questions in which Cholly wonders what he can do to be a better father. Phyllis Klotman observes that the rape may very well be the only expression of love that Pecola receives.[45] The rendition of incest is filtered through a third-person narrator that closely adheres to the consciousness and experience of Cholly, leaving Pecola silenced throughout the scene, uttering only one sound—"a hollow suck of air in the back of her throat."[46] Because Pecola is characterized throughout the narrative as "no more than a sigh," the reader is invited, much like in *Invisible Man*, to focus on the father's perspective.[47] Whatever Morrison's reasons for this may be, she succeeds in writing an account of incest that challenges the leading psychiatric textbook by not showing the daughter as seductive and the father as gratified.

Additionally, the topic of incest does come up again later in the novel when Morrison introduces her readers to Soaphead Church, whose chapter is juxtaposed between Cholly's and Pecola's. Soaphead Church, "an old man who loved things," who is said to have dabbled in the "budding field of psychiatry," is as strange as his name.[48] The narrator explains that no one remembered where the "Church" came from; they assumed it was from his days as a guest preacher. Everyone, however, knew that the "Soaphead" part was in reference to his embodied funk: "the tight, curly hair that took on and held a sheen and wave when pomaded with soap lather. A sort of primitive process."[49] A "cinnamon-eyed West Indian with lightly browned skin," Soaphead is a self-proclaimed psychic and hoodoo spiritualist.[50] He is the one Pecola seeks out after the incest results in pregnancy, asking for blue eyes, essentially to be beautiful. Like Cholly, he was traumatized by abandonments—his mother's early death and his wife's desertion. The first mention of him comes before Cholly's chapter, when the reader hears about his reputation for molesting young girls. When Frieda is inappropriately touched by Mr. Henry, Claudia questions what Mr. Henry did to Frieda, asking if he "picked" at her, "like Soaphead Church."[51] With the proliferation of perverse father figures—Cholly, Soaphead, and Mr. Henry—Morrison further illustrates that the sexual violation of young females is an extensive problem.[52]

Through the interracial and racially conscious character of Soaphead, Morrison extends her critique of white supremacy beyond the United States to include its effects on British colonized islands in the West Indies, where some were deluded into thinking that incest and inbreeding with the whiter members of their family were preferable in the quest to lighten up their lines, to get rid of the funkiness. Soaphead comes from a long line of people who are products of miscegenation. Proud of their diverse bloodlines, Soaphead's family claims a "Sir Whitcomb," a "decaying British nobleman," as their patriarch.[53] This British "nobleman" impregnated an enslaved black woman, who then hoped for social advancement after birthing a light-skinned child. Sir Whitcomb's descendants are grateful to him for introducing the white strain into the family in the early 1800s. In an effort to maintain their white traits, "some distant and some not so distant relatives married each other."[54] In other words, incest was accepted, if not encouraged. In response to the psychiatric book's normalizing of cousin and sibling incest, Morrison shows the fruits of the efforts: a misanthropic misfit who has come to deny all his urges save for his attraction to little girls.

PECOLA'S VOICE

Just how much the worse Pecola is from the experience is revealed in a chapter told from her point of view. For all the book did to undermine the medical understanding of incest, it was not without its critics—including Morrison herself, who views her first novel as "something of a failure."[55] In an interview with Stephen Colbert on November 19, 2014, Morrison was asked if she was ever tempted to rewrite any of her books and if there is anything she would have done differently. Singling out *The Bluest Eye* from her oeuvre, Morrison replied that she made a "fairly substantial mistake" in "not doing justice to one of the characters." Not naming Pecola Breedlove, Morrison is certainly referring to this girl, a character she says she did not like. She laments that she never paid her much attention.

In her afterword, Morrison has also expressed her disappointment with her rendering of, or failure to render, Pecola's perspective, especially during the incest scene. She identifies the book's main flaw as

> the silence at its center: the void that is Pecola's "unbeing," . . . It should have had a shape—like the emptiness left by a boom or a cry. It required a sophistication unavailable to me, and some deft manipulation of the voices around her. She is not *seen* by herself until she hallucinates a self. And the fact of her hallucination becomes a kind of outside-the-book conversation.[56]

Because Pecola is a rather tangential presence throughout the text, the work has been criticized in recent years for not being feminist enough. Commenting on the relationship between voice and empowerment, some have faulted the novel for not offering Pecola's private thoughts in first-person narration until madness descends; in other words, for silencing the dispossessed protagonist while seeking to redress power relations. Pin-chia Feng thinks that the work ultimately fails because, narrated mostly by Claudia, it omits Pecola's perspective.[57] Contending that the story is over before Pecola begins to speak, Janice Doane and Devon Hodges are dissatisfied with the experimental chapter where, they claim, Pecola fails to find a voice.[58] Monica Michlin criticizes the novel's "ambiguous" structure that silences the child, "in what could be read as an additional move of abuse and victimization."[59] She adds, "the fact that Pecola does not survive psychically and that the story is told by everyone *but* her is one of the things that feminist writers have necessarily revised since."[60]

Pecola's voice is unfortunately muted during the incest scene, as she utters no words and makes one ambiguous action—gripping Cholly's wrists; it is never quite clear if she does so out of disgust to push him off of her or out of desire to hold him there. Also, a fourth of the novel is told from a third-person perspective of the male characters with consecutive pages detailing their traumatic experiences. The reader is privy to Cholly's conflicted emotions and difficult questions. Had Morrison ended with his chapter, I too would have been disappointed and read the novel as another form of objectifying and victimizing the daughter figure by privileging the male perspective.

And yet, Morrison's novel does not end there. Unlike Ellison but like Fitzgerald, Morrison's work contains the daughter's voice, an entire chapter in which Pecola attempts to author her story of trauma. At the time Pecola breaks her silence, no one is there to bear witness, but, by piecing together vague conversations and community gossip, Claudia testifies and bears witness to Pecola's traumatic story. As the psychological costs of Pecola's "beauty" become apparent, access into her thoughts and voice—albeit divided voice—are nonetheless present at the end of the text. Just as she had granted perspective to Cholly, who is an otherwise invisible man, Morrison also gives voice to Pecola and, as Fitzgerald had done, presents a realistic portrayal of a female character suffering from complex post-traumatic stress disorder brought on by father–daughter incest.

At the time the book was published, official recognition of PTSD in the medical community was still ten years on the horizon, not included in the *DSM* until 1980. And yet, Morrison validates not just PTSD but anticipates CPTSD through her characterization of Pecola, who struggles with not just feeling like herself since the incest, but questions her sense of self. Many who experience chronic trauma present with additional symptoms alongside those of formal PTSD, including maladaptation to stressful situations and misperceptions of their self-concept. Unlike PTSD, which is typically the result of a traumatic event of time-limited duration, such as a hurricane or car accident, CPTSD captures severe prolonged psychological harm and makes one more susceptible to psychological fragmentation, revictimization, and losing a sense of safety, trust, and self-worth. The loss of a coherent sense of self most pointedly differentiates CPTSD from PTSD. Morrison's use of the word "unbeing" when describing Pecola in her afterword provides a clue that this is a character who suffers from CPTSD.

In the dialogue between Pecola and what one may consider her dissociated alter or an imaginary friend, Morrison illustrates her protagonist's disjointed self, which was overwhelmed as a result of the incest and other traumatic factors that led to that Saturday afternoon, and how those experiences could not be integrated into her existing mental framework. As a coping mechanism, Pecola banishes them from her consciousness, but not successfully, as we see when the trauma returns as fragments that get relived and repeated in her psyche. During her attempt to narrate her painful experience, the reader finds out that Sammy ran away for good, Pecola no longer attends school, and she has finally gotten, or thinks she's gotten, what she wanted all along—the bluest eyes. We also hear that she was revictimized, a characteristic of CPTSD: the incest happened more than once, at least twice. Significantly, we learn all this information from Pecola herself.

In this twelve-page section, Morrison offers a realistic depiction of a victim who has dissociated her traumatic experiences in self-defense. It is Pecola's last-ditch attempt to minister to her wounded self. Typical of many incest victims, Pecola faints after the first rape and experiences visual and auditory hallucinations, delusional thinking, and high paranoid anxiety. Much like her hallucination, her loss of consciousness lends support to what many trauma theorists think happens as a result of a traumatic event: "Pecola's fainting depicts not only the somatic reactions that occur in extreme states of shame—which include physiological responses such as 'fainting, dizziness, rigidity of all the muscles'—but also the physical and mental paralysis experienced by the trauma victim."[61] Morrison represents Pecola's response with almost clinical precision, anticipating recent discussions about the social and political context of family trauma.

Her chapter provides information about her present state and also her past experiences, perhaps the most important being a second occurrence of incest. In the conversation, the alter ponders Cholly's sexual power over Pauline, which quickly turns into a question about how Pecola let Cholly sexually violate her. When asking why she didn't tell her mother, the alter states, *"I don't mean about the first time. I mean about the second time, when you were sleeping on the couch."*[62] Instead of denying the incest, Pecola corrects her: "I wasn't sleeping! I was reading!"[63] Another question is posed: *"So that's why you didn't tell her about the second time?"*[64] Pecola admits, "She wouldn't have believed me then either."[65] Although Pecola rushes on to other topics (Sammy, her blue eyes), the reader may have a difficult time overlooking Pecola's disclosure. Unlike the details of that Saturday afternoon when Cholly "staggered home reeling drunk," Morrison withholds information of the second offense.[66] Aside from suggesting that Cholly is a repeat offender, she leaves it to readers to judge him and to decide the moral repercussions of incest happening more than once, along with our assessments of Pauline, who fails to believe her daughter.

Keeping within Pecola's character, Morrison does not give her the language to describe the second time, thus remaining unable to work through her trauma. As we've seen throughout most of the book, notably during the first incest scene, Pecola is a character who lives outside of language. Morrison explains in her afterword that Pecola "does not have the vocabulary to understand the violence or its context."[67] When we get to her chapter, it should come as no surprise that the exchange she has with herself is at times incoherent. Morrison's experimental Pecola chapter, as Michael Awkward and others observe, gives new meaning to W. E. B. DuBois's theory of double consciousness, "this sense of always looking at one's self through the eyes of others, of measuring one's soul by the tape of a world that looks on in amused contempt and pity."[68] In this chapter, we see Pecola go from no voice to two. Pecola looks at herself through the eyes of white society and those in her community who have internalized its standards; she is left questioning if her eyes are blue enough, forever asking for beauty and acceptance. She is unable to tell her story and fails to find her voice in madness. The best she can do is struggle to reconcile her dissociated other into a whole. By the novel's end she becomes almost as indecipherable as the third rendition of the unpunctuated, indistinguishable Dick and Jane primer paragraph that opens and is dispersed throughout the book.

RESHAPING THE TRUEBLOOD MOLD

Michael Awkward was the first to rightly cite the intertextuality between *The Bluest Eye* and *Invisible Man*. In "'The Evil of Fulfillment': Scapegoating and Narration in *The Bluest Eye*," he convincingly argues that Morrison's first novel is a conscious revision of the Trueblood tale as it indicates that the construction of identity is not only racialized and classed but also gendered, and that the violent sexual initiation of the daughter is just as important as that of the father: "Morrison writes her way into the Afro-American literary tradition by foregrounding the effects of incest for the *female* victims in direct response to Ellison's refusal to consider them seriously" (emphasis added).[69] Morrison offers a feminist reading of Ellison's depiction of father–daughter incest, exposing the dangers of adhering to patriarchal phallocentrism steeped in sexism, racism, and classism that his Trueblood chapter only begins to address. Awkward sees Morrison "taking Ellison to task for the phallocentric nature of his representation of incest which marginalizes and renders as irrelevant the consequences of the act for the female victim."[70] Unlike Awkward, who argues that Morrison "rejects" her male ancestors Ellison (along with James Baldwin) to clear canonical space for herself, I see her work as signifying on *Invisible Man* as it simultaneously pays tribute to—yet critiques—the novel. I employ Henry Louis Gates's definition of "signifyin,'" the African American literature term for intertextual readings whereby "black writers read and critique other black texts as an act of rhetorical self-definition."[71]

Evidence exists in Morrison's text to support the assertion that hers is a conscious revision of Ellison's, including the similarity between the last names Trueblood and Breedlove and the fact that both incest accounts include similes comparing breath to a balloon. In *Invisible Man,* Ellison writes, "I heard the sharp intake of breath, like a toy-balloon suddenly deflated"[72] ; in *The Bluest Eye,* Morrison writes, "a hollow suck of air in the back of her throat. Like the rapid loss of air from a circus balloon."[73] Both also include a variation of the phrase "I am what I am." In Ellison's novel, the protagonist says, "I yam what I am!" after scarfing down yams[74] ; in Morrison's novel, Soaphead writes in his letter to God, "'I am who I am.' Like Popeye? I Yam What I Yam?"[75]

Revisiting the connection between *Invisible Man* and *The Bluest Eye*, Doane and Hodges find more similarities than differences between the two and maintain that Morrison, as Ellison had, creates sympathy for the father and refuses to blame him entirely for Pecola's fate. They observe that *The Bluest Eye* has been praised for its thoughtful understanding of the father's point of view and conclude that the female victim's perspective remained unspoken, "unsayable," as late as 1970, stating "we should not forget how hard it was for Morrison to tell Pecola's story or how hard it may still be to recognize the complexity of Morrison's effort to break a culturally enforced silence."[76] Morrison's ability to represent and humanize Cholly may be explained by the literary tradition of sympathetic fathers, such as Jim Trueblood and Dick Diver. Similarly, the narrative troubles with telling the female victim's story from her perspective is understandable given the model of Matty Lou.

Like Ellison, Morrison is driven to understand how a racist, classist culture has denied people humanity. A central theme in black American literature, invisibility is taken up in *The Bluest Eye* as Morrison explores the conditions under which her characters—both male and female—are rendered invisible. Both novels force the reader to look at black male characters like Trueblood and Cholly who, with reference to the dominant culture's construction of masculinity, have been emasculated or feminized by being positioned as passive victims of white male aggression.

More importantly, Morrison writes about those she calls in her afterword the "most delicate" and "most vulnerable" members of society—poor black girls.[77] When Pecola, who thinks that whiteness is the answer to all of her problems, goes to Mr. Yacobowski's store to buy Mary Jane candies, which bear the image she hopes to acquire by ingesting, the narrator tells us that the blue eyes of Mr. Yacobowski reluctantly look toward Pecola as his hand hesitates in offering her the candy. Morrison illustrates how invisibility is visited on Pecola because she is black and poor (as is Trueblood) and also because she is female. The vacant stare of Mr. Yacobowski suggests that nothing in society would allow a white male storeowner, even one whose name indicates that he is not entirely white in the American sense, to give a poor black girl a look of approval or acceptance. Pecola internalizes her outsider position so much that she reactively wishes herself into invisibility. Hearing her parents argue, she prays to God, "Please make me disappear."[78] She wishes for all but her eyes to fade away. Rendered invisible by and scapegoated from the black community, much like Trueblood, Pecola and her plight seem just as tragic, if not more so.

Even more troubling than Pecola's encounter with Mr. Yacobowski is the maternal denial she experiences. Uncannily conversant with the "three whores" she befriends who are more maternal than her own mother, Pecola exchanges little to no words with Pauline, whom she always calls Mrs. Breedlove.[79] Their first exchange comes midway through the novel, when Pecola is visiting her mother at work and drops a berry cobbler all over the floor. Instead of comforting the burned Pecola, Pauline hits her, dealing a blow so hard it knocks her to the floor, and then she proceeds to yell at her to get out of the house as she hugs the white girl whose family she works for.[80] Later, at the end of the incest scene, Pauline again denies Pecola the love and affection she so craves when she looms over her daughter as she regains consciousness following her husband's violation.[81] Unlike Kate Trueblood, Pauline beats her daughter upon finding out about the incest, according to the townswomen.[82] A victim of domestic violence herself, Pauline lets her home become a den of abuse for her daughter.

Pecola becomes invisible, even to her own mother, who deems her ugly upon birth.[83] In the conversation with her dissociated self at the novel's end, Pecola admits that her mother refuses to see her: "even Mrs. Breedlove doesn't say anything to you. Ever. Sometimes I wonder if she even sees you."[84] Depriving her daughter of the maternal support that would increase her chances of adopting successful coping strategies, Pauline breeds not love, but insecurity and self-doubt. Like Ellison's, the novel encourages readers to struggle with the ways its black characters were made invisible and metaphorically raped by whiteness.

Clearly Morrison did not set out to put the pieces of Pecola's life together—that's evident from the narrative's disjointed form. Instead, she wanted to engage the reader and show that Pecola's fate is not solely the result of a drunken father or misanthropic magician or callous mother—and to do so in a way that did not "dehumanize the characters who trashed" her.[85] Morrison leaves the difficult task of connecting the pieces of Pecola's life to her reader.

As disappointing as the silent and silenced Pecola may be for some readers, the fact that Claudia tells Pecola's story suggests a glimmer of hope. For this reason, I agree with Stephanie Demetrakopoulos and others, who don't read *The Bluest Eye* as a complete tragedy. Demetrakopoulos states, "there is a redemption in the fact that this story of incest has been told finally from a female point of view, told so well, and, I believe, for the first time in human history in this depth and completeness."[86] *The Bluest Eye* is also the story of Claudia, Pecola's childhood friend who develops an individual voice as she attempts to understand why she survived and Pecola did not. Awkward and other critics have observed that Morrison gives to Claudia the resources and strengths—such as a stable family, an ability to articulate a narrative, and a desire to combat racism—which Pecola lacks. As our main first-person narrator, Claudia attempts to understand the complexity of the issues surrounding father–daughter incest and struggles to figure out whether Cholly is a villain, victim, or both.

Claudia understands that the deaths of Pecola's baby and of Cholly are perhaps the most humane outcome.[87] She is most concerned, however, with her friend's life and how these events could happen to someone so much like herself. By the end, Claudia assumes some of the responsibility for Pecola's demise. She sums up Pecola's life with the sentence, "A little black girl yearns for the blue eyes of a little white girl, and the horror at the heart of her yearning is exceeded only by the evil of fulfillment."[88] By this point she realizes that Pecola's demise was caused by more than the fatal love of her father; the entire community had a hand in raping her. After revealing just how much others depended on Pecola to make themselves look and feel better, Claudia explains that Pecola leaves their town and retreats into madness.

If Claudia reaches any conclusions about the incest, it is that Cholly loved his daughter. She reasons, "He, at any rate, was the one who loved her enough to touch her, envelop her, give something of himself to her."[89] Her words complicate traditional views of father–daughter incest. Likewise, we'll never know how Cholly's touch was received by Pecola. Morrison has said that she couldn't focus exclusively on the young girl because it was too depressing. In her afterword, she explains that she thought the novelty "would be in having this story of female violation revealed from the vantage point of the victims or could-be victims of rape—the persons no one inquired of (certainly not in 1965): the girls themselves."[90] And because Pecola does not possess the language to author her story, "gullible, vulnerable girlfriends, looking back as the knowing adults they pretended to be in the beginning, would have to do that for her, and would have to fill those silences with their own reflective lives."[91] Doing perhaps the next best thing by having Claudia as the main narrator, Morrison's novel suggests that the shift in incest discourse was on the horizon.

Writing a fragmented, nonchronological account of the physical violation and psychological destruction of eleven-year-old Pecola, a "little-girl-gone-to-woman" who longs for white beauty, Morrison shows the interconnectedness of racism, rape, classism, and imperialism.[92] For breaking the silence of taboo topics both within and beyond the black community, *The Bluest Eye* "is now seen as a landmark in American literature, signaling a shift away from the white male-dominated literary establishment."[93] As Justine Tally puts it, Morrison didn't just move from the margins to the center of the literary canon; she moved the center.[94] The novel that significantly departed from dominant male-authored representations and challenged the psychiatric community's understanding of father–daughter incest inspired a whole generation of black and white women, such as Alice Walker, Gloria Naylor, Toni Cade Bambara, and Dorothy Allison to tell their own stories. As I show in my remaining chapters, dealing with familial rape more realistically than previous works, *The Bluest Eye* was instrumental in enabling incest victims to claim narrative as a vehicle for working through their trauma.

NOTES

1. Christopher Bigsby, *Writers in Conversation*, Vol. 1 (Norwich: Arthur Miller Centre for American Studies, 2000), 251.
2. As many have noted, Morrison's title indicates a search for identity, as *eye* and *I* are homonyms.
3. Toni Morrison, *The Bluest Eye* (1970; New York: Plume, 1994), 214.
4. Seward, quoted in Adam Langer, "Star Power," in *Toni Morrison: Conversations*, ed. Carolyn C. Denard (Jackson: University Press of Mississippi, 2008), 211.
5. Harvey Young and Jocelyn Prince, "Adapting *The Bluest Eye* for the Stage," *African American Review* 45, no. 1–2 (Spring/Summer 2012): 149.
6. Morrison, *The Bluest Eye*, 216.
7. Ágnes Surányi, "*The Bluest Eye* and *Sula*: Black Female Experience from Childhood to Womanhood," in *The Cambridge Companion to Toni Morrison*, ed. Justine Tally (Cambridge: Cambridge University Press, 2007), 11.
8. Quoted in Elissa Schappell, "Toni Morrison: The Art of Fiction," in *Toni Morrison: Conversations*, ed. Carolyn C. Denard (Jackson: University Press of Mississippi, 2008), 73.
9. For example, Morrison's 1977 *Song of Solomon* won the National Book Critics' Circle Award for fiction and the American Academy and Institute of Arts and Letters Award, and her 1987 *Beloved* received the Pulitzer and in 2006 was voted by *The New York Times* the best piece of fiction written in the United States in the last twenty-five years. Interestingly, the winner for the previous twenty-five years was Ralph Ellison's *Invisible Man*. Justine Tally, "Introduction: 'All Necks are on the Line,'" in *The Cambridge Companion to Toni Morrison*, ed. Justine Tally (Cambridge: Cambridge University Press, 2007), 2.
10. Nancy Peterson, "Introduction: Reading Toni Morrison—From the Seventies to the Nineties," in *Toni Morrison: Critical and Theoretical Approaches* (Baltimore: Johns Hopkins University Press, 1997), 3; Karen Stein notes that when Morrison's work first appeared, at least one critic argued that she was limiting her canvas by focusing on black characters: this critic contended that Morrison "was wasting her talents writing about the African American community rather than about 'the universal human condition' (which usually means the white community)." Stein, *Reading, Learning, Teaching Toni Morrison* (New York: Peter Lang, 2009), 15.
11. Marc C. Conner, "Introduction: Aesthetics and the African American Novel," in *The Aesthetics of Toni Morrison: Speaking the Unspeakable*, ed. Marc C. Conner (Jackson: University Press of Mississippi, 2000), x.
12. J. Brooks Bouson, *Quiet as It's Kept: Shame, Trauma, and Race in the Novels of Toni Morrison* (Albany: State University of New York Press, 2000).
13. Robert B. Stepto, "'Intimate Things in Place': A Conversation with Toni Morrison," in *Toni Morrison: Critical Perspectives Past and Present*, ed. Henry Louis Gates Jr. and K. A. Appiah (New York: Amistad, 1993), 378.
14. Quoted in Bouson, *Quiet as It's Kept*, 24.
15. Toni Morrison, "10 Questions for Toni Morrison," *TIME.com*. *Time*, May 7, 2008.
16. Pam Houston, "Pam Houston Talks with Toni Morrison," in *Toni Morrison: Conversations*, ed. Carolyn Denard (Jackson: University Press of Mississippi, 2008), 256.
17. Morrison, *The Bluest Eye*, 83.
18. Ibid.
19. Ibid., 105.
20. Ibid. 19.
21. Houston, "Pam Houston Talks with Toni Morrison," 256.

22. Quoted in Bessel A. van der Kolk, afterword in *Treating Complex Traumatic Stress Disorders: An Evidence-Based Guide*, ed. Christine A. Courtois and Julian D. Ford (New York: Guilford, 2009), 455.
23. D. James Henderson, "Incest," in *Comprehensive Textbook of Psychiatry*, vol. 2, 2nd ed., ed. Alfred M. Freedman, Harold I. Kaplan, and Benjamin J. Sadock (Baltimore: Williams & Wilkins, 1975), 1533.
24. Ibid., 1537.
25. Ibid.
26. Ibid.
27. Ibid. For more information regarding that study, see Joseph E. Davis's *Accounts of Innocence: Sexual Abuse, Trauma, and the Self*, 277–278n20.
28. Morrison, *The Bluest Eye*, 6.
29. Ibid., 17.
30. Ibid., 18.
31. Ibid., 159
32. The reader can infer that the ages are not accidental and serve to reinforce the idea that traits, good and bad, are passed on—are bred—into the next generation.
33. Morrison, *The Bluest Eye*, 156.
34. Ibid., 160.
35. Ibid., 147.
36. Ibid., 148.
37. Ibid., 150–51.
38. Ibid., 161.
39. Ibid., 215.
40. Ibid., 160.
41. Ibid., 162.
42. Ibid.
43. Ibid., 215.
44. Quoted in Stein, *Reading, Learning, Teaching Toni Morrison*, 38.
45. Phyllis Klotman, "Dick-and-Jane and the Shirley Temple Sensibility in *The Bluest Eye*," *Black American Literature Forum* 13, no. 4 (1979): 124.
46. Morrison, *The Bluest Eye*, 163.
47. Ibid., 67.
48. Ibid., 164, 170.
49. Ibid., 167.
50. Ibid.
51. Ibid., 99.
52. See James Mayo, "Morrison's *The Bluest Eye*," *The Explicator*, 60, no. 4 (Summer 2002): 231–34, for a compelling argument that Claudia was molested by Soaphead.
53. Morrison, *The Bluest Eye*, 167.
54. Ibid., 168.
55. Quoted in Linda Wagner-Martin, *Toni Morrison and the Maternal: From* The Bluest Eye *to* Home (New York: Peter Lang, 2014), 21.
56. Morrison, *The Bluest Eye*, 215.
57. Pin-Chia Feng, *The Female* Bildungsroman *by Toni Morrison and Maxine Hong Kingston* (New York: Peter Lang, 1998).
58. Janice Doane and Devon Hodges, *Telling Incest: Narratives of Dangerous Remembering from Stein to Sapphire* (Ann Arbor: University of Michigan Press, 2001).
59. Monica Michlin, "Narrative as Empowerment: *Push* and the *Signifying* on Prior African-American Novels on Incest," *Études Anglaises* 59, no. 2 (2006): 181.
60. Ibid.
61. Bouson, *Quiet as It's Kept*, 43.
62. Morrison, *The Bluest Eye*, 200.
63. Ibid.
64. Ibid.
65. Ibid.

66. Ibid., 161.
67. Ibid., 214.
68. Quoted in Bouson, *Quiet as It's Kept*, 14.
69. Michael Awkward, "The Evil of Fulfillment': Scapegoating and Narration in *The Bluest Eye*," in *Toni Morrison: Critical Perspectives Past and Present*, ed. Henry Louis Gates Jr. and K. A. Appiah (New York: Amistad, 1993), 201.
70. Ibid. In addition to Awkward, John N. Duvall discusses Morrison's revision of Ellison's novel, focusing on the character of Soaphead Church. He reads Soaphead's letter to God, in which he challenges God's authority, as representing Morrison's desire to usurp Ellison's authority. Duvall, "Naming Invisible Authority: Toni Morrison's Covert Letter to Ralph Ellison," *Studies in American Fiction* 25, no. 2 (1997): 241–53.
71. Gates, *Figures in Black: Words, Signs, and the "Racial" Self* (New York: Oxford University Press, 1987), 242. Ellison used the term "vernacular process" to convey a similar concept. It is the means by which one takes an inherited style and combines it with an improvised one to create something entirely new." Quoted in Jennifer Howard, "Ralph Ellison's Never-Ending Novel," *The Chronicle Review*, May 9, 2010.
72. Ellison, *Invisible Man*, 49.
73. Morrison, *The Bluest Eye*, 163.
74. Ellison, *Invisible Man*, 266.
75. Morrison, *The Bluest Eye*, 180.
76. Doane and Hodges, *Telling Incest*, 44, 45.
77. Morrison, *The Bluest Eye*, 210.
78. Ibid., 45.
79. Ibid., 50.
80. Ibid., 109.
81. Ibid., 163.
82. Ibid., 189.
83. Ibid., 126.
84. Ibid., 198.
85. Ibid., 211.
86. Stephanie Demetrakopoulos, "On Morrison's Bleak Vision and Its Redemption," in *Toni Morrison's* The Bluest Eye, ed. Harold Bloom (New York: Infobase Publishing, 2010), 66.
87. Like Ellison's novel, which tells us (twice) that "the end is in the beginning" (6 and 571), Morrison's "book can be seen to open with its close" in that Morrison provides the plot details on the first two pages of her work (in some cases, the plot is given away on the book's cover) (214). But unlike Ellison who suggests that the Trueblood name live on, Morrison kills off baby and Cholly, suggesting an end to the Breedlove line.
88. Morrison, *The Bluest Eye*, 204.
89. Ibid., 206.
90. Ibid., 214.
91. Ibid.
92. Ibid., 31.
93. Langer, "Star Power," 211.
94. Tally, "Introduction: 'All Necks,'" 1.

FOUR

"White Trash" Trauma in Allison's *Bastard Out of Carolina*

Commenting on how struck she was by Morrison's first novel, Dorothy Allison said, "Besides James Baldwin, nothing ever hit me as hard as Toni Morrison's *The Bluest Eye* . . . it was about incest, about that terror, and it was about suicide."[1] The novel resonated with her because of the "speech," "rhythms," "language," and most familiarly, the emphasis on poverty.[2] In Pecola's story of shame, social contempt, and sexual violation, Allison saw her own. And like *The Bluest Eye,* which was the first novel to have a little black girl as a protagonist, Allison's 1992 *Bastard Out of Carolina* charts the coming-of-age of a character little seen in canonical literature—a girl from "white-trash" origins. Allison's novel shares with Morrison's the breaking of a cultural silence surrounding child abuse because it shows what can happen when a father internalizes class hatred and unleashes his frustrations on his daughter. This semiautobiographical book marks a significant departure from Morrison's, Ellison's, and Fitzgerald's accounts of father–daughter incest in that the story of sexual violation is told entirely from the perspective of the female victim herself. In this harrowing *Bildungsroman,* protagonist Ruth Anne Boatwright, better known as "Bone," authors a story that illuminates the complex trauma surrounding domestic violence, which culminates in a twelve-page graphic rape scene at the novel's end. Detailing Bone's coming-to-speech, Allison enables the traumatized subject to claim narrative and her physical body as ways of working through trauma.

Between the publication of *The Bluest Eye* and *Bastard Out of Carolina,* many important historical events happened, not the least of which was Second-Wave feminism, which Allison credits as saving her life: "The only way I ever began to write was because there was a women's movement. If there had not been a women's liberation movement in the early

'70s, I would not only have not started writing. I would not be alive."[3] In addition to teaching Allison that women's lives were important, the movement organized the first speak outs on rape and "offered a new language for understanding the impact of sexual assault."[4] In 1971, Florence Rush spoke at the first conference on rape. She called attention to the fundamental moral flaws of prominent studies of sex offense victims and offenders.[5] Moreover, there was an outpouring of pivotal articles and books published in the 1970s and early 1980s that made a strong case for understanding rape and incest as political issues, most notably Susan Griffin's "Rape: The All-American Crime" (1971), Susan Brownmiller's *Against Our Will: Men, Women and Rape* (1975), Ellen Weber's "Incest: Sexual Abuse Begins at Home" (1977), Florence Rush's "The Freudian Cover-up" (1977), Sandra Butler's *Conspiracy of Silence* (1978), Louise Armstrong's *Kiss Daddy Goodnight* (1978), and most importantly for this study, Judith Herman and Lisa Hirschman's *Father–Daughter Incest* (1981).[6] Furthermore, statistics were gathered that revealed the prevalence of sexual abuse. The most reliable data came from sociologist and human rights activist Diana Russell who performed a study in the early 1980s of 930 randomly selected San Francisco women that found that one in four had been raped, and one in three had been sexually abused in childhood.[7] Russell was among the first to call incest the "secret trauma," and to state that a minimum of one in every six women in this country had been incestuously abused.[8] And yet, despite the nation's growing awareness of rape and incest, the 1970s saw a staggering increase (about 15 percent every year) in reported cases of rape—"cases estimated moreover to be only a small percentage of the total actual occurrences."[9] As Elaine Showalter remembers, these feminists "described a violence against women that was confirmed by each day's newspaper, each night's TV news."[10]

Although published in the 1990s, Allison's novel is not set during Second-Wave feminism. Instead, it takes place just a decade after *The Bluest Eye*, during the 1950s, before public awareness and institutional reform regarding child abuse. As Amanda Charlene Lee notes in "Forgotten Child: *Bastard Out of Carolina* and the History of Child Sexual Abuse": "It was not until the sixties, a decade too late to help Bone and real children like her, that child welfare officials revisited the matter with any seriousness."[11] In other words, Allison has Bone come of age in the 1950s, the decade that saw "the dying remains of an America without proper social or legal protection for its abused children" and in the poor-white town of Greenville, South Carolina, one of the states most resistant to change.[12] For example, in the 1950s, South Carolina went so far as to enact "a substitute parent law" that denied "aid to children whose mothers had even a casual, short term relationship with a man" who was not the biological father.[13] It wasn't until five years after *Bastard* is published that UNICEF declared what feminists of the 1970s already sensed: violence against women and girls is the most pervasive abuse of human rights in the world.

Allison has said that in *Bastard Out of Carolina* she set out to do two things: "to put in print everything [she] understood that happens in a violent family where incest is taking place" and to tell "the complicated, painful story of how [her] mama had, and had not, saved [her] as a girl."[14] Her book is one of the first to explore at length the role of the mother in father–daughter incest, as Allison tries to come to terms with how the mother's actions or inactions further traumatized the daughter. However, instead of portraying "Mama" Anney Boatwright as a collusive mother, Allison reflects on why the mother doesn't leave her abusive husband and finally chooses him over her daughter. Following Allison's lead, I examine in this chapter the traumas experienced by several figures in the narrative: "Daddy Glen" Waddell, "Mama" Anney Boatwright, and Bone herself, all of whom are marked by classism and institutional misogyny. In recreating her own family, Allison exposes how the unequal power relations of patriarchy and capitalism enable father–daughter incest. I also examine how Aunt Raylene, who assumes the maternal role by the novel's end, helps Bone transition from victim to survivor and what the novel tells us about the body's role in psychological trauma.

One of many female-authored incest narratives published in the 1990s, *Bastard* became a best seller and spawned an award-winning (although for Allison, disappointing) film. Despite its southern roots, it has been translated into more than a dozen languages and published in more than a dozen countries. Like Fitzgerald's *Tender Is the Night,* Allison's novel was ten years in the making. The novel that began as a poem in 1974 (titled "To the Bone") was bid on by two female editors; no male editors were interested. Carol De Santi at Dutton got the contract and gave Allison a $37,000 advance, a significant sum considering Allison had $200 to her name before publishing the book. It established Allison as a major contemporary author and received many accolades: it was a finalist for the 1992 National Book Award; it won the Ferro-Grumly prize, the ALA Award for Lesbian and Gay Writing, and the Bay Area Book Reviewers Award for fiction.

Allison had published with feminist, lesbian, and gay newspapers, periodicals, and presses for almost two decades, but the publication of *Bastard* moved her work to a mainstream press and readership. It received flattering reviews in *The New York Times Book Review,* the *San Francisco Chronicle,* and *The Village Voice.* It was even discussed favorably in Katie Roiphe's "Making the Incest Scene," an otherwise scathing attack on contemporary writers of incest narratives.[15] Although it was mainly received as a novel written in the tradition of Southern regionalist fiction that told the story of working-class families, many reviewers also emphasized the issue of sexual abuse. The first in her family to graduate from high school, Allison also reached another milestone: her novel established her as a major contemporary American author credited with altering the literary landscape, and her book "has become a touchstone in scholarly treatments of class, gender, sexuality, trauma, and violence in contemporary literature."[16] Depicting dire poverty in rural Appalachia, it pioneered the genre of working-class literature. And representing father–daughter incest with painful accuracy, Allison's novel spearheaded the explosion of incest memoirs of the late 1990s.[17]

For Allison, a major concern is to break the culture of silence surrounding sexual abuse and to express the insidious manifestations of trauma leading up to the time-limited event of incestuous rape. Since the age of five, Bone suffers many forms of severe abuse at the hands of her stepfather, culminating in rape. Sexual assaults frame the narrative with numerous accounts sprinkled throughout. The first mention of abuse comes early—readers are not even forty-five pages into the three hundred-page novel, when we first encounter Glen molesting Bone. She comes dangerously close to being raped in the front seat of Daddy Glen's Pontiac while her mother gives birth to a stillborn son. The first half of this story charts Bone's descent into victimhood. The events leading up to the rape scene show that Bone's body, much like Pecola's, has been marked by the threat of violation long before the rape even occurs. As it tells the tale of the damage done to Bone, the female incest victim who is disempowered by age, gender, and class, *Bastard* also reveals the systems of oppression that act on Bone and the women of her family, which constitute female bodies as objects that are always susceptible to rape and the way this constant, implied menace is constitutive of female identity. Allison, who relinquishes a straightforward narrative for a meandering middle in which Glen takes a back seat to Bone's search for identity, exposes the material realities of economic oppression and the romanticized view of heterosexuality to show the vulnerabilities they create.

Like *Invisible Man* and *The Bluest Eye*, *Bastard Out of Carolina* focuses on identity and the powerful effects of naming, evident in the novel's first line: "I've been called Bone all my life, but my name's Ruth Anne."[18] As we quickly learn, our protagonist's troubles go way beyond an unusual nickname. Because Anney goes into labor after being knocked unconscious as a result of a drunk-driving accident (her brother-in-law is to blame), she is unable to provide a name for her baby daughter. And because Bone's Aunt Ruth and Granny could not write legibly, Bone's first name wound up being spelled three different ways: "Ann, Anne, and Anna."[19] However, Anney is more troubled by the fact that there is no man to give Bone a last name, as Granny ran him out of town "for messing with her daughter."[20] Despite her efforts to make it appear that Bone is not fatherless in a patriarchal culture, Anney fails and is left with two babies and three uncertified copies of Bone's birth certificate—all by the age of nineteen. To compensate, Anney agrees to marry Glen, with one of her first thoughts of him being that he would "make a good daddy."[21] Blinded by her desires for a respectable, legal familial relation, her actions backfire and one of the novel's ironies is that her marriage to Glen, which she thinks will protect her and her girls from class prejudice, actually makes it easier for the abuse and incest to happen. The union between Glen and Anney grants Glen legal right to Bone's body.

Like Ellison's Truebloods and Morrison's Breedloves, the Boatwrights struggle with their identity as they are described as far from the ideal white American family. As pointed out by Matt Wray and Annalee Newitz in *White Trash: Race and Class in America*, there is a distinction made between "white trash" and "poor white," in which the former entails a racial category. Whereas *poor* implies an economic designation, *trash* includes debasement in economic, sexual, moral, and intellectual terms. White trash has come to be a descriptor of not just a class, but a racial, group: white trash has functioned as a "classist slur" and a "racial epithet that marks out certain whites as a breed apart, a dysgenic race unto themselves."[22] At times, Bone remarks on the connection between racial and class oppression: when her friend, Shannon, says *nigger*, Bone hears "the tone pitched exactly like the echoing sound of Aunt Madeline [of Glen's family] sneering 'trash' when she thought I wasn't close enough to hear."[23] Moreover, brief references to Bone's Cherokee great-great-grandfather further emphasize the Boatwrights as disenfranchised descendants of the Native Americans, who were stripped of their home, language, and land; in effect, were victims of cultural rape.[24] Not coincidentally, Allison has Bone be the special inheritor of this legacy: she has "black Indian eyes" and only Bone "got that blue-black hair."[25]

Providing an insider's view of white-trash experience and father–daughter incest, *Bastard* speaks previously unspoken truths about culturally marginalized figures. One difficulty for early critics was how to talk about poor-white culture and father–daughter incest without reinforcing stereotypes of poor southerners as sexually perverse, dirty, drunk, and lazy. In other words, how does one address these topics without suggesting that incest and inbreeding happen only in poor, rural families? Allison herself has even said in jest, "What's a South Carolina virgin? 'At's a ten-year-old can run fast."[26]

J. Brooks Bouson observes that the novel "ends up legitimating, at least in part, the popular view that white-trash culture is a central site of social pathology and abjection."[27] Allison admits that to a degree her novel does reinforce standard images of white-trash culture, saying "Some of that stuff is true."[28] Without making excuses for the behavior of her family members, Allison shows how insidious forms of trauma can dehumanize which, in Glen's case, leads to violence, and, in Anney's case, leads to her turning a blind eye. Allison suggests, much as Morrison had, that violence can be learned from domination because these metaphorically emasculated, socially impotent fathers come to resemble their oppressors. And yet, *Bastard* also challenges the popular view that white-trash culture is a central site of social pathology and abjection by having Glen not come from the poor white class: his family is comfortably and consciously middle class, part of a patriarchal Southern culture that prides itself on property ownership. For example, Glen's father owns a dairy and his brothers are lawyers and dentists. Moreover, their wives are housewives, enjoying the luxury of not having to work outside the home and frowning on women who do.

Since its publication, critics have discussed how the novel both confirms and transcends stereotypes of poor-white southerners. Provoking a steady stream of literary analysis, *Bastard* has been approached from many lenses. Critics over the last two decades have commented on its postmodern sensibility, narrative strategies and storytelling, southern locale, depictions of gender, sexuality, race, and region, the character of Shannon Pearle (Bone's friend or, as some have argued, her alter ego), Bone's fantasies and vivid descriptions of masturbation, the curious undertones of Bone's budding lesbianism, and Allison's genre-bending. Chapters on the novel have appeared in at least six books published in the twenty-first century: Sonya Andermahr's *Trauma Narratives and Herstory*, John N. Duvall's *Race and White Identity in Southern Fiction*, Bouson's *Embodied Shame: Uncovering Female Shame in Contemporary Women's Writings*, Laura Di Prete's *"Foreign Bodies": Trauma, Corporeality, and Textuality in Contemporary American Culture*, Deborah Horvitz's *Literary Trauma: Sadism, Memory, and Sexual Violence in American Women's Fiction*, and Gillian Harkins's *Everybody's Family Romance: Reading Incest in Neoliberal America*. In *Class Definitions: On the Lives and Writings of Maxine Hong Kingston, Sandra Cisneros, and Dorothy Allison*, Michelle M. Tokarczyk discusses how socioeconomic class shapes these writers and their works. The first (and to date only) collection of essays exclusively on Allison was published in 2004: *Critical Essays on the Works of American Author Dorothy Allison*, edited by Christine Blouch and Laurie Vickroy, contains eight essays on Allison's work, three of which focus entirely on *Bastard*.

PUTTING INTO PRINT FATHER–DAUGHTER INCEST

Like Morrison and Ellison, Allison explores how a classist society contributes to the problem of father–daughter incest. And like them, she depicts her father figure as something other than a villain. In her first-person account, told retrospectively by Bone, Allison asks what causes some fathers to commit incest. In the case of Glen Waddell, his pathology takes the form of paternal incest because of the pressures of trying to compensate for what his father sees as his failures in a capitalistic and patriarchal society. In contrast to the men in his family, Glen works in menial, low-paying jobs. At seventeen, when he first meets Anney, he is a truck driver. Pointed out by Bone, "Skinny, nervous little Glen Waddell didn't seem like he would amount to much, driving a truck for the furnace works, and shaking a little every time he tried to look a man in the eye."[29] The precocious Bone increasingly understands that Glen's insecurities stem from his inability to live up to his father's middle-class standards. To compensate, Glen does what his society has taught him to do; he turns to women to reassert a masculinity defined by domination.

In a troubling scene, we see not only how women are exchanged in this community but Glen's ulterior motives for pursuing a Boatwright woman. From the beginning we know that Glen is attracted not just to Anney but to her brothers' bad-boy reputation. Seemingly aware of this, Anney's brother Earle plays matchmaker and brings Glen to the White Horse Café where she works. Earle makes sure the meeting takes place after an appropriate lapse of time since the death of Anney's first husband (and the father of Bone's sister Reese). Earle's ownership of Anney is illustrated when, seeing Glen glare at his baby sister who is "no bigger than a girl," Earle gets "hot-angry" and tells Glen to watch himself.[30] Even more unsettling is Glen's reaction: he determines to marry Anney for a number of not-so-noble reasons. Marriage, he thinks, will provide access to patriarchal privilege, and marrying into a family less fortunate than the Waddells is an act of rebellion that allows Glen to disgrace his family. Further, the union will secure Glen's ties to the legend of the Boatwright boys, who are feared and even oddly respected by the rest of the town for their bad tempers and violent ways. Like Morrison, whose narrative strategies spotlight Cholly's thoughts, Allison also portrays the perpetrator's perspective: "He would have her, he told himself. He would marry Black Earle's baby sister, marry the whole Boatwright legend, shame his daddy and shock his brothers. He would carry a knife in his pocket and kill any man who dared to touch her."[31] Glen's dependency on the Boatwrights shows his internalization of the ideals of a sexist, elitist, patriarchal society. Flexing his masculinity, he comes to see himself as the rightful owner of the female bodies of his new family members.

By providing glimpses into Glen's relationship with his father, Allison exposes the complex trauma he experiences, blurring clear distinctions between victim and victimizer. Statements about Glen's need for love abound in the novel. Although well aware of his black-sheep, "bastard," status, he continues to brag about his family, visiting them "at least once every other month."[32] He always promises Anney and the girls that they won't stay long, but a young Bone knows that "he would not have the nerve to leave before his father had delivered his lecture on all the things Glen had done wrong in his long life of failure and disappointment."[33] Even Bone notes the regression in Glen's demeanor when he is around his father: "Around his father, Glen became unsure of himself and too careful. He broke out in a sweat, and his eyes kept flickering back to his daddy's face as if he had to keep watching or miss the thing he needed most to see. He would pull at his pants like a little boy and drop his head if anyone asked him a question."[34] Furthermore, Anney tells her sister Ruth, "I an't never seen a boy wanted his daddy's love so much and had so little of it. All Glen really needs is to know himself loved."[35] Foregrounding issues of classism, Anney is quick to identify Glen's father as the cause of his insecurities.

Glen fails as a son, husband, and father. Unable to meet his father's expectations, he struggles financially. He has married beneath his class, cannot hold a steady job, cannot make good on the rent, and on at least one occasion, cannot feed his family. In a memorable scene, Anney resorts to giving her daughters soda crackers and ketchup with salt and pepper after Glen is laid off from yet another job. The scene ends with what the reader assumes is Anney leaving the house to prostitute herself. Added to Glen's list of disappointments is his inability to produce a son of his own, and thus achieve the myth of fatherhood. When Glen Jr. dies in childbirth, his failures in a capitalistic and patriarchal society collide. Perhaps not coincidentally, Glen Jr. dies at the same time that Glen first molests Bone in the hospital parking lot. Juxtaposing these two traumatic events, Allison suggests that the death of Glen's son is retribution for taking the virginity of a girl who is now legally his daughter. Unable to father his own son and carry on the Waddell name, Glen cannot even afford to buy a burial site. According to Bone, this marks the turning point when Glen's grief turns to rage. From that day, Glen becomes obsessed with patriarchal independence, making the family move away from Anney's family and ultimately embarking on numerous moves, living "in no one house more than eight months," dodging creditors along the way.[36] Much like Cholly, Glen moves his family to the socially disgraced level of "outdoors."

Despite her sympathetic portrayal of her stepfather, Bone does not excuse the abuse even though she realizes that Glen is mistreated by his own father. She sees firsthand how tightly intertwined poverty and abuse are, but she is increasingly aware that Glen chooses to oppress. She knows that Glen is no stranger to the hunger and rage Bone feels while in the company of the more privileged. Yet she also begins to understand that despite what Glen has suffered because of his father, his history of abuse should not permit him to victimize her. Bone whispers, "I don't care if his daddy does treat him bad. I don't care why he's so mean."[37] By the novel's end, she painfully understands the difference between the Waddells' abuse of Glen and Glen's abuse of Bone: the Waddells attack Glen verbally; his abuse of Bone is emotional, physical, and sexual.

BEARING WITNESS: THE ROLE OF THE MOTHER

At the heart of *Bastard* is the story of Anney Boatwright, who is fifteen years old when she becomes a mother, making the novel about Anney's coming-of-age in addition to Bone's. Anney's ideals of what a woman should be like are shaped by her sisters' and society's beliefs, enlarging Allison's vision to criticize the Boatwright women and constructions of femininity in general. Glen isn't the only one to internalize patriarchal and capitalistic norms: Anney, along with most of her sisters, has bought into the standards as well. As Morrison comments on the tragic results of internalizing white value systems, Allison critiques the Boatwright women's dependency on heteropatriarchal practices. In a culture where women are old at twenty-five and men never mature, Allison has said that women in her family were born to suffer and "to keep silent": "Even in this book with these strong women they all believe that suffering is what they are supposed to do. And they pass it on to their children."[38] As Pauline and Cholly breed insecurity and self-doubt in Pecola, so do the Boatwrights breed suffering and uncertainty into their daughters.

For many readers, Anney emerges as a woman who unquestionably embraces Glen's possessiveness, and thereby revictimizes her daughter. Consumed with Bone's illegitimacy, a stamp of shame she wishes to erase, Anney hastily marries Glen. Throughout the narrative, she questions, not Glen's actions, but what Bone had done to provoke him. For example, after Glen's routine bathroom beatings, Anney questions what Bone had done to make him so angry: "Oh, girl. Oh, honey. Baby, what did you do? What did you do?" and again, "Why, honey? Why did you have to act like that?"[39] Likewise, Bone notes, "When Daddy Glen beat me there was always a reason, and Mama would stand right outside the bathroom door. Afterward she would cry and wash my face and tell me not to be so stubborn, not to make him mad."[40] Anney at one point says that she should buy Bone vitamins because she claims that she can't understand how her daughter is always bruising herself.

Instead of blaming her for a series of bad choices, which some readers might do, Allison reveals the lack of freedom Anney has in making choices and the economic factors that prevent her from exposing the familial secret of child abuse and leaving her abusive husband. Bone has a precocious understanding of her mother's motivation and recognizes that her mother is a product of "a patriarchal system that rewarded settled women with a small dose of respectability and, most importantly, threatened them with more hardship if they became single."[41] For example, in South Carolina, if Bone's mother and stepfather stay married for seven years, legitimacy would be conferred on Anney's daughters.[42] The stigma against having a child out of wedlock and being a single mother explains why Anney, who hates that her daughter is a bastard, makes humiliating annual trips to the courthouse to get Bone's birth certificate legitimized and even why Anney marries Glen to her family's dismay and has her heart set on staying wed. Anney, who does move out temporarily, is ultimately unable to leave Glen, even after witnessing the rape of her daughter with her own eyes.

Bone tells of her mother's complex trauma, including her mother's hunger for a man's love. After Reese's father, Lyle Parsons, is killed in a car accident, Bone notes that her mother cries herself to sleep and "more than anything else in the world she wanted someone strong to love her."[43] Likewise, Anney sheds many tears after she and Glen temporarily break up after her daughter's bruises are exposed to the family. In addition to dealing with her pain by weeping, Anney also responds by stonewalling Bone. Because of her devoted longing for a man who will validate her self-worth along with her daughter's legal status, Anney dismisses the protests of her family members who try, unsuccessfully, to warn her against marrying Glen. Great Aunt Maybelle voices her distrust of Glen; Uncle Beau doesn't like him because he doesn't trust a man who doesn't drink. Even Granny expresses her concerns about Anney marrying Glen: "That boy's got something wrong with him. . . . He's always looking at me out the sides of his eyes like some old junkyard dog waiting to steal a bone. And you know Anney's the bone he wants."[44] At this point, even the wise Granny fails to see that Bone is the bone he wants.

As we see in the novel, Anney is not the only one to long for heterosexual validation. Most of the Boatwright women have internalized patriarchal ideals to devastating effects. They believe that their ultimate worth comes from remaining attractive and bearing children for their husbands. For example, after Bone's Aunt Alma discovers her husband has been cheating, she separates from him—but only for a while: "when the baby got sick and the boys started running around at night, she gave it up and moved back in with him."[45] Alma eventually excuses Wade's behavior, claiming, "I guess he an't no worse than any other man."[46] He's certainly not unlike Bone's great-grandfather who left the family several times for other women. From observing the heterosexual relationships of her family members, Bone learns at a young age the unequal power dynamics in which men are granted certain freedoms, as she puts it, "could do anything," whereas women grow old, mothering the men they marry.[47] Bone comments on the stark differences between the women and men in her family:

> My aunts treated my uncles like overgrown boys—rambunctious teenagers whose antics were more to be joked about than worried over—and they seemed to think of themselves that way too. They looked young, even Nevil, who'd had his teeth knocked out, while the aunts—Ruth, Raylene, Alma, and even Mama—seemed old, worn-down, and slow, born to mother, nurse, and clean up after the men.[48]

By observing her aunts, Bone learns that the female body "was born to be worked to death, used up, and thrown away."[49] Anney's appearance is emphasized throughout the novel, as her beauty wanes during her marriage to Glen. The men at the diner who once talked about how pretty Anney is start to talk about how pretty she had been.[50] Similarly and not coincidentally, when Alma separates from Wade, she looks "better than ever": "Her face was smooth and relaxed, her skirt loose on her soft hips."[51] But when she goes back to him, she assumes her tired, haggard looks. Repudiating a sentimental view of poverty, Allison shows how these women literally embody their hardships. She also gestures toward a larger truth: healthy heterosexual relationships are impossible when masculinity and femininity are constituted in and through structures of oppression.

Allison illustrates how Western standards of female beauty weigh on these women, who instruct Bone on how important looks really are. Aunt Alma teaches her that "love had more to do with how pretty a body was than anyone would ever admit."[52] Her sentiments are echoed by her sister Ruth, worn out in part by excessive child-bearing, who thought that a woman's ultimate validation came through having children for her husband. Repeating Ruth's words to Bone, Anney says, "Being pregnant was proof that some man thought you were pretty sometime."[53] Anney goes on to tell Bone that "the more babies she got, the more she knew she was worth something."[54] Although she says she wanted to hit Ruth when she told her that, Anney, as Bone begins to understand, has also internalized standards of oppression and wants the love of a man, at all costs. Bone remains unsure throughout the story about "love for a man not already part of the family," and is indoctrinated into a culture that celebrates beauty and marriage.[55] It is therefore no surprise when, as her abuse escalates, she wishes to be beautiful and questions "why couldn't I be pretty? I wanted to be more like the girls in the storybooks, princesses with pale skin and tender hearts."[56] Echoes of Pecola Breedlove are heard as Bone starts to internalize unattainable standards of beauty and convince herself that no part of her is beautiful and therefore she is deserving of Glen's abuse.

Even Ruth, who glimpses that all the signs of abuse are present and who speaks with the wisdom of a dying woman, is so committed to patriarchal norms that even in her final days, she still excuses male behavior. In a poignant scene Bone attempts to break her silence and tell Ruth about the abuse. Bone blurts out, "Daddy Glen hates me."[57] Ruth agrees that "Glen don't like you much," and that he's jealous of Bone's relationship with Anney.[58] However, like Anney and her other sisters who infantilize men, Ruth quickly excuses Glen's behavior, claiming that it's typical: "There's a way he's just a little boy himself, wanting more of your mama than you, wanting to be her baby more than her husband. And that an't so rare, I'll tell you." "Men," she continues, "are just little boys climbing up on titty whenever they can. Your mama knows it as well as I do. We all do."[59] After explaining the ways of men to Bone, Ruth presses the question about Glen touching her. It is no wonder, however, that she denies the abuse. Ruth hesitatingly questions, "has Daddy Glen ever . . . well . . . touched you?"[60] While placing her hand on Bone's parted legs, Ruth, who had been so forthright in her explanation about men, tiptoes around the issue and blushingly asks, "Down here, honey. Has he ever hurt you down there?"[61] Unsurprisingly, Bone whispers no, which she repeats, and then she attempts to end the conversation by reducing Glen's abuse to normal disciplining: "He just looks at me hard. Grabs me sometimes. Shakes me."[62] With Ruth's euphemistic description and flushed cheeks, it seems that even if Bone had been ready to tell the truth, her family was not ready to listen.

BONE'S RAPE

There comes a day, however, when Bone's family can no longer ignore the abuse: the horrific rape scene placed at the end is a turning point for Bone, who, unlike the dissociated Pecola, finds her voice and starts to hold her parents accountable for their actions. In what is arguably the most chilling scene in *Bastard*—and there are plenty of them—Anney comforts and hugs Glen, not Bone, after he brutally rapes her while Anney stands by watching. As the bruised and bloodied Bone regains consciousness, she notes that her mother "was holding him, his head pressed to her belly."[63] Withholding access to Anney's thoughts, Allison diverges from the other authors of this study discussed thus far by providing Bone's running internal monologue before, during, and after the novel's climactic rape scene.

"The afternoon Daddy Glen showed up," completes Bone's indoctrination into a patriarchal culture as it conveys father–daughter incest as an expression of patriarchy, a systematic organization of regulated power in which women are oppressed by men.[64] Allison's is the first book in this study to devote many pages—twelve consecutive pages—to detailing the traumatizing rape of the confused and terror-stricken twelve-year-old daughter, making the reader share in her pain and despair. Like the beginning of Trueblood's tale, this scene starts innocently enough with Bone at her Aunt Alma's house playing with her puppies and making peanut butter sandwiches to take with her on a picnic. Glen's rape of Bone while she is cleaning up in the kitchen evokes Cholly's rape of Pecola. At this point in the novel, Bone, along with her mother and sister, are living with Aunt Alma because Aunt Raylene discovered the domestic abuse, calling it to the attention of the entire family.

Bone, who is accustomed to retreating into silence, stands up to her father in this scene, challenging Glen with her words. Much like we've seen in the Trueblood narrative and the Warren account, the father focuses on the daughter's sexual development, trying to make her assume some of the blame. A significant change, however, occurs in Bone when she whispers to Glen the following words: "No. . . . I don't want to live with you no more. Mama can go home to you. I told her she could, but I can't. I won't."[65] Glen responds by telling Bone that he is her "daddy," and will tell her what she can and cannot do. But Bone, who is becoming more confident in her voice, repeats "No" three times, adding to the third denial, "I'd rather die than go back to living with you."[66] Bone, who had held her secret for so long, too afraid to lose her mother's love, who "would work as hard as he did to make sure she never knew," finally has the fortitude to say the words that both she and Glen fear the most: "I'll tell Mama."[67]

However, Bone doesn't have to tell her mother anything since Anney is there to see Bone get raped. Bone divulges details, explaining how Glen violently enters her body, casting her as the seductress saying, "You've always wanted it. Don't tell me you don't. . . . I'll give you what you really want."[68] After the rape, a bleeding, cursing Bone passes out briefly, and like Pecola, awakens to the sight of her mother. The outcome for Bone is just as upsetting as it was for Pecola, who tells her alter that her mother refused to believe the incest had occurred. As in *The Bluest Eye,* the rape scene does not end with the mother rescuing her daughter. Instead, Anney consoles Glen.

"Is it more traumatic for [Bone] to experience Daddy Glen's physical violence or to watch her mother comfort him," asks Ann Cvetkovich.[69] This is a question with which Allison clearly struggles. Commenting on society's collective mother-blaming, Louise Armstrong notes, "the very violence of our reactions against our mothers, our greater fury with them, shows not how much at fault they were, but rather how much *more* we needed from them, how much more we were conditioned to expect."[70] The reader knows that Bone mainly keeps quiet about the abuse because she fears losing her mother's love, something Glen threatens her with. Like Glen, resembling his oppressors who keep him in a subservient state, Bone had come to identify as a victim who assumed fault. But during the rape scene she starts to care less about her mother and admits that she hates her for choosing Glen. In her anger, Bone asks, "Could she love me and still hold him like that?" taking another step from victim to survivor as she begins to doubt not just her mother's love but her need for that love.[71]

FROM VICTIM TO SURVIVOR

Bastard Out of Carolina is an account of childhood sexual abuse, but it is also a story of survival, and Allison indicates that masturbation, lesbianism, and narrative can help victims work through trauma. A striking feature of the novel is Allison's emphasis on Bone's masturbatory fantasies, which can be read as attempts at narrativization. These scenes, which are at times uncomfortably erotic in their explicit descriptions of the sexually abused, particularly vulnerable working-class female body, show how engaging the body can be therapeutic.

Although many trauma scholars and clinicians have long realized the importance of narrative in working through trauma, just recently we have begun to place corporeality as central to traumatic representation. One of psychological trauma's biggest paradox is that "the wound of trauma seems both distinct from and yet inextricably bound up in that of the body."[72] As I mention in the Fitzgerald chapter, for decades, many clinicians contended that traumatic symptoms were caused by *physical* ailments. For example, in the 1860s, British physician John Erichsen thought that the symptoms from railway accidents were caused by shock or concussion of the spine. Similarly, after dealing with World War I soldiers, the British psychologist Charles Myers credited their distress to the effects of exploding shells.

Freud, however, recognized that many of these World War I soldiers were behaving like his female patients who had been diagnosed with hysteria. Furthermore, he glimpsed at the truth that these illnesses were psychological—not physical—in origin. Yet, Freud's theories of trauma, which Caruth draws on, focuses on the image of a bodily wound. Caruth then problematically moves between bodily and psychological wounding without clearly differentiating between them. In a footnote, she admits, "it would be interesting to pursue the complexity of the relation between mind and body as it might be rethought through the problem of trauma."[73] In recent years, Kathryn Robson, Laura Di Prete, and others take up this neglected project and build on Freud's and Caruth's work to emphasize the relation between the body and psyche.

Trauma's double status of body/mind, physical/psychic, exterior/interior, has troubled not only Freud and Caruth but also some contemporary trauma theorists, who are skeptical of neurophysiological theories of trauma and note the dangers of shifting the focus of research from the mind back to the body. In their quest to position the problem within the culture, they advocate moving away from locating the pathology within the individual's body. For example, Dominick LaCapra questions the "overly functionally specific model of the brain."[74] Likewise, Ruth Leys contends that focusing too much on the physical would be at odds with a conceptualization of trauma that accounts for social values and political realities.

As LaCapra and Leys note, contextualizing trauma within a social and political framework is critical. However, the role of corporeality should not be overlooked when formulating an approach to the study of psychological trauma and the post-traumatic. In her 2006 study on corporeality and textuality in contemporary American texts, which includes a chapter on *Bastard*, Di Prete convincingly argues,

> Any theoretical reflection on the ways of narrating trauma—including debates on representational distance, objectivity, and faithfulness to the psychic dynamics at work—cannot exclude corporeality as one of the central figures of this telling. Writing trauma means . . . speaking and writing the body, and returning to the body as a medium of self-expression and—crucially—self-empowerment.[75]

For Bone engaging the body is beneficial: masturbation allows her to work through trauma by reclaiming a body that has suffered many forms of injury. Remarkably, Allison is able to write about incest without desexualizing the female body and denying her sexual desires. Bone's masturbatory repetition simultaneously acts out the trauma and creates authority and agency for herself. Bone comments on the paradoxical situation—she is both "ashamed for masturbating to the fantasy of being beaten" but empowered in her ability to defeat her stepfather: "it was only in my fantasies with people watching me that I was able to defy Daddy Glen."[76] In her fantasies, the "people watching" parallel Pecola's dissociated alter in that they bear witness to Bone's trauma and show how divided personalities may be helpful, at least temporarily, for those who are enduring severe trauma. Bone is at times unable to separate her sexual desire from the experience of being abused, and Allison has been criticized for her controversial linking of childhood sexual abuse with practices of sadomasochism. But Bone works through, and at times seemingly masters, her sexual abuse by repeating it in fantasy. Through masturbation she is able to recreate the punishment so that she pleasurably relives and phantasmatically controls the event.

In her exploration of masochistic tendencies and trauma, Lynda Hart observes, "whereas the sexual abuse survivor is most clearly recognizable to others through *dissociative* symptomologies, the S&M practitioner acts out these scenes in ways that repeat, reorganize, and integrate them into her present. Dissociation is replaced by *consciousness* of associations."[77] In her fantasies, Bone "embraces the erotics of power," and "moves toward a precarious, delicate borderline that tests and transgresses the line between fantasy and reality."[78] Hart further notes

> For those women whose 'selves' have been constituted in large part by a traumatic history of sexual abuse, this borderline is often not a place to which they travel in order to risk the repetition of oppressive social structures; rather, it is the place where they find themselves located in order to repeat and transform their histories with a difference.[79]

Simply put, Hart believes in the therapeutic value of S&M.

Critic Michelle Tokarczyk sums up the problem: "Although Bone's physical and sexual abuse are graphically depicted, Allison likely upset a number of readers more with her descriptions of Bone's masturbation with a chain as she fantasizes that Daddy Glen is beating her or that she is being burned."[80] The five main accounts of Bone's masturbation reveal her desires, wishes, and passions, which are entrenched in sadomasochism. Sprinkled throughout the narrative are accounts of Bone's masturbatory pleasures, which are fueled by fantasies of fire, violation, dry sticks, and even, as Tokarczyk notes, a chain. Allison has said that Bone "becomes excited by some of the things [Daddy Glen] does."[81] For example, Bone orgasms while fantasizing that she is tied to a blazing haystack, or left to starve to death as blackbirds peck at her body.

Charting the progression in these masturbatory accounts, we see that Bone, who at first is defeated by her stepfather, is later able to stand up and conquer him. As the abuse escalates, so does Bone's masturbation. In her second account, she no longer dreams about fire, but instead, she imagines others bearing witness to Glen's beatings, which her mother and aunts fail to do. In this second and one of the longer accounts, the constructive potential of her fantasies becomes an exhibitionist form of empowerment, and her craving for someone to see her abuse becomes painfully evident: Bone tells us that those who watched her heroic endurance admired and loved her while hating Glen.

In addition to having others bear witness to her violation, Bone also fantasizes about her mother as she longs for her mother's love, evident when she rocks against her hip. In this scenario, Bone is a child, five or younger, strapped around her mother's body. In her mother's arms, she feels loved. Bone's age in her dream is significant because Glen's abuse started when she was five. However, Glen is not a part of this fantasy. Longing for the comfort her mother fails to provide, Bone uses masturbation as a way to reconnect with her. Tanya Horeck, who has reflected at length on how sexual violence is linked to fantasy, finds the abandonment by Anney to be more traumatic than the prolonged sexual and physical abuse by Daddy Glen and argues that Bone's masturbatory fantasies are staged less in response to Glen than to her mother.[82] In this final fantasy Anney certainly provides for Bone in a way she never did in real life, and makes good on the promise she once made to her young daughter—that she "wouldn't let nothing happen to my little girl."[83] In these masturbatory fantasies, Bone constructs an alternative ending to her abuse—one in which her masturbation becomes fused with the dream of comfort that in reality her mother cannot provide. Allison has said that "The huge issue for any incest survivor is learning to enjoy sex," and having Bone masturbate throughout the course of the novel suggests that the healing process must engage the body.[84] Allison has Bone move from passivity to activity by learning to enjoy her body, turning the senseless abuse into gratifying acts. The masturbation may also serve as a healthy alternative to heterosexual sex.

Along with the potential to heal herself through masturbatory fantasies, another saving grace for Bone is the character of Aunt Raylene who, we learn in the last chapter, is a lesbian. Unlike her sisters, Aunt Raylene does not adhere to patriarchal practices such as marriage and pregnancy; nor does she feel less of a person for being born into poverty: "For all she was a Boatwright woman, there were ways Raylene had always been different from her sisters. She was quieter, more private, living alone with her dogs and fishing lines, and seemingly happy that way."[85] In stark contrast to her sisters, Raylene has rented the same house for most of her adult life. Commenting further on her peculiar ways, cousin Butch tells Bone that "Raylene had worked for the carnival like a man, cutting off her hair and dressing in overalls. She'd called herself Ray."[86] In one of the novel's final disclosures, Raylene confesses to Bone that she ran off to the carnival, "yeah, but not for no man."[87] She seems to understand Anney's dilemma in having to choose between husband and daughter because Raylene made the woman she loved choose between herself and the woman's child. Significantly, it is during her stay with Raylene when Bone decides never to live again in the same house with Glen, and it is her aunt who finds the bruises on Bone and makes the abuse known to the rest of the family at Ruth's funeral. Unlike her mother and other aunts who inundate Bone with not-so-subliminal messages about how to grow up to be a housewife and mother, Raylene instills a sense that heteropatriarchal ideologies can be resisted. She teaches Bone to question a system that defines women as selfless wives who mother their husbands sometimes to the neglect of their children.

Allison drops subtle hints of Bone's budding lesbianism throughout the novel; however, the lesbian theme is understated in *Bastard*, becoming more prominent, but still ambiguous, in the final chapter. In the concluding scene, as she delivers Bone's birth certificate "blank, unmarked, unstamped," freeing Bone of the bastard status, Anney leaves her daughter in the care of Raylene.[88] The irony is that she gains legitimacy through disinheritance—in addition to having no father, Bone is now left without her birth mother. As Bone rests her head on Raylene's shoulder, she questions who her mother is and had been before she was born. She understands that their lives are intertwined. Bone questions what she'll be like when she reaches fifteen, twenty, and thirty, and if she would be "as strong as [her mother] had been, as hungry for love, as desperate, determined, and ashamed?"[89] Instead of questioning why Anney doesn't leave Glen, Bone here probes a slightly different question—what makes her stay—as she seems to have some understanding that her mother is a part of a misogynist and classist society that encourages a woman to value a husband over her daughter. However, instead of final judgment, Bone offers honest questions, much as Cholly does in *The Bluest Eye*. She wonders about her mother as well as her own emerging identity. As Bone draws Raylene closer to her, she notes that she knows who she is going to be: "I was who I was going to be, someone like [Raylene], like Mama, a Boatwright woman."[90] Strikingly, after Anney relinquishes custody of Bone to Aunt Raylene, Bone identifies with her mother, reaching toward an understanding of her tortured past.

Although uncertain if Bone's sexuality will be formed in reaction to her mother's heterosexual subordination or her aunt's autonomy, it is clear that in tracing her heritage through the women in her family, Bone is becoming comfortable with her "bastard" status, imagining a life that challenges the patriarchal order in which femininity is traumatizing. Allison's final sentence, "I wrapped my fingers in Raylene's and watched the night close in around us," suggests that Allison enables queer possibilities for her protagonist.[91] The image Allison leaves us with—Bone tilting her head to lean on Raylene's shoulder, trusting her and her love—may indicate that lesbianism offers Bone an alternative to the dangers of heterosexuality and a way out of the cycle of abuse.

And yet, Allison's critics (Cvetkovich, Katrina Irving, and Nick Melczarek) argued that her first novel was not lesbian enough. Unmistakably feminist, *Bastard* is unclear about the role lesbianism plays in Bone's development. An out lesbian who has written explicitly about homosexual sex in other works, Allison has said that "being a lesbian is part of why I survived," but she did not set out to write the lesbian Bildungsroman in *Bastard*[92] : "The book is not about growing up queer successfully, and I got the real strong impression from talking to people was, what they hoped I would write would be the lesbian biography."[93] Perhaps Allison leaves Bone's sexuality ambiguous because she did not want to link incest with lesbianism and thereby imply that it is the only recourse to father–daughter incest. If that were the case, she's said, we'd have a lot more lesbians.[94]

An important lesson Raylene teaches Bone is to author a different version of her story, one that turns senseless violence into meaningful artwork. Literally collecting trash out of the river she lives near, Raylene illustrates to Bone the power of transformation. For Bone, storytelling has always been a part of her life, and she has witnessed how it holds the potential to alter reality. She explains, "All the Boatwrights told stories, it was one of the things we were known for, and what one cousin swore was gospel, another swore just as fiercely was an unqualified lie."[95] Granny, an avid storyteller, illustrates to Bone how easy it is to merge fact with fiction:

> She would lean back in her chair and start reeling out story and memory, making no distinction between what she knew to be true and what she had only heard told. The tales she told me in her rough, drawling whisper were lilting songs, ballads of family, love, and disappointment. Everything seemed to come back to grief and blood, and everybody seemed legendary.[96]

This reconstruction of reality mesmerizes young Bone, who learns that tragedy can be rewritten as legend. Even Glen recognizes the power of storytelling and views Granny's tales as threats to his patriarchal control. Glen dismisses Granny, instructing Bone and Reese to stop listening to her. "Your granny is the worst kind of liar," Glen exclaims; "That old woman wouldn't tell the truth if she knew it."[97] In place of Granny's stories, Glen tells the girls about the Waddell family as he claims them as his own: "I'll tell you what's true. You're mine now."[98]

However, from the time of the rape on, Bone has no intention of allowing Glen to author her story. The tales of grief and blood that Granny tells resonate with Bone's own reality. Well into her abuse, Bone starts to tell frightening stories of "boys and girls gruesomely raped and murdered, babies cooked in pots of boiling beans, vampires and soldiers and long razor-sharp knives."[99] These descriptions can be read as a cry for help, but they also suggest that in creating fictional stories, Bone is learning to gain critical distance from her trauma and to reconstruct reality. At a crucial moment during the rape scene, in which Bone's innocence is irrevocably damaged, she studies Glen's face with the purpose of turning it into a narrative of her identity. As she stares into his eyes, she likens his face to "a road map, a route to be memorized, a way to get back to who I really was."[100] Focusing on this critical part of the scene, Tania Friedel comments on how important fitting this experience into her mental scheme is for Bone, and by implication, for all incest victims in their transition to survivor: "By fixing Daddy Glen's face, and all the shame and trauma it signifies for her, in her memory, Bone will be able to assimilate it all into narrative language, a story she can tell herself about herself and that she will be able to use to transform emerging feelings of shame into a source of empowerment."[101] Despite the enormity of the obstacles she faces, Bone knows that reinventing herself through narration and putting a different ending on her version than the one her stepfather wants will aid her in authoring her own story and taking back a part of herself.

AUTOBIOGRAPHICAL TRACES: "NOT BIOGRAPHY AND YET NOT LIES"

Perceptive critics pointed out, and Allison candidly acknowledged, that Bone is a thinly veiled Dorothy Allison. Allison, who labors to humanize without idealizing her characters, patterned Bone's family after her own: specifically, her aunts and uncles are modeled after Allison's mother's family. Portraying her flawed characters realistically, she has said that she is driven by compassion and a desire to get at why these people are the way they are, including Glen. Like Morrison, Allison steps out of her gender and presents Glen as somewhat sympathetic, even though Allison has said that the flaw of the novel is her characterization of him.[102] She didn't think she managed to understand and love him, much like Morrison's claims regarding her depiction of the silent Pecola. Acknowledging the stereotypes that have been foisted on her and her loved ones, Allison states:

> I show you my aunts in their drunken rages, my uncles in their meanness. And that's exactly who we are said to be. That's what white trash is all about. We're all supposed to be drunks standing in our yards with our broken-down cars and our dirty babies. Some of that stuff is true. But to write about it I had to find a way to pull the reader in and show you those people as larger than that contemptible myth. And show you why those men drink, why those women hate themselves and get old and can't protect themselves or their children. Show you human beings instead of fold-up, mean, cardboard figures.[103]

Allison's story resists representing her people as case studies. "One temptation," Allison has said, "is to make the Boatwrights something off Tobacco Road. Just dirt poor slutty horrible, you know, stealing and wenching and all that bullshit."[104] In the novel most of the uncles do think they have the right to stay drunk from sunset on Friday until dawn on Monday. They also are members, however, of a close-knit family who genuinely love each other. For example, even though Bone notes that her uncles go to jail as early and often as some people go to school, these same uncles make gifts, such as coin purses and hair barrettes, for their nieces during their stints at the county farm.

Bone's parents are based on Allison's own. Glen reincarnates her stepfather. Although not much is documented on him, Allison revealed that he raped her from the time she was five years old: "The man raped me. It's the truth. It's a fact. I was five, and he was eight months married to my mother."[105] The scene in the fourth chapter in which Glen molests Bone in the hospital parking lot while Anney has a miscarriage is based on actual events. In an interview with Marilyn Strong, Allison confided that her stepfather gave her gonorrhea when she was twelve, which left her sterile.[106] Most likely, he also sexually violated her sisters, although she said she doesn't have any right to tell their stories.[107] To this day, he lives in denial, claiming he never touched her: "When contacted by *San Francisco Focus*, Allison's stepfather denied he ever physically or sexually abused her. 'Everything she says against me is untrue. I never touched her at all. I did everything I possibly could for that girl all my life.'"[108] Despite the fact that her stepfather has called her a liar, she is sensitive and even sympathetic to Glen's character. Insisting that "the first rule of writing is to love your characters," "Even the one you hate. You have to get inside them," Allison was asked if she loved the Daddy Glen character. She said, "Of course. I had to make somebody I could almost understand."[109] She writes from a place of compassion as she humanizes Glen and, as Morrison had, shifts the responsibility for father–daughter incest away from the indictment of any one individual.

"The woman that I made Bone's mother, Anney, was so much of my own mother," Allison has said.[110] The first chapter, which details the circumstances surrounding Bone's violent birth—a drunk driving accident, an unconscious teenage mother, and the word *illegitimate* stamped on her birth certificate—happened to Allison, whose mother was a grade-school drop-out, working as a waitress, and one month past fifteen when she first gave birth.[111] Unconscious during Bone's delivery, Allison's mother remained metaphorically unconscious to her daughter's abuse and refused to bear witness to her trauma. Allison says that for all of her mother's life, "She could not say the words—incest, violence, betrayal. She couldn't say: I knew he was fucking you. She could only say: I never meant for those things to happen. She'd say 'those things.' And she'd say: I know you'll never be able to forgive me."[112] Not surprisingly, Allison's mother is unable to put the experience to words, which suggests that, even though she knew what was happening, naming the incest was impossible for her. However, Allison seems to understand why her mother was so evasive, and through writing *Bastard*, she arguably comes to forgive her for ignoring the abuse.

The compulsive need for heterosexual validation exacerbated by Southern poverty confined Allison's mother, along with her sisters and other women. Allison's mother remarried, in part, out of economic necessity. In her novel, Allison also displays the compulsive need for heterosexual validation to which her mother, aunts, and many other women fell prey. Aware of the harshness of South Carolina's laws in the 1950s regarding unwed mothers, she notes that many women in her culture wished to marry to escape the ingrained shame of class prejudice.[113] "I think the shame [my mother] felt was one of the reasons she stayed with my stepfather. She wanted to be respectable," Allison comments.[114] She has also emphasized the hold that her stepfather had on her mother, with marriage reinforcing his claims to patriarchal privilege as he assumed the role of head of the family: "My stepfather broke her, broke her in a way that she couldn't imagine life without him."[115] Still living with Allison's abusive stepfather, her mother died at just fifty-six after suffering from cancer for thirty of those years. Tokarczyk reports that "In her final days, Allison's mother apologized to her for the abuse she had endured; trying to explain that she never wanted their lives to be so horrifying, that she always hoped things would get better."[116] Acknowledging her mother's love for herself and her sisters, Allison says she "fought desperately to get us through our childhood intact, but she failed utterly."[117] To show the strength of Bone and to focus on the complexity of Anney's character and why she failed, Allison explains: "I had to forgive my mother, really forgive her in order to show a child who couldn't forgive her."[118] Dramatizing her stepfather's violence and her mother's neglect, Allison refuses easy dichotomies of victim and perpetrator. It becomes clear that she is not out to seek revenge but that "forgiving rather than hating marks Allison's aesthetic."[119]

If the events Allison recounts actually happened, why does she turn to fiction to tell them? She anticipates this question when saying that "The element of fiction" provided "the necessary distance."[120] Her statement is in line with what critical theorists such as Cathy Caruth, Shoshana Felman, and Ronald Granofsky have argued with respect to trauma: "literary symbolism allows for a 'safe' confrontation with a traumatic experience."[121] If Allison fictionalized her account for personal reasons, her timing was also apt; in the early nineties when the novel was released, mainstream presses were starting to publish books about incest and sexual trauma in what would come to be seen as a publishing explosion. Allison thus pioneered a trend, well before the tell-all memoir outpouring. In fictionalizing her story, she was also able to draw out the broader cultural implications of a personal story, conveying a keen sense of ethical and political urgency.

In *Bastard*, Allison reconstructs her own story of abuse, giving Bone the strength that she claims she didn't possess at that age. She makes Bone get angry at thirteen, which she thinks will save her, unlike the author, who did not get angry until she was in her twenties.[122] Effectively rewriting her own story, Allison is pleased with the ending of her book in which Bone begins to claim a sense of herself and "goes to live with somebody who will teach her not to give her life away to a man who won't value it."[123] Through storytelling, she is able to counter the physical and economic domination of a patriarchal society that at one point crippled her.

Even though Allison is optimistic about the healing potential of fiction, which to her describes a better world than the one she knew, some of her critics are more skeptical. Harkins explains that there is a catch to telling one's story of incest: Allison is granted agency but it is by telling the story of a violated feminine sexual innocence.[124] Similarly, Horvitz questions how one can preserve memories of brutality without repeating them.[125] Acutely aware of the pain it took to author her story, Allison insists that writing is redeeming. To her, it is a form of resistance and a subversive way to uncover the class structure and the abuse that such inequities breed. Storytelling became a strategy for Allison not only to comment on social oppression but also to make sense out of her own life.

Allison's work is transgressive in that it questions the legitimacy of patriarchal, legal family structures that sometimes do not protect children as they claim. In rewriting the poor, violated female body—traditionally an easy target for patriarchal control—as a site of resistance and psychological healing, she transforms the disabling effects of traumatic experience to an empowering story of survivorship. Allison has written, "Behind the story I tell is the one I don't. Behind the story you hear is the one I wish I could make you hear. Behind my carefully buttoned collar is my nakedness, the struggle to find clean clothes, food, meaning, and money. Behind sex is rage, behind anger is love, behind this moment is silence, years of silence."[126] Claiming "there was no meaning in what my stepfather did to me," Allison broke her silence and made meaning out of a senseless experience.[127] Through the act of storytelling Bone helps save herself; through the act of writing Allison learns to survive the trauma that she captures so powerfully in her first novel. Like the story of the impoverished Pecola Breedlove, in which Allison saw her own experience, the story of Bone inspired a generation of female authors to share their own accounts of sexual violation. As we'll see in the next chapter, some of these writers relinquish the label *fiction* to achieve a more effective representation of father–daughter incest.

NOTES

1. Quoted in Minnie Bruce Pratt, "Dorothy Allison," *Progressive* 59, no. 7 (1995): 30.
2. Ibid., 31.
3. Quoted in Mae Miller Claxton, *Conversations with Dorothy Allison* (Jackson: University Press of Mississippi, 2012), x.
4. Judith Lewis Herman, *Trauma and Recovery* (New York: Basic, 1992), 30.
5. In *Accounts of Innocence: Sexual Abuse, Trauma, and the Self*, Joseph E. Davis provides a succinct overview of the literature on adult-child sexual relations before the mid-1970s, which often denied or minimized the harm: "Early writings in anthropology were largely concerned with the incest taboo and its explanation. Biologists studied the effects of inbreeding and posited various theories of biological disturbances as causative factors in sexual offenses. Sociologists produced a small but influential number of research studies on incest. The psychiatric literature, by contrast, was large, with one strand concerned principally with incest, especially father–daughter incest, and another strand concerned with a much broader range of sexual offenses. The criminology and legal literatures, too, were considerable, and focused on a wide range of legally defined or socially proscribed sexual offenses, contact and noncontact, in and outside the family." Davis, *Accounts of Innocence: Sexual Abuse, Trauma, and the Self* (Chicago: University of Chicago Press, 2005), 29–30.
6. Davis notes that "by one count, more than thirty books on child sexual abuse appeared between 1978 and 1982." *Accounts of Innocence*, 279. The first autobiographical book was published in 1979. The first film appeared in 1976: "Incest: The Victim Nobody Believes" even won a New York Film Festival Award and paved the way for other documentaries that informed the public of incest's prevalence.
7. Quoted in Herman, *Trauma and Recovery*, 30.
8. Diana E. H. Russell, *The Secret Trauma: Incest in the Lives of Girls and Women* (New York: Basic, 1986), 16.
9. Elaine Showalter, "Rethinking the Seventies: Women Writers and Violence," *The Antioch Review* 70, no. 1 (2012): 164.
10. Ibid., 163; Oprah Winfrey's contribution to putting sexual violence on the political map should not be overlooked. In the 1980s she was an instrumental figure in opening up a public space in which women shared first-person accounts of sexual violence on television.
11. Amanda Charlene Lee, "Forgotten Child: *Bastard Out of Carolina* and the History of Child Sexual Abuse," *Proteus* 30, no. 1 (2014): 21.
12. Ibid., 17.
13. Katrina Irving, "'Writing It Down So That It Would Be Real': Narrative Strategies in Dorothy Allison's *Bastard Out of Carolina*," *College Literature* 25, no. 2 (1998): 102.

14. Dorothy Allison, *Skin: Talking About Sex, Class & Literature* (Ithaca: Firebrand, 1994), 54, 34.
15. Katie Roiphe, "Making the Incest Scene," *Harper's*, November 1995, 65, 68–71.
16. Michael LeMahieu, "An Interview with Dorothy Allison," *Contemporary Literature* 51, no. 4 (2010): 651.
17. Other father–daughter incest narratives published during this time period include Jane Smiley's *A Thousand Acres* (1991), Mary Gaitskill's *Two Girls, Fat and Thin* (1991), Marilyn French's *Our Father* (1994), Russell Banks's *The Sweet Hereafter* (1991), and Sapphire's *Push* (1996).
18. Dorothy Allison, *Bastard Out of Carolina* (New York: Plume, 1992), 1.
19. Ibid., 3.
20. Ibid.
21. Ibid., 13.
22. Matt Wray and Annalee Newitz, *White Trash: Race and Class in America* (New York: Routledge, 1997), 2.
23. Allison, *Bastard Out of Carolina*, 170.
24. Peggy Dunn Bailey, "Female Gothic Fiction, Grotesque Realities, and *Bastard Out of Carolina*: Dorothy Allison Revises the Southern Gothic," *Mississippi Quarterly* 63, no. 1–2 (2010): 282.
25. Allison, *Bastard Out of Carolina*, 25, 27.
26. Dorothy Allison, *Trash* (New York: Plume, 1988), 12.
27. J. Brooks Bouson, *Embodied Shame: Uncovering Female Shame in Contemporary Women's Writings* (Albany: SUNY Press, 2009), 36.
28. Quoted in Amber Hollibaugh, "Telling a Mean Story," *The Women's Review of Books* (July 1992): 16.
29. Allison, *Bastard Out of Carolina*, 10–11.
30. Ibid., 11.
31. Ibid., 13.
32. Ibid., 99.
33. Ibid.
34. Ibid.
35. Ibid., 132.
36. Ibid., 64.
37. Ibid., 209.
38. Quoted in Hollibaugh, "Telling a Mean Story," 16.
39. Allison, *Bastard Out of Carolina*, 107, 234.
40. Ibid., 110.
41. Michell Tokarczyk, *Class Definitions: On the Lives and Writings of Maxine Hong Kingston, Sandra Cisneros, and Dorothy Allison* (Selinsgrove: Susquehanna University Press, 2008), 168.
42. Irving, "Writing It Down," 98.
43. Allison, *Bastard Out of Carolina*, 10.
44. Ibid., 37.
45. Ibid., 91.
46. Ibid.
47. Ibid., 23.
48. Ibid.
49. Ibid., 206.
50. Ibid., 120.
51. Ibid., 86.
52. Ibid., 32.
53. Ibid., 230–31.
54. Ibid., 231.
55. Ibid., 32.
56. Ibid., 206.
57. Ibid., 122.

58. Ibid., 123.
59. Ibid.
60. Ibid., 124.
61. Ibid.
62. Ibid.
63. Ibid., 291.
64. Ibid., 280.
65. Ibid.
66. Ibid.
67. Ibid., 118, 282.
68. Ibid., 285.
69. Ann Cvetkovich, "Sexual Trauma/Queer Memory: Incest, Lesbianism, and Therapeutic Culture," in *Incest and the Literary Imagination*, ed. Elizabeth Barnes, 329–57 (Gainesville: University Press of Florida, 2002), 346.
70. Louise Armstrong, *Kiss Daddy Goodnight: A Speak-Out on Incest* (New York: Pocket Books, 1978), 234.
71. Allison, *Bastard Out of Carolina*, 291.
72. Kathryn Robson, *Writing Wounds: The Inscription of Trauma in Post-1968 French Women's Life-Writing* (New York: Rodopi, 2004), 31.
73. Quoted in Robson, *Writing Wounds*, 31.
74. Dominick LaCapra, *Writing History, Writing Trauma* (Baltimore: Johns Hopkins University Press, 2001), 109.
75. Laura Di Prete, *"Foreign Bodies: Trauma, Corporeality, and Textuality in Contemporary American Culture* (New York: Routledge, 2006), 11.
76. Allison, *Bastard Out of Carolina*, 113.
77. Lynda Hart, *Between the Body and the Flesh: Performing Sadomasochism* (New York: Columbia University Press, 1998), 186.
78. Ibid., 202.
79. Ibid.
80. Tokarczyk, *Class Definitions*, 175.
81. Quoted in Carolyn Megan, "Moving Toward Truth: An Interview with Dorothy Allison," *The Kenyon Review* 16, no. 4 (1994): 79.
82. Tanya Horeck, "'Let Me Tell You a Story': Writing the Fiction of Childhood in Dorothy Allison's *Bastard Out of Carolina*," *New Formations* 42 (2000): 54.
83. Allison, *Bastard Out of Carolina*, 142.
84. Quoted in Alexis Jetter, "The Roseanne of Literature," *New York Times* magazine, December 17, 1995, 57.
85. Allison, *Bastard Out of Carolina*, 178.
86. Ibid., 179.
87. Ibid., 263.
88. Ibid., 309.
89. Ibid.
90. Ibid., 309.
91. Ibid.
92. Quoted in Strong, "Talking Trash," 97.
93. Quoted in Hollibaugh, Telling a Mean Story," 16.
94. Dorothy Allison, *Two or Three Things I Know for Sure* (New York: Dutton, 1995), 45; In "Sexual Trauma/Queer Memory," Ann Cvetkovich agrees that sexual abuse is one factor among many in someone's sexual orientation. Cvetkovich, "Sexual Trauma/Queer Memory," 334.
95. Allison, *Bastard Out of Carolina*, 53.
96. Ibid., 26.
97. Ibid., 52.
98. Ibid.
99. Ibid., 119.
100. Ibid., 288.

101. Tania Friedel, "The Transformational Power of Shame: Masturbation, Religion, and White Trash Myths in *Bastard Out of Carolina*," in *Critical Essays on the Works of American Author Dorothy Allison*, ed. Christine Blouch and Laurie Vickroy (Lewiston: Edwin Mellen Press, 2004.), 36–37.
102. Strong, "Talking Trash," 97.
103. Quoted in Hollibaugh, "Telling a Mean Story," 16.
104. Quoted in E. J. Graff, "Dorothy Allison: Novelist Out of Carolina," *Poets and Writers Magazine*, January/February 1995, 46.
105. Allison, *Two or Three Things*, 39.
106. Strong, "Talking Trash," 96.
107. Graff, "Dorothy Allison: Novelist Out of Carolina," 47.
108. Strong, "Talking Trash," 62.
109. Ibid., 97.
110. Quoted in Hollibaugh, "Telling a Mean Story," 16.
111. Allison, *Skin*, 15.
112. Quoted in Hollibaugh, "Telling a Mean Story," 16.
113. Irving, "Writing It Down," 102.
114. Strong, "Talking Trash," 95.
115. Quoted in Jetter, "The Roseanne of Literature," 56.
116. Tokarczyk, *Class Definitions*, 168. For a fuller account of her last days with her mother, see "Skin, Where She Touches Me," in *Skin: Talking About Sex, Class and Literature*.
117. Quoted in Strong, "Talking Trash," 64.
118. Quoted in Hollibaugh, "Telling a Mean Story," 16.
119. Tokarczyk, *Class Definitions*, 192.
120. Quoted in George Garrett, "No Wonder People Got Crazy as They Grew Up," *New York Times* July 5, 1992: 3.
121. Di Prete, *"Foreign Bodies,"* 5.
122. Megan, "Moving Toward Truth," 73.
123. Quoted in Strong, "Talking Trash," 95.
124. Gillian Harkins, "Telling Fact from Fiction: Dorothy Allison's Disciplinary Stories," in *Incest and the Literary Imagination*, ed. Elizabeth Barnes (Gainesville: University Press of Florida, 2002), 303.
125. Deborah Horvitz, "'Sadism Demands a Story': Oedipus, Feminism, and Sexuality in Gayl Jones's *Corregidora* and Dorothy Allison's *Bastard Out of Carolina*," *Contemporary Literature* 39, no. 2 (1998): 238.
126. Allison, *Two or Three Things*, 39.
127. Allison, *Skin*, 218.

FIVE

The Failure of Bearing Witness

The Politics of Truth Telling and Kathryn Harrison's The Kiss: A Memoir

"Trash," *Washington Post* critic Jonathan Yardley called it.[1] "Trash with a capital 'T,'" agreed James Wolcott in the *New Republic*.[2] These reviewers were not referring to the subject of Dorothy Allison's *Bastard Out of Carolina*. Allison's semiautobiographical account of father–daughter incest seemingly confirmed what most readers suspected—father–daughter incest is confined to the homes of poor, southern, "white-trash" families who lack the rationality and morality necessary to control their impulses. Despite problematizing such pattern by having the abuse initiated by a man whose family is middle class, Allison's book was, for the most part, received as an acceptable tale of incest. The same cannot be said of Kathryn Harrison's now infamous 1997 memoir titled *The Kiss*, published five years after *Bastard* and the target of Yardley, Wolcott, and many other reviewers during the three-year period following its release. These reviews often excoriated not just the subject matter but also its author.

"Not her maiden voyage into writing about the perils of sexuality," *The Kiss*, one can rightly say, was self-plagiarized.[3] The three-time novelist had published a good part of the material she uses in *The Kiss*, including the incest, in her first novel titled *Thicker Than Water*, released in 1991 to modest sales and critical success. The positive reviews suggested that Harrison arrived on the literary scene with her first novel. It was not until Harrison confirmed what her first book's discerning reviewers glimpsed—Isabel is Harrison once flimsily removed—that Harrison became a publishing event. In *The Kiss*, which provides a true account of paternal incest told from the perspective of a member of the white, upper-middle class New York literati, Harrison stripped the account of its fictional cloak, baring her family's deepest, darkest secret, which proved too much for the reviewers.

The following discussion examines how Harrison's depiction of father–daughter incest differs from the expected stories. It also considers the reviewers' scathing comments as manifestations of complex trauma, using textual analysis to illustrate how scenes from the memoir refute charges leveled by the critics. I look at how the portrait Harrison constructs of her father reveals him to be an insecure man longing for power. Similarly, her mother is portrayed as a collusive mother who desires freedom from motherhood. Instead of accusing either parent, however, Harrison attempts to understand how her childhood emotional deprivation evolved into a sexually abusive, adult relationship. What she exposes in her memoir should make us question those who read the book/her life as having a happy ending. It should also make us reconsider what the reviewers identified as the book's failure.

As trauma theorists point out, transforming experience through writing—what literary critic Suzette Henke calls "scriptotherapy"—can have therapeutic value.[4] In *Trauma and Recovery*, Judith Herman argues that altering memory through writing can be helpful; she states that to successfully work through trauma one should convert traumatic memory, which unconsciously repeats the past, into narrative memory, which narrates the past as past. Hence, she claims that a goal of therapy is "to put the story, including its imagery, into words" because the "*physioneurosis* induced by terror can apparently be reversed through the use of words."[5] The authorial effort to reconstruct a story of psychological debilitation could offer potential for mental healing and begin to alleviate symptoms common to those suffering from trauma. Writing, in these cases, becomes a protective space that encourages critical distance. Herman and Henke see much value in narrative recovery, meaning both the recovery of past experience through narrative articulation and the psychological reintegration of a trauma victim. And yet, Harrison uses the perpetual present tense, which suggests that she is unable to narrate the past as past. The book can be read as a depiction of complex trauma that is characterized by habitual, current action.

Along with its inability to convey the trauma as a past event, *The Kiss* did not succeed on another level. Herman, along with Dori Laub and Shoshana Felman, maintain that another important piece to the healing process exists—having others bear witness to the trauma. Many of the memoir's reviewers were unwilling to do that. As Harrison has said, the book "certainly pissed people off in a way that I had never experienced before."[6] In fact the memoir's prepublication frenzy made critics cringe, many of whom went on to author cutting critiques that questioned the book's veracity and compared Harrison to a modern-day Lolita.[7] What we then witness, in seeing the critics fail to attest to her story of incest, is another manifestation of the complex traumas of patriarchy. In addition to what is revealed in the memoir, the ensuing controversy and the reviewers' refusal to bear witness to Harrison's trauma expose the tumultuous, abusive social network that continues to create, yet deny, father–daughter incest.

Aside from being a memoir, Harrison's sparse book differs from the other works explored in this study in significant ways. The incest for *Tender Is the Night*'s Nicole, *Invisible Man*'s Matty Lou (if there was incest at all), *The Bluest Eye*'s Pecola, and *Bastard Out of Carolina*'s Bone occurred when the girls were young. Not so for Harrison. The incest did not begin for her until her father, who had been kicked out of her life when she was a toddler, reunited with her when she was twenty years old, a week after her twentieth birthday, to be exact. Unlike the other daughters, Harrison did not grow up with her father. Her parents, who met as teenage virgins, had a shotgun wedding and divorced before Harrison turned one. For twenty years, her father visited his daughter only twice—one time when she was five and the other when she was ten. Instead of the abuse we see Bone endure, Harrison's experience is more of a tryst—with a four-year run—not ending until her mother loses her battle with breast cancer. Instead of documenting the father's advances and focusing on his thoughts and words, as we read in *Invisible Man* and, to a lesser extent, in *The Bluest Eye*, Harrison's memoir neither probes the father's perspective nor gives him voice. He isn't even granted a name. Unlike Fitzgerald, who includes letters written from Nicole to Dick, as I discuss in the first chapter, Harrison mentions that she saved her father's letters, all "839 pages" of them, but she does not reproduce a single word from any of them.[8]

In place of her father's point of view, the work grapples with the daughter's role as collaborator, accomplice, and agent. For example, the book opens with the collusive "we": "We meet at airports. We meet in cities where we've never been before. We meet where no one will recognize us."[9] In so doing, the memoir raises difficult questions about how one can be both victim and collaborator. Many reviewers pointed out that the experience is portrayed more as an affair than as abuse. For example, in his coyly titled "Dating Your Dad," James Wolcott writes, "the father–daughter incest it recounts is not childhood exploitation, but a consensual act between two adults."[10] He then comments on Harrison's age, saying she was "old enough to know better."[11] It's true: the words *abuse*, *rape*, and even *incest* do not appear in the memoir. And Harrison is twenty years old, legally of age.

Nonetheless, *The Kiss* does not understate the horrors of incest and restrict its damages to child victims. At twenty, Harrison, stuck in the liminal zone between childhood and adulthood, is still vulnerable and craves parental acceptance. As a result, she acquiesces to the affair. Moreover, in *Interrogating Incest* Vikki Bell states that the crime of incest is less about the daughter's age than about the "gendered power dynamics of a male-dominated society that depicts women and children as possessions of the male."[12] As portrayed in the memoir, it is the father who is in control, something they will argue about; he insists that they continue meeting, requests that they have sex, and makes it clear that it is an all-or-nothing relationship. In "The New Face of Incest? Race, Class, and the Controversy over Kathryn Harrison's *The Kiss*," Mako Yoshikawa points out that the book "deserves credit for driving it home to us that incest is a traumatic event even if the victim is grown, even if her father is not someone she has long leaned upon."[13] Yoshikawa applauds Harrison's brave work, which pictures the blonde Harrison on its cover, for expanding our definition of incest while still showing the abusive power it entails.

The debate stirred by Harrison's book may be of greater significance than the book itself. The hostile reactions certainly tell us more about the political climate than the memoir does. Reviewers were deeply disturbed by its confession and in no uncertain terms told Harrison to shut up. For example, at the end of Cynthia Crossen's *Wall Street Journal* review patronizingly titled "Know Thy Father," where she criticizes memoirists and pities Harrison's father, she dispenses what she calls "two wise but widely ignored words of advice for Ms. Harrison and her brethren: Hush up."[14] Reviewer Jonathan Yardley, not known for welcoming women's writing, voices similar concerns to Crossen's, wishing for the discussion of father–daughter incest to cease. He ends his scathing review in which he calls *The Kiss* "trash from first word to last," with the sentences, "The temptation to go on and on about this book, piling one abusive paragraph upon another, is extreme, but must be resisted. Space is short in this newspaper. Let's save it for something worth my words and your time."[15] Strangely, not heeding his own advice, he goes on to write two more pieces about Harrison's *The Kiss*. In his hostile review, Wolcott suggests that some secrets, evidently incest, should be kept secret: "Secrets are an integral part of privacy, a personal identifying mark or a family bond."[16] He goes on to quote the narrator of Saul Bellow's *The Bellarosa Connection*: "Deeply experienced people—this continually impresses me—will keep things to themselves."[17] Wolcott's nod to Bellow's narrator is a not-so-disguised way of saying essentially what Crossen said—shut up already. Additionally, Karen Lehrman from the *Post* charged Harrison with "literary overexposure": "Just like wearing a miniskirt that's too short or a blouse that's unbuttoned too low."[18] Mary Gordon and Catharine Stimpson are indeed right to detect a dose of misogyny in the reviews and the responses they generated, one of which is titled "James Wolcott Smacks Kathryn Harrison in the Kisser."[19]

Despite attracting much negative attention from many reviewers and making for quite the literary event, the memoir did not provoke nearly as much scholarly debate. To date, one can still easily mine the scholarly articles and essays. Currently, no book-length studies are devoted to *The Kiss: A Memoir* or to Kathryn Harrison. Some of the articles and essays comment on the book's critical reception as I do here. For example, in "After Lot's Daughters: Kathryn Harrison and the Making of Memory," Laura Frost argues that the reviewers were troubled mainly with Harrison's violation of genre conventions. She maintained that these reviewers were, in part, lashing out at the genre of memoir, the ever-so-popular literary form of the 1990s they felt was overused, abused, and inferior to the craft of fiction writing. Memoirs of the 1990s occupied an ambiguous space between autobiography and fiction. Traditionally, as Kate Douglas writes in "'Blurbing' Biographical: Authorship and Autobiography," readers of memoir expected testimonial authenticity, the "recording [of] authentic experience."[20] In the last twenty years, as memoir theorist Paul John Eakin notes, they got creation instead—literary experimentation and innovation. The pervasive initiative among memoir writers was to establish autobiography and memoir as imaginative art, with special emphasis on invention and storytelling. For example, in the creative nonfiction genre that emerged at this time with Harrison at its forefront, reconstructed dialogue, the use of metaphor, and foreshadowing devices abound. Frost explains that memoir is "the genre that most obviously raises questions of referentiality and authorial presence."[21] Considered by some to be a narcissistic narrative of solipsism, the memoir, both the genre itself and this particular book, can be defined as "a reflective and highly constructed representation of the self that engages with and draws on conventions of *fiction* and incorporates other cultural material" (emphasis added).[22]

Harrison's memoir ignited a heated discussion about the form as few others had. By the time of its publication, reviewers had tired of the confessional, testimonial form of discourse that is at times self-absorbing and self-indulgent, even likening the explosion of creative nonfiction to "a rampant publishing orgy."[23] For instance, Crossen reduces *The Kiss* to a book about "a woman who can't get over herself."[24] Well aware that everything one writes has elements of autobiography and that the boundaries between fact and fiction are always uncertain, Harrison has acknowledged that "you have to have suspense, you have to shape it. It is certainly as much a crafted thing as fiction is."[25] However, most reviewers of *The Kiss* took *memoir* to mean *autobiography* and charged Harrison with dramatizing and flouting autobiographical conventions and even purposely misrepresenting events in the book.

The memoir backlash began almost concurrently with the memoir boom in the early 1990s, and perhaps it should come as no surprise that female memoirists, particularly female memoirists like Harrison who disclosed too much regarding the structures of patriarchy, drew the harshest critiques. The criticism *The Kiss* received exposed the gendered politics of autobiographical acts. It was a rather predictable pattern that we saw with the female confessional poets as the work of Sylvia Plath and Anne Sexton was initially dismissed as "disgustingly autobiographical."[26] For example, *The New York Times*'s Christopher Lehmann-Haupt wrote that Sexton's "tortured confessions seemed to be personal yelps rather than universal cries."[27] With the memoirs of the 1990s, Harrison's book was part of what Lehrman saw as "a disconcerting trend in women's writing."[28]

Tobias Wolff, a memoirist himself and sympathizer of Harrison, argued that *The Kiss* was an easy target for reviewers to vent their frustrations with memoirs. He recognizes the literary merit of the genre, stating, "I wanted to know how a man of flesh and blood, not of fiction, made sense of what had been done to him."[29] Instead of seeing Harrison's memoir, like Wolff, as a cathartic release, a way of working through trauma, the reviewers found it devoid of art and an easy avenue for Harrison to cash in on her woes. For instance, Yardley's second negative review announces that memoir is "'The Kiss' of Death for Literature."[30] Additionally, Crossen contends that "Memoirs are literature's slipperiest slopes: They require neither the rigor of journalism nor the imagination of fiction."[31] And, commenting on the book's marketing and financial success, reviewers Adam Begley and Stephen Moss mockingly write, "beware a woman scorned—especially if she is clutching a publishing contract."[32]

However, it's unlikely that just the genre of memoir troubled these reviewers. As Eakin states in "Breaking Rules: The Consequences of Self-Narration," one does not make front-page news for violating literary traditions.[33] Moreover, in his response to Wolff's charges that Yardley and company were really criticizing the genre of memoir, Yardley states that he "loves" memoirs, has even written in his thirty-five-year writing career what may be rightly labeled a memoir.[34] Clearly it was something else that struck a nerve. In addition to the form that Harrison's narrative took, the content distressed them. They were concerned with the taboo subject Harrison was so unflinchingly revealing. Put simply, they had a difficult time trusting her. For example, in "Pants on Fire! Who Really Believes Kathryn Harrison's Incest Tale?" Mary Eberstadt questions "why we should believe that this story is true."[35] Likewise, Yardley questions the validity of the events in Harrison's memoir.[36] Eberstadt's and Yardley's line of reasoning sounds eerily similar to that used by the False Memory Syndrome Foundation, who discredit the truth of father–daughter incest, insisting that therapists plant false memories of incest in the minds of their female patients.

Eberstadt and Yardley were not alone in their quest to track down the truth. Jeff Giles of *Newsweek* went so far as to contact Harrison's father. In "The Father Won't 'Kiss' and Tell," (as in, shame on the daughter for doing that) Giles regretted to inform the public that Harrison's father "never explicitly denied the affair."[37] His contribution shows the great lengths some were willing to go, as late as 1997, to undermine the daughter's story by letting the father have the last word.

THE INCESTUOUS FATHER AND COLLUSIVE MOTHER

Sympathizing with the father, Crossen, along with most of the reviewers, excuses his behavior by stating that Harrison's father is mentally ill, "so obviously sick that one's natural revulsion is tempered by pity."[38] Yet, Harrison's father is depicted as a highly intelligent white man, armed with a PhD and camera. He is a full-time minister and a part-time photographer. He can "outwit most psychiatrists," and has succeeded in fooling a second wife and children.[39] However, to write him off as a mental case would be a justification, rationalizing the pain he inflicts on his daughter. The reviewers remarked that Harrison supplies no good reason why she, or any woman for that matter, would fall in love with a man she describes as physically unattractive. Strikingly, she describes him in feminine, almost maternal, terms. Although saying that he is a "good-looking man," her focus is on his obesity ("I have to stretch to get my arms around him"), disconcertingly visible man breasts, voluptuous arms, and bloodshot eyes—which would make Harrison seem like the perverse one for being attracted to him.[40] They criticize her for not furnishing her father with a name, going so far as to wonder if she called him dad in bed.[41] They delight in the double entendres that result when talking about the book: the story "then climaxes—sorry, no other word will do—with the reappearance of her father and his seduction of the not-unwilling her."[42] And most troubling, they feel let down by the lack of sex scenes, calling those subtle scenes more chaste and coy than disturbing. *Vanity Fair*'s contributing editor Michael Shnayerson even accused the book's silences as being "a tease."[43]

It's true that in place of graphic sex with her father, Harrison supplies condensed fragments of the events juxtaposed without clear references. The chapter that opens, "It begins when I'm twenty," where readers expect to learn the details of their ten-year reunion, ends with what readers are also likely to expect—forced penetration.[44] But instead of reading about how her father took her virginity, we encounter a humiliating scene where her mother takes her to a gynecologist's office to have her fitted for a diaphragm. Presumably, she is trying to protect her daughter from a similar fate to her own—becoming a teenage mother. The doctor explains that she can't be fitted for one unless her hymen is broken. He questions, "You don't want to do that, do you?"[45] Briefly hesitating, Harrison's mother says yes and watches as her college-bound daughter is stabbed with "a series of graduated green plastic penises."[46] Interestingly, it is her mother, not her father, who deflowers her, something the critics were quick to note.

In addition to the breaking of her hymen, the event that deeply affects Harrison lives up to the freakish foreshadowing of the book's title—the kiss. At the end of their ten-year reunion, just as her father's plane is boarding, he initiates a kiss that seemingly sets a spell in motion. Harrison at first tries to resist his kiss and escape his grasp, but she is unsuccessful, as she will be for the next four years. She does include a brief scene in which her father performs cunnilingus in his mother's house ("he opens my legs and puts his tongue between them" is the extent of the description), but the initial airport kiss seems to haunt her the most. Couched in fairy-tale language, she describes the kiss's long-term effects:

> In years to come, I'll think of the kiss as a kind of transforming sting, like that of a scorpion: a narcotic that spreads from my mouth to my brain. The kiss is the point at which I begin, slowly, inexorably, to fall asleep, to surrender volition, to become paralyzed. It's the drug my father administers in order that he might consume me. That I might desire to be consumed.[47]

Despite the emphasis that Harrison places on the kiss, the reviewers had rather little to say about the initiating traumatic event. Wolcott does mention it, but he makes light of the situation by calling it "a Roto-Rooter tongue probe."[48] Instead of being a kiss of enchantment, it is one of disenchantment; instead of awakening a sleeping beauty, it puts Harrison in the depths of sleep, and judging from the hypnotic, trance-like, somnambulistic writing style, pits from which she has not fully emerged.

But if the kiss blinds Harrison to the incest, which allows it to go on for four years, it opens her father's bloodshot eyes even wider than they were when he first met her after those ten years. When he first lays eyes on his grown-up daughter, he instructs her not to move: "Just let me look at you."[49] And look he does, in a way that no one had ever looked at her before. His eyes turn on his daughter with "absolute attention," something that her mother's eyes, which are frequently closed, fail to do.[50] Finally, it seems that Harrison has been awarded the attention she felt she never got, even after years of playing the good daughter, being high school valedictorian, acing Latin exams, and petitioning to take unusually high course loads in college.

Just as we've seen in *The Bluest Eye* with Pecola, Harrison yearns for someone to acknowledge her existence and to love her. One of the memoir's most gruesome scenes clearly shows her longing for attention. In this scene, her grandmother's Persian cat has a litter of kittens five years after Harrison's mother moves out, leaving her in the care of her grandparents. Harrison is promised whichever kitten she wants but the catch is she can't touch them until they're old enough to open their eyes. An impatient Harrison kneels by their box every day until she can no longer stand it. One day she pries the kittens' eyes open. Harrison writes, "I laid one in my lap and, with one thumb on the upper lid, the other on the lower, I carefully pulled its eyes open, separating one delicate membrane of flesh from the other."[51] She performs this procedure on all five of the kittens. A day later their eyes are swollen shut and when Harrison tries to clean the yellow crust away, a worm of pus shoots out. Finally telling her grandmother that she thinks something is wrong with the kittens' eyes, she cannot bring herself to explain what happened.

The kitten scene contains much metaphor and symbolism, literary devices that the reviewers were not expecting in a memoir. The closed-eyed kittens represent Harrison's mother, who is usually sleeping, and even Harrison's estranged father. The violation of the kittens' eyes is comparable to the sexual and emotional violation Harrison experiences by her father. It also stands for the revenge of her mother that she accomplishes via the father–daughter incest. Her inability to wait for the kittens' eyes to naturally open mirrors her powerlessness to resist the temptation of her father. Not telling the truth to her grandmother can be interpreted as a failure to speak out about the incest.

Eberstadt finds this scene to be "the single most emetic passage in all the book."[52] Instead of recognizing the conflicted emotions that the scene conveys, however, Eberstadt suggests that this scene illustrates how corrupt Harrison is—a kitty tormentor who keeps feelings of guilt at bay to continue doing disgusting things. Undoubtedly, this is a terrible scene that shows a darker side of Harrison. But one may wonder why Eberstadt finds this scene more disturbing than the airport kiss scene, or any of the other scenes in the book where Harrison's father exerts control over her and her body. For example, using language evocative of Glen's (from *Bastard*), Harrison's father says that he will show her who she is, a task accomplished by making her meet his parents. The meeting of the paternal grandparents includes her grandfather placing his hand on her thigh and her father performing oral sex on her in her grandmother's house. Despite all of these unsettling scenes, Eberstadt conspicuously singles out the kitten scene, where Harrison is clearly the perpetrator, as the "emetic" one.

In the wake of the memoir's promotion and publication, the assaults on Harrison seemed endless and vacillated between criticizing her writing to attacking her person. Adding insult to injury, in "Doing Daddy Down," Elizabeth Powers questions whether Harrison is well read, particularly in Greek mythology and Freudian theory: "Like many contemporary authors, Harrison does not appear to be very well or very deeply read: it is hard to tell from this memoir whether she is even familiar with the Oedipus story."[53] Does one need to be well versed in the Oedipus myth to write a father–daughter incest memoir? A deeper reading, however, suggests that Harrison is well acquainted with the Oedipus story. Perhaps it is Powers who is guilty of a superficial reading. Harrison evokes the mythic precursors of Oedipus Rex and Tiresias, not just to emphasize the themes of sight and blindness, but also to expose the flaws of Freud's Oedipus complex in that before Harrison begins the sexual affair with her father, she desires her mother, undermining Freud's theory that the child is attracted to the opposite-sex parent and wishes to eliminate the same-sex parent. In the alternative storyline Harrison offers, the daughter first falls in love and stays in love with the same-sex parent. Ultimately, Harrison's father–daughter incest story is about her mother. Harrison's mother, who knows of the affair, speaks the truth when she says to her daughter, "You know . . . this isn't about *you*. It's about *me*."[54]

The reviewers were offended by Harrison's depiction of her minister father; however, they had very little to say about the disclosures regarding her mother, who at first glance embodies the textbook definition of the collusive mother. In *Father–Daughter Incest*, Herman and Hirschman give the portrait of the mother of paternal incestuous families as represented in popular men's magazines, which was disappointingly similar to that in the psychiatric literature. Neither source holds back on saying what is wrong with the mother. She is typically sexually unavailable to her husband, emotionally distant from her daughter, and rendered powerless in her family. Although they state that the professional authors would not be so blunt as to say that she's "no good in bed," their language—"frigid, hostile, unloving women"—"barely disguises the same judgment."[55] Because the father has lost access to the mother as his normative sexual partner, her "frigidness" is blamed for causing the incestuous relationship to develop. Because of her powerlessness, devaluation, and economic dependence in the traditional, male-dominated family structure, the mother is unable to protect her daughter. Ironically, as Armstrong points out in *Rocking the Cradle*, from the perspective of popular culture and even some of the professionals in the field of psychiatry, father–daughter incest is thought to illustrate the extreme failure of *maternal* protectiveness.[56]

Harrison strives throughout her narrative to understand her mother and father, rather than simply blaming them for being cold and aloof. Like Anney from *Bastard*, Harrison's mother had her adolescence taken from her as a result of teenage pregnancy. Both women are dependent on the attention of men and react with ambivalence toward what they perceive to be the degrading and dispiriting role of mother. Yet, despite feeling unmothered, the daughters unconditionally love their mothers and cannot forsake them. Like Allison, Harrison devotes her book to her mother: "Beloved, 1942–1985."[57] Both books are written after their mothers die of cancer. Harrison makes clear that her mother was in a powerless position most of her life, in which her weakness is most poignantly shown through her inability to combat her husband's and her own parents' domination.

The main reason Harrison's parents divorce is because her maternal grandparents find her father not good enough for their daughter, a judgment that is based on class and ethnicity. Harrison explains that her mother and father became parents at seventeen, "without money, with no more than high school educations."[58] As she says, they were still children themselves and unfit for the kind of responsibility that followed. Harrison's grandfather is most concerned with how her father will financially provide for the family, doubting his ability to support them. Without a college degree, her father takes a job as an encyclopedia salesman. Commenting on the class division between her parents, Harrison outlines her father's humble origins that make him susceptible to her grandparents' contempt: "German immigrant ancestors, the miscegenation of his Native American grandmother, not one but two missionary grandfathers, his own parents' broken marriage, not to mention their relatively modest circumstances."[59] His inferior status is further highlighted in its contrast to that of her wealthy Jewish maternal grandparents, who were born in London and lived all over the world. Harrison's father admires, if not fears, the grandparents' "entitled European condescension, their wealth and property and the solid history implied by antiques that were passed down, not acquired."[60] Not only is Harrison's father's financial situation a problem, but so too is his religion. He is a non-Jew *and* a preacher. Harrison's grandparents teach their daughter that a life with that man, a life as "a preacher's wife," would be a fate worse than death—one of poverty.

Neither Harrison's mother nor father has a say in their relationship. The decision for Harrison's parents to divorce comes from Harrison's grandfather, who tells her father in no uncertain terms that it is over between him and his daughter. Exempting him from financial responsibility, such as child support, her grandfather also excuses her father from being a father, not letting him hold his daughter and forbidding him to visit. Harrison's grandfather then assumes the role of nurturing father, providing for her, "singing her to sleep every night, teaching her to ride a bicycle, counseling her about her education (and paying for it, as well as a year abroad to travel), and letting her help him garden."[61] In her grandparents' house, her father's "name is never spoken, his existence is not acknowledged."[62] Her grandmother goes so far as to cut his face out of every picture, erasing him from the family.

The emasculation of Harrison's father is not limited to Harrison's maternal side. It is compounded by the treatment he receives from his own parents and grandparents. Harrison knows very little about her paternal grandfather. But the three things she learns are disconcerting. Her philandering paternal grandfather was so handsome in his youth that women he didn't even know followed him down streets. (Once, in an attempt to tag along with his father, Harrison's father ran into a parking meter and knocked himself out because, instead of paying attention, he was watching the women watch his father.) Additionally, Harrison's grandfather shot a man in his yard just for looking at his wife. And finally, Harrison tells us that her grandfather is slowly dying of prostate cancer because he refuses treatment, evidently preferring death to the loss of his testicles. She sums it up succinctly when she says, "So this is the way my father understands his father, and thus his own manhood: mythic sexual appeal, violent sexual jealousy, fatal sexual vanity."[63] It seems that her father, not unlike Glen Waddell, is still very much that little boy trying to follow his father but falling miserably short.

The influence on his mother's side is just as troubling. Raised by his missionary grandmother while his mother worked as a secretary, Harrison's father felt overpowered by his maternal grandmother who insisted that he become a preacher. He does become a man of God, but he resents his grandmother and the servitude she imposes on him. Harrison explains that he begrudges "the *castration* implied by the robes he's forced to wear (he calls them skirts)" (emphasis added).[64] Like Cholly Breedlove of *The Bluest Eye*, who redirects his hatred from the white men to Darlene, Harrison's father targets others—Harrison's mother and grandmother, who took away his wife and daughter, and his own mother, whom he thinks failed to protect him from her mother. This may explain, without excusing, why he feels it necessary to violate his daughter in his mother's house. Commenting on the experience, a reflective Harrison realizes that the setting has to do with power: "He needs to do it at his mother's house. He needs the power granted by her presence, and he needs to thwart that power."[65]

As much as her father wanted to be part of her life, her mother wanted *not* to be, and her negligence is allowed by her parents. Like Anney of *Bastard*, Harrison's mother remains willfully unconscious of the incest, absenting herself from the situation. Both mothers literally move away from their daughters. Harrison's mother is a far cry from a traditional, idealized mother. In fact, her actions can be seen as rebelling against not just her own parents but against typical feminine and maternal roles. While in Harrison's maternal grandparents' house, her mother sleeps whenever she can, preferring unconsciousness to being a mother. When Harrison is six years old, her mother moves out, leaving her daughter in the care of her parents. In her attempt at an independent life, she moves into a nearby apartment, telling her family what street it is on, but supplying neither house nor phone number. Years later, Harrison understands that her mother wished to be free from the burdens of motherhood: "she does not want to be summoned by fevers or nightmares or lost teeth."[66] In short, she wants what her parents grant her ex-husband—the freedom from parental responsibility.

Harrison neither fully blames her mother for poor parenting and negligence, nor does she excuse her for turning a blind eye to the abuse. She hints that her mother has been a victim of emotional abuse in her own family, especially controlled by Harrison's maternal grandmother. Tellingly, Harrison won't let her grandmother be buried on top of her mother. Trying to get to the root of her childhood emotional deprivation and the resulting father–daughter incest, Harrison suggests how crucial yet fragile mother-daughter relationships are in patriarchal societies. When the bond between mother and daughter is strong, it most efficiently wards off paternal incest; when it is weak, it makes the daughter most susceptible to sexual abuse. Rearing and nurturing children in a patriarchal society falls on the mother, who is expected to be caring, attentive, and ready to place her child's needs before her own. But as Adrienne Rich explains in *Of Woman Born: Motherhood as Experience and Institution*, to properly perform these selfless tasks, to be a "good mother," requires that the mother demonstrate a "strong sense of *self*-nurture."[67] This "strong sense of *self*-nurture," however, is what oppression—whether patriarchal or racial or economic—undermines, correctly observes Paula Bennett in her essay on incest and maternal deprivation.[68] Instead of passing on a healthy sense of self-worth, the mother often transfers to her daughter her own sense of deprivation and helplessness. In Harrison's case, she inherits sexual submissiveness and degradation from her mother. Similarly, her father's second wife is also too weak to stop her husband's affair. She simply asks that he spare her any evidence of it. Because they are powerless to his demands, such women cannot nurture or protect Harrison. In a patriarchal society, mothers are seen as unworthy of children's profoundest love and loyalty, which often are reserved for fathers. Seeking in men—in this case, in her father—what her mother cannot provide results in competition. In this oppressive society, women are pitted against each other in an unnecessary and often dangerous rivalry.

Instead of—or in addition to—presenting herself as a victim of incest, Harrison suggests that she is out to get revenge, but, despite what the reviewers claim, the revenge is more on her mother than on her father. Ironically, through the sexual affair with her father, Harrison is able to "penetrate" her mother, to use her word. Harrison uses her father to finally get the attention she so craves from her.[69] Both daughter and father know what they are doing, though. When talking about love, they admit that they have "a subject more consuming than love: *Her*. Love's object. My mother. His wife."[70]

Harrison claims that it takes kissing the bodies of two corpses—her maternal grandfather's and, not surprisingly, her mother's—to break the spell cast by her father. Prior to kissing her mother, she performs a symbolic castration by cutting her hair to tell her dying mother that the incest is over. Having clung to her long hair as a symbol of sexuality, Harrison explains that her father was as dedicated to her hair as she was, having been the one to trim it for the past few years. The real release and acknowledgment, however, come in the dream Harrison has of her mother, which she describes in the last two pages. Instead of the nightmares she often dreams, this one is tranquil. In it they "look closely at each other."[71]

Harrison ends her memoir with the image of mother and daughter looking into each other's eyes with acceptance and recognition. As her father's influence fades into the background, Harrison is left with a dream of her mother. Illustrating her undying love for her mother, her concluding words show how hurt mother and daughter were by the incest. In a moment of fantastic reconciliation, they reach an understanding of each other, something not accomplished in their lifetime.

AN UNAVOIDABLE BOOK

In "Innocence Betrayed," Susan Cheever argues, "The real shock is that this is a book with a happy ending."[72] Christopher Lehmann-Haupt takes this assertion a step further in "Life with Father: Incestuous and Soul-Deadening," and insists Harrison's mysterious healthy survival is the major flaw of the memoir.[73] He assumes, as Lisa Alther notes, that if Harrison's claims are true, then she should be too traumatized to tell the tale. Instead of remaining silent, she goes on to write her story—in best-seller fashion, no less. Lehmann-Haupt's assertion raises several questions. Did Harrison really survive the trauma? How does one define survival? What is the proper form for telling a story of trauma? Is there ever one? Or, should victims of father–daughter incest heed the words of Crossen and "hush up"?

The fact that Harrison (like Bone) goes on to author the book suggests that she has made some progress in working through her trauma, at least enough to gain critical distance to put words to the events. Yet, as questioned in the previous chapter, can one demonstrate agency when writing a story of female violation? Moreover, can one represent memories of horrific experiences without repeating them? And, to borrow from feminist theorist Rosaria Champagne, can one ever be healed in a sick society?[74] Harrison's closing scene recounts a positive dream she had of her mother on February 7, 1995, when she seems to reach some kind of closure, but this does not mean that Harrison is free from nightmares. Her entire memoir, like Pecola's dissociated chapter toward the end of *The Bluest Eye*, is written from the perspective of someone suffering from CPTSD. For example, on the first page, she writes that "we are out of time as well as out of place."[75] Again, she comments on the timelessness of her experience in the middle of the memoir when she writes "a time out of real time."[76] Laub notes, "The traumatic event, although real, took place outside the parameters of 'normal' reality, such as causality, sequence, place and *time*" (emphasis added).[77] Because the shattering experience results in a distorted memory, the chronology of the memoir is appropriately nonlinear, recursive, and in the present tense.

In addition to feelings of dislocation and timelessness, Harrison experiences physical symptoms common to those with CPTSD. Not surprisingly, she experiences a split between body and mind when her father performs oral sex on her in his mother's house. She writes about her dissociation: "What he does feels neither good nor bad. It effects so complete a separation between mind and body that I don't know what I feel. Across this divide, deep and unbridgeable, my body responds independently from my mind."[78] She is not fully conscious of the sexual experiences. In a telling passage, she reflects on her inability to recall her feelings during the sexual experience with her father despite the fact that she can remember exact details, such as the socks he wears, the lines surrounding his eyes, and the hair on his hands. Able to remember fine details surrounding the sexual affair, she is unable to recall her feelings, which at least partly explains the restraint of the memoir's style and the omission of the act of incest that many reviewers criticized.

But whereas her mind fails to supply these memories, her body keeps score. In other words, she has corporealized her feelings. Eberstadt notes that what we learn of Harrison is that she is very sick. Presenting her more as a hypochondriac than as someone suffering from CPTSD, Eberstadt rattles off Harrison's ailments: "(in alphabetical order only) amenorrhea, amnesia, anorexia, asthma, bulimia, dehydration, depression, insomnia, narcolepsy, pneumonia, rashes, and shingles."[79] Added to this list are "coughing fits, sore throats, an inability to breathe, suicidal longings, and acts of self-mutilation."[80] Eberstadt reminds us that this is quite a lot for a very short book. One may want to remind Eberstadt that this is more than a book—this was/is Harrison's life. Harrison is aware that her mental distress is manifested through her bodily symptoms. Not coincidentally, the summer her father visits she comes down with shingles caused by "physical or emotional stress."[81] Not enough to cancel her trip to see her father, the shingles nevertheless alert Harrison to the severity of their budding relationship. Realizing what clinicians Herman, Bessel van der Kolk, and others have maintained, Harrison writes "What a memory the body has, events recorded in our bones, our blood, our nerves."[82] Emotionally, Harrison "feel[s] nothing"; physically, the abuse takes its toll.[83]

Robert Coles, distinguished life-long advocate for the voiceless, child psychiatrist, Harvard professor, prolific writer, and author of *The Moral Intelligence of Children*, among other books, originally wrote a blurb for *The Kiss*, praising it for its literary achievement and for its author's courage. The endorsement read, "This book offers an account of a moral victory—the re-emergence of a thoughtful, disciplined, knowing sensibility" (which was posted on the site http://kathrynharrison.com/the-kiss.htm, but has since been taken down). However, when he found out that Harrison is the mother of two young children (as of 2000, three young children), he retracted his statements. According to Warren St. John of the *New York Observer*, Coles explains that "he had not realized Ms. Harrison had young children of her own who would have to cope with her public revelations"[84] It seems that for Coles and others, because Harrison is a mother of young children, she should not publish a memoir of this sort. Coles may have had good reasons to withdraw his endorsement; he may have been attempting to protect Harrison's children from a phenomenon known as intergenerational trauma in which symptoms are passed on from one generation to the next. However, the implication of his retraction can also be seen as an attempt to maintain the myth of childhood sexual innocence and to perpetuate a conspiracy of silence that retraumatizes the victims, the latter of which is discussed in my first chapter. Coles's concerns, along with Lehmann-Haupt's assertion, beg the question: is silence really the answer?

For Harrison, silence was not an option. In an interview with the *New York Observer*, she told the reporter, "I've been writing this book in my head for years."[85] By the time she sat down to put words to paper, she completed it in a mere four weeks. In an interview with *The Seattle Times*, Harrison admits that "rather than one I set out to write," "*The Kiss* was a book I couldn't avoid."[86] Voicing no regrets about going autobiographical, she further explains:

> It was a book that came out of a decade of thought. There was a point in my life as a writer and as a human being in which I reached a kind of clarity and an ability to be honest with myself about what my relationship with my father had been. And I knew as a human being and as a writer that it would be a real mistake to back away from that, and the only apparatus I have as a human being for understanding things is writing.[87]

After writing *Thicker Than Water*, she felt as though she had betrayed her experience, "which was so much more complicated and complicit."[88] As she's said: "the moment I finished the first novel I resented having novelized the story. I felt that I had betrayed it and betrayed my own story by turning it into fiction and by dampening it."[89] Moreover, Harrison felt that she was complicit in the silencing of father–daughter incest by cloaking it in fiction: "I had unwittingly complied with the social imperative that you always hear about incest, that I made it up." [90] Although she's said that she "never considered writing nonfiction" when she began her literary career, she authored *The Kiss* to face up to herself, not necessarily to expose her father and mother.[91] She chose memoir as an avenue to tell the truth about her complicated ordeal, giving readers a glimpse into the difficulty she has working through her trauma.

Certainly, as Wolcott states, it is one thing to write about trauma; another matter to publish it.[92] It seems that in addition to asserting aesthetic and psychological mastery over trauma, Harrison's published work becomes a testament to the therapeutic value of articulating painful experiences. Much like Dylan Farrow, her decision to go public with her memoir, the transgressive act of publishing, suggests a political consciousness to break the taboo of talking about incest. In *Survivor Rhetoric: Negotiations and Narrativity in Abused-Women's Language*, Christine Shearer-Cremean and Carol L. Winkelmann comment on the necessity to tell one's impossible story of trauma, emphasizing the *political* importance for such telling. They write: "the atrocious stories of male violence against women must come to voice in order for women to secure their full human rights."[93] Giving voice to her story of incest, Harrison challenges the patriarchal and hierarchical discourses that seek to silence her and deny her full rights.

Despite what Lehmann-Haupt says, the memoir did not "fail" because Harrison lived to tell about it, went on to marry (a fellow novelist, former deputy editor of *Harper's*, and current vice president and senior editor at Scribner), have children, and establish her place as a successful writer; rather, it failed in the eyes of the reviewers because it did not integrate unspeakable acts into a narrative that meets conventional expectations—as Dorothy Allison's did. These expectations stipulate that a political critique of this kind can be neither too overt nor come from a white, middle- to upper-class, highly educated woman.[94] This was a book that Harrison couldn't avoid, but that the reviewers certainly wanted to. Why? In "When the Daughter Tells Her Story: The Rhetorical Challenges of Disclosing Father–Daughter Incest," Brenda Daly, who has herself authored a story about father–daughter incest, supplies an answer: "It is important to keep in mind, when reviewers and critics attack women who write trauma narratives, especially those disclosing father–daughter incest, that reviews or critical essays are sites of ideological struggle about control of, and representation of, women's bodies." [95] The controversy over Harrison's *The Kiss* speaks to this ideological struggle and to the politics of truth-telling in that most of the reviewers who endorse patriarchy felt threatened by Harrison's truthful account of the social order's horrors. They glimpsed the truth that we live in a society that allows and even encourages such violence, and they lashed out in fear of exposure.

When *Bastard Out of Carolina* met with success, Allison thought she must have done something wrong to garner such accolades. As critics praised the book, and at year's end selected it as a National Book Award finalist, Allison was hesitant to uncork the champagne.[96] With only $200 left to her name when she published *Bastard*, she said, "I saw myself as a living affront to a kind of literature that I despise. How could the people who were the pantheon of that literature think I did something right? I thought I must have screwed up bad." [97] Allison loathes literature that adheres to a masculinist canon and echoes heteropatriarchal, racist, classist discourse. According to her, it is often written by men, judged by men, and passed off as universal.[98] This canon repeats what has been said before, and, in universalizing the experience it portrays, denies the humanity of those who dwell outside of its gates. Tellingly, *The Kiss* outraged the gatekeepers of literature, many of whom perpetuate the unjust social order. Harrison's book expanded our conceptualization of father–daughter incest and indicated that one of its own could be its victim. What the reviewers identified as the failure of the book is perhaps Harrison's true success.

NOTES

1. Jonathan Yardley, "Daddy's Girl Cashes in: Kathryn Harrison Writes a Shameful Memoir of Incest," *Washington Post*, March 5, 1997, D2.
2. James Wolcott, "Dating Your Dad," *New Republic*, March 31, 1997, 32.
3. Kera Bolonik, "About Kathryn Harrison," *Ploughshares* 35, no. 2/3 (2009): 174.
4. Suzette A. Henke, *Shattered Subjects: Trauma and Testimony in Women's Life-Writing* (New York: St. Martin's, 1998), xv.
5. Judith Lewis Herman, *Trauma and Recovery* (New York: Basic, 1992), 177, 183.
6. Quoted in J. David Bellamy, "An Interview with Colin and Kathryn Harrison," *The Iowa Review* 37, no. 1 (2007): 172.
7. Nicci Gerrard, "A Family Affair, We Have Sinned . . . ," *The Observer Review*, April 13, 1997," 6.
8. Kathryn Harrison, *The Kiss: A Memoir* (New York: Avon, 1997), 156.
9. Ibid., 3.
10. Wolcott, "Dating Your Dad," 33.
11. Ibid.
12. Vikki Bell, *Interrogating Incest: Feminism: Foucault and the Law* (London: Routledge, 1993), 140.
13. Mako Yoshikawa, "The New Face of Incest? Race, Class, and the Controversy over Kathryn Harrison's *The Kiss*," in *Incest and the Literary Imagination*, ed. Elizabeth Barnes, 358–76 (Gainesville: University Press of Florida, 2002), 368.
14. Cynthia Crossen, "Know Thy Father," *Wall Street Journal*, March 4, 1997, A16.
15. Yardley, "Daddy's Girl Cashes in," D2.
16. Wolcott, "Dating Your Dad," 35.
17. Ibid.
18. Quoted in Eula Biss, "The Voice Box: Our Opera of High and Low," *Columbia: A Journal of Literature and Art* 45 (2008): 153.
19. Quoted in Adam Begley, "When a *Kiss* Ain't Just a Kiss: Robert Coles, Blurbist, Repents," *New York Observer*, April 7, 1997, 31.
20. Kate Douglas, "'Blurbing' Biographical: Authorship and Autobiography," *Biography* 24, no. 4 (2001): 817.
21. Laura Frost, "After Lot's Daughters: Kathryn Harrison and the Making of Memory," *Auto/Biography Studies* 14, no. 1 (1999): 52.
22. Marshall, "The Daughter's Disenchantment," 404.
23. Quoted in Emily Hipchen, "Genetic Sexual Attraction and the Creation of Fatherhood: Making Daddy (Infamous) in *The Kiss*," *The Journal of the Midwest Modern Language Association* 42, no. 2 (2009): 16.
24. Crossen, "Know Thy Father," 16.
25. Quoted in Bolonik, "About Kathryn Harrison," 176.
26. Carolyn G. Heilbrun, "Contemporary Memoirs: Or, Who Cares Who Did What to Whom?" *The American Scholar* 68, no. 3 (1999): 39.
27. Quoted in Heilbrun, "Contemporary Memoirs," 39.
28. Quoted in Biss, "The Voice Box," 154.
29. Tobias Wolff, "Literary Conceits," *New York Times*, April 6, 1997, 19.
30. Jonathan Yardley, "'The Kiss' of Death for Literature?" *Washington Post*, March 10, 1997, B2.
31. Crossen, "Know Thy Father," 16.
32. Quoted in Douglas, "'Blurbing' Biographical," 822.

33. Paul John Eakin, "Breaking Rules: The Consequences of Self-Narration," *Biography* 24, no. 1 (2001): 115.
34. Jonathan Yardley, "Thanks for the Memoirists," *Washington Post*, April 14, 1997, D2.
35. Mary Eberstadt, "Pants on Fire! Who Really Believes Kathryn Harrison's Incest Tale?" *Weekly Standard*, March 24, 1997, 31–32.
36. Yardley, "Daddy's Girl Cashes in."
37. Jeff Giles, "The Father Won't 'Kiss' and Tell," *Newsweek*, April 28, 1997, 81.
38. Crossen, "Know Thy Father," A16.
39. Harrison, *The Kiss*, 94.
40. Ibid., 67.
41. Wolcott, "Dating Your Dad," 34.
42. Yardley, "Daddy's Girl Cashes in."
43. Quoted in Biss, "The Voice Box," 153.
44. Harrison, *The Kiss*, 32.
45. Ibid., 42.
46. Ibid.
47. Ibid., 70.
48. Wolcott, "Dating Your Dad," 33.
49. Harrison, *The Kiss*, 51.
50. Ibid., 62.
51. Ibid., 90.
52. Eberstadt, "Pants on Fire!" 32.
53. Elizabeth Powers, "Doing Daddy Down," *Commentary* 103, no. 6 (1997): 39.
54. Harrison, *The Kiss*, 98.
55. Judith Lewis Herman and Lisa Hirschman, *Father–Daughter Incest* (Cambridge: Harvard University Press, 1981), 43.
56. Louise Armstrong, *Rocking the Cradle of Sexual Politics: What Happened When Women Said Incest* (Reading, MA: Addison-Wesley Publishing, 1994), 123.
57. *Thicker Than Water* is even more explicitly about her mother, particularly her long and painful death. The father–daughter incest is present in the last fourth of the novel. Kathryn Harrison, *Thicker Than Water* (New York: Random, 1991).
58. Harrison, *The Kiss*, 16.
59. Ibid., 23.
60. Ibid., 23–24.
61. Hipchen, "Genetic Sexual Attraction," 12.
62. Harrison, *The Kiss*, 5.
63. Ibid., 121.
64. Ibid., 126.
65. Ibid., 128.
66. Ibid., 14.
67. Adrienne Rich, *Of Woman Born: Motherhood as Experience and Institution* (New York: Norton, 1976), 245.
68. Paula Bennett, "The Mother's Part: Incest and Maternal Deprivation in Woolf and Morrison," in *Narrating Mothers: Theorizing Maternal Subjectivities*, ed. Brenda O. Daly and Maureen T. Reddy (Knoxville: University of Tennessee Press, 1991), 126.
69. In *Thicker Than Water*, she is even more frank: "Of course I could never have hated my mother so much, enough to allow her husband to fuck me, had I not loved her so desperately. I would have done anything to get her attention." Harrison, *Thicker Than Water*, 238.
70. Harrison, *The Kiss*, 78.
71. Ibid., 206.
72. Susan Cheever, "Innocence Betrayed," *New York Times Book Review*, March 30, 1997, 11.
73. Christopher Lehmann-Haupt, "Life with Father: Incestuous and Soul-Deadening," *New York Times*, February 27, 1997, C18.

74. Rosaria Champagne, *The Politics of Survivorship: Incest, Women's Literature, and Feminist Theory* (New York: New York University Press, 1996), 210.
75. Harrison, *The Kiss*, 3.
76. Ibid., 101.
77. Dori Laub, "Bearing Witness or the Vicissitudes of Listening," in *Testimony: Crises of Witnessing in Literature, Psychoanalysis, and History*, ed. Shoshana Felman and Dori Laub (New York: Routledge, 1992), 69.
78. Harrison, *The Kiss*, 128.
79. Eberstadt, "Pants on Fire!" 32.
80. Ibid.
81. Harrison, *The Kiss*, 118.
82. Ibid.
83. Ibid., 170.
84. Warren St. John, "Kathryn Harrison's Dad Responds to Her Memoir," *New York Observer*, April 21, 1997, 9. In "When a *Kiss* Ain't Just a Kiss: Robert Coles, Blurbist, Repents," Adam Begley provides a fuller explanation of the events of, and his own role in, Coles's "public repentance": The eminent Robert Coles, whose blurb, gushy as blurbs must be, blessed Ms. Harrison's book, has recanted. I faxed him a copy of James Wolcott's gleeful, hilarious and virulently nasty attack on *The Kiss* in *The New Republic*, which concludes with a slap at "psychologist and saint Robert Coles." Mr. Coles read the article and admitted that he deserved Mr. Wolcott's censure. "I accept the criticism," said Dr. Coles. "I *should* be reprimanded." (31) Now seeing the book as inviting "misery and humiliation" upon Harrison's children, Coles added, "My God, what are those children to think—*what are they to think*? And why would the mother of those children want to put that down so that all the families of the kids her children play with are going to know?" Begley, "When a *Kiss* Ain't Just a Kiss," 31. Begley further explains that Coles received the galleys of *The Kiss* when he was busy teaching a Harvard seminar in which Morrison's *The Bluest Eye* is regularly assigned. Coles claims he got so "swept up" in reading and discussing the book with his students that he wrote the blurb without considering the fact that Harrison's book is based on real life and that she is a mother. Ibid.
85. Quoted in Giles, "A Father," 62.
86. Quoted in Yoshikawa, "The New Face of Incest?" 374.
87. Quoted in Julie Lewis, "Secret Souls of New York," *Weekend Australian*, February 12, 2000, R10.
88. Quoted in Gerrard, "A Family Affair," 6.
89. Quoted in Bellamy, "An Interview," 171.
90. Quoted in Bolonik, "About Kathryn Harrison," 175.
91. Ibid., 174.
92. Wolcott, "Dating Your Dad," 35.
93. Christine Shearer-Cremean and Carol L. Winkelmann, introduction to *Survivor Rhetoric: Negotiations and Narrativity in Abused Women's Language*, ed. Christine Shearer-Cremean and Carol L. Winkelmann (Toronto: Univ. of Toronto Press, 2004), 11.
94. See Elizabeth Wilson's "Not in This House: Incest, Denial, and Doubt in the White Middle Class Family" for a discussion of the history of middle-class attitudes toward the sexual abuse of children and reasons why the denial of incest persists.
95. Daly, "When the Daughter Tells Her Story," 158–59.
96. Jetter, "The Roseanne of Literature," 57.
97. Quoted in Jetter, "The Roseanne of Literature," 57.
98. Both Allison and Harrison are young enough to have grown up with Second-Wave feminism. But unlike Allison, who has been vocal about her endorsement of feminism, Harrison's stance is not nearly as clear. In an interview with Patricia O'Connell, Harrison expresses her suspicion with any group, including feminists, "who are very sure only *they* know what's really going on." Patricia A. O'Connell,

"Kathryn Harrison: Her Harrowing Psychological Novels Are Fiction, but Seem Vividly Real," *Publisher's Weekly,* March 1, 1993, 34. However, the language she uses—incest is not the taboo; talking about it is—echoes feminist language.

SIX

Convicting the Victim

Stacey Lannert's Redemption *and the "Little-Known Psychological Problem" of Child-Abuse Parricide*

Like Kathryn Harrison, Stacey Lannert had a difficult time proving that she was a victim of father–daughter incest. While many were hurling insults at Harrison for printing her autobiographical account of father–daughter incest for the world to read, Lannert was serving hard time for being unable to prove that she killed her father in self-defense. Just before daybreak on July 5, 1990, an eighteen-year-old Stacey shot her forty-three-year-old father Tom Lannert while he was sleeping on the couch. The fatal wound was delivered in the head at point-blank range. For a fifteen-year sentence, the prosecuting attorney wanted Lannert to say she killed her father for his money. But Lannert was one of the only people to know the truth; she did it because she had been incestuously abused for close to a decade. Refusing to plead guilty, Lannert was convicted of first-degree murder on October 30, 1992. By December, Judge Steven H. Goldman handed down the mandatory sentence of life in prison without the possibility of probation or parole, a conviction upheld on appeal and harsher than the one given to Charles Manson. In his post-trial report, Goldman wrote, "The sentence is severe for a twenty-year-old. It is also somewhat surprising considering the sexual abuse by the victim's father . . . a conventional life sentence would be more appropriate from a comparison standpoint."[1] So why didn't Stacey Lannert receive a conventional life sentence? And is justice really served when Lannert and other victims of child abuse who commit parricide are convicted of first-degree murder?

Those questions, along with how this family disintegrated into lethal violence weigh heavily on the reader of Lannert's 2011 memoir, *Redemption: A Story of Sisterhood, Survival, and Finding Freedom Behind Bars*. This chapter discusses what the jury did not know about the Lannerts and argues that Stacey did not receive a sentence fitting for her crime. As Fitzgerald's and Morrison's novels point out the shortcomings of the psychological community, Lannert's memoir calls attention to the corrupt legal system she was under for eighteen years of her life. Both books reveal that the professions that are supposed to be ones of healing and justice are instead part of the problem and further serve to retraumatize the victims. To that end, it raises questions about culpability as it argues that our legal system has failed to protect those most in need. In *Rocking the Cradle of Sexual Politics: What Happened When Women Said Incest*, Armstrong agrees that incest

> should be enforced as a crime just like wife-beating. Because when the battered wife kills her battering husband they're pretty good at enforcing that as a crime. True. And when kids kill their fathers (or arrange to have it done) they do a pretty good job with that too.[2]

As we see with the Missouri case of *State v. Lannert*, that is also unfortunately true.

Strikingly, Lannert's memoir is not written by a writer like the other works in this study. Although Lannert received help from *Glamour* reporter Kristen Kemp, this book, which was reviewed favorably, is not authored by a professional, partly explaining why it has not received critical attention. Instead, the chronological account is a plain-spoken, candid, chilling attempt at breaking a silence that paralyzed and ultimately resulted in her taking the life of her father. As with Harrison's memoir, Lannert's cover includes a picture of herself—a blonde-haired, blue-eyed, attractive, thirty-some-year-old woman wearing a pink cardigan and a pearl necklace with matching earrings. This is not the typical portrait of a father–daughter incest victim, let alone of a murderer. On the cover, there's another picture, also atypical. In the upper-left-hand corner is a family shot, featuring a young, smiling Tom Lannert, a bit glazy-eyed, with his daughters by his sides and his wife standing behind him. Tellingly, wife and mother Deborah's head is cut out, indicating her estrangement from the family. As we learn in the book, Tom and Deborah had marital problems for most of Stacy's childhood. Like Harrison's mother, Deborah was an absent parent. The three family members whose faces we do see appear to be happy. And from the picture, the Lannerts look like a normal, white, middle-class, Midwestern family. But the words on the cover and in the rest of the memoir tell a much different story than the picture-perfect life. Adjacent to the family photo the text reads, "At age 18, I shot and killed my sexually abusive father and was sent to prison for life. . . . " Before her memoir most readers knew that

Lannert took her father's life. It was much later that she admitted why it happened—the sexually abusive part.

In the chapter that documents her time in custody, Lannert explains why it took her so long to speak about the brutal abuse and to admit that she was raped approximately three times a week for ten years. As she writes in her narrative, she was unable to tell Detective Schulte, who hinted that he knew she was abused, that she is an incest victim: "I could barely tell a guidance counselor that my father hurt me, and when I did, it didn't matter. The word *rape* was not yet in my vocabulary. It was too heavy, harsh, and loaded. It was too embarrassing and dirty. I could barely speak, let alone tell a husky stranger—a man—what I had been through. I didn't have the words."[3] In addition to telling her high school guidance counselor, Lannert attempted to inform her babysitter, psychologist, and even her mother who herself was sexually abused by her father—all to no avail. Repeating what she said about being unable to use the word *rape*, Lannert writes later in her book that she had a difficult time revealing the abuse to her lawyer: "I couldn't explain the details of a lifetime of abuse"; "I couldn't tell . . . how I got a scar on my wrist. I couldn't tell anyone what Tom Lannert did to me on my eighteenth birthday."[4] She couldn't tell them that Tom raped her with the gun she bought to protect herself and that he had pulled the trigger to what turned out to be an unloaded gun with it inside of her. She also did not have the words to explain that the initial aggressor was Tom, who, just hours before his death, raped her sister, Christy, for the first time and who, in a fit of rage, fired at Stacey's head the same .22 that would later kill him. The first part of her memoir provides those words that Lannert and the jury did not have when they needed them the most—when she was fighting for her freedom.

As we saw in Allison's book, this reluctance to break the silence regarding father–daughter incest is quite common.[5] In at least one parricide case where the daughter killed her abusive father, she was ready to plead guilty of first-degree murder rather than recount the past.[6] The daughter's unwillingness to tell about her abuse is partly explained by psychologist S. V. McLeer, who noted that children sexually abused by fathers, in addition to being "more likely to exhibit PTSD than children abused by other adults or by older children" experience a peculiar bonding with their father.[7] A theory of traumatic bonding, state psychologists M. DeYoung and J. A. Lowry, may be used to explain some of

> the commonly confusing dynamics involved in incestuous relationships, such as the child's unwillingness to disclose the abuse, strong emotional ties to the incest perpetrator, and a history of behavior that may increase the risk of further victimization. They suggest that due to the traumatic bond, cognitive distortions may arise concerning issues of blame, responsibility, power, and trust.[8]

These sexually abused children often do not talk about their past because of shame and embarrassment.

> Although they may feel that sexual behavior with a parent is wrong, they are often forced to choose between believing themselves or believing others who are important to them. These children may find it necessary to surrender their perceptions and to give up control of themselves for psychological, and sometimes physical, survival.[9]

In addition to being threatened by their abusers to not tell, there are numerous other psychological reasons that make seeking and getting help the exception and not the rule for children like Lannert. Aside from the obvious financial dependence, these children often fear abandonment and resort to self-blame. Moreover, these abused children often stay because they fear that other family members would be abused in their absence, which Tom threatens to do when Stacey goes to live with her mother in Guam. Runaways are likely to be further victimized on the streets. There are even legal repercussions for running away from home. For example, in some states, if juveniles run away several times, they could be found in contempt of court and held in a detention facility. Children are commonly reluctant to talk about their victimization—even to authorities—because they know that those who report abuse are often not believed. And, of course, there is the implicit family oath to remain quiet, that family matters are private and that a father has absolute power to discipline his children as he sees fit.

Even after finding a pair of Lannert's bloody underwear tucked in the basement stairs, her mother, who had been molested by her father as an adolescent and whose mother turned a blind eye, convinces herself that Stacey is not being abused but has merely started menstruating. When asked by her maternal grandmother Marilyn, with her mother in the car, if her father ever touches her, Lannert responds, "Ewww. No! My daddy would never do that!"[10] Lannert writes, "I didn't have words for this topic, not out loud and not even in my head. Ask any child this question point blank, and she will deny it."[11] Much like Bone when questioned by her Aunt Ruth about being molested, Lannert knows that even if she does say yes, it is unlikely that her family members would do anything about it. Denial by other family members places added responsibility on the child to solve the problem. Often, these children become the protectors of their abused younger siblings, as Stacey does for her sister. Furthermore, Tom repeatedly warns Stacey that no one would believe her if she told. Telling her guidance counselor and others seemed to confirm it. And so, it should come as no surprise that when questioned by two male detectives about what led to her father's death, she does not have the words to express the ten years of abuse she endured. In her statement to the police, Lannert does admit that her father had sexually abused her. But as she notes, she was unable to provide the details of her father's abusive behavior and her "words could only scrape the surface of what really happened between" them.[12]

Even if Stacey detailed the truth about her years of abuse, would it have mattered to the court? Author of "Abused Children Who Kill Abusive Parents: Moving Toward an Appropriate Legal Response," Susan C. Smith notes that too often the psychological landscape of child-abuse parricides is not addressed in courts: "Results such as that in *Lannert* do not 'take into account all of the facts and circumstances surrounding the parricides, and emphasizes only the narrow goals of preserving human life and limiting self-help."[13] The law's dismissal of the child abuse leading to parricide, as demonstrated in the *State v. Lannert* case, exposes complex social and legal problems and reinforces the conspiracy of silence surrounding father–daughter incest.

PARRICIDE

"Few crimes are as shocking or intensely personal as the killing of one's parents," states Kathleen Heide, a psychotherapist, scientist, and leading expert in the field of parricide who has conducted assessments of more than 100 adolescent homicide offenders and written three books on the topic.[14] And yet, it should come as no surprise that most daughters who kill their fathers were sexually abused by them. Paul Mones, a Los Angeles attorney who since 1980 has been a pioneer in dedicating his career to defending adolescent parricide offenders, maintains that "over 90 percent of youths who kill their parents have been abused by them."[15] Heide notes that juvenile involvement in parricide is high in relation to the proportion of juveniles arrested for homicide.[16] Although "the large majority of parricides are committed by white middle- or upper-class boys between 16 and 18 years of age,"[17] the rate of females committing homicide has been increasing each year since 1984 and some report that female killers, though smaller in number, are more likely than males to kill a family member.[18] Mones states that children often resort to this desperate measure when they see an abusive parent attack the other parent or a sibling.[19] Some studies found that females received harsher sentences for their offenses, perhaps because a girl who commits a crime may be seen as more deviant than a boy who commits the same crime; she may also be considered less amendable for rehabilitation. However, most of these youths of both genders were identified as having minimal or no prior trouble with the law and rearrests were rare.[20] Furthermore, "case reports indicate that boys and girls who killed fathers were unlikely to have histories of severe mental illness, but they have typically had long histories of being victims and witnesses to abuse by their fathers."[21] In her four studies of girls who killed their fathers, Heide found that all of the girls were sexually abused by their fathers.[22] Speaking from experience,

Lannert sums up the reason why: "women kill because they're afraid they'll be killed."[23]

When Lannert was navigating the legal system for killing her father, child-abuse parricide was thought to be, in the words of the Washington Supreme Court, a "little-known psychological problem."[24] In 1941, Frederic Wertham was the first mental health professional to explore adolescent parricide, some twenty years before child abuse was recognized as a serious problem in the United States. In the wake of Wertham's case study, fewer than a dozen others followed until the 1990s (Heide's first book on the topic was published in 1992) leaving many questions unanswered including why these children take the life of the person who has given them life. In 1990, when Stacey killed her father, courts were just "waking up to the problem. Kids just don't take these actions unless something is very, very wrong."[25]

Our courts have historically denied the legal protection to abused children they were intended to offer. These children were victimized at least two times: first by their abuser, then by the legal system's failure to recognize the validity of their defense. As late as the 1990s, many states had "transfer" legislation that allowed or even required the child to be prosecuted and punished as an adult, even when studies found that the societal consensus was to try them in juvenile court.[26] In fact, in some states, the youths could even be given the death penalty.[27] Traditionally the courts have viewed the homicides as random acts of violence instead of what they often really are—acts of self-defense. For example, judges and attorneys were found to be "naïve and brutally insensitive to a fact on which all child abuse experts agree—the attacks visited on a child are qualitatively different from the violence one adult perpetuates on another."[28] Customarily "the courts have not considered words, no matter how vile or insulting, to constitute adequate provocation. Similarly, the courts generally have not viewed trivial blows, even if technically a battery, as qualifying as sufficient provocation to cause a reasonable person to engage in a killing frenzy."[29] In short, the doctrine of self-defense, whose classic definition holds that the defendant prove that she reasonably believed she was in imminent danger of death or substantial bodily harm, is problematic in these cases. It was formulated almost a thousand years ago to address combat situations between men, particularly one-time assaults between strangers. As Heide notes, "it did not take into consideration differences in physical size and strength between men and women and between parents, particularly fathers, and their children."[30] Nor does it take into account the cumulative effect of a series of abusive or provocative acts, as it often requires immediate, and not just imminent, danger. In most jurisdictions, an honest belief on the part of the defendant that she was in danger is simply not enough.

To establish a claim of self-defense in most jurisdictions, defendants must prove the following: that they were not the aggressor (in this case, that the parent was attacking the youth), they reacted with only the amount of force necessary to repel the attackers, and they reasonably believed they were in *immediate* danger of unlawful or deadly bodily harm and that retreating at that moment without sustaining serious injury or death was extremely remote. The burden of proof falls on, in this case, Lannert and other victims who must show that they were in danger and were legitimately standing their ground. The doctrine of self-defense does not include the psychological state of the defendant, who very well could be suffering from complex trauma and has reached a point where he or she believes to be in danger of being killed at any time and who sees no other way out of an intolerable situation. Because abused children often perceive the imminence of danger differently from nonbattered children, expert testimony is a "critical factor in helping jurors understand why an abused youth feared for his or her life at the time the youth killed the parent."[31] Only an expert can delineate the specific psychological traits of abused children and how they impact the child's actions, or more appropriately, his or her reactions and why the distinction between immediate and imminent danger is a blurred line.

It was not until as late as 1982 in *Jahnke v. State* when a court even *considered* the killing of a parent as an act of self-defense or as having a legitimate case for justifiable homicide. The Wyoming Supreme Court was the first to address the question of admissibility of expert testimony on what is called psychological "battered child syndrome" (BCS) as part of a self-defense claim. The widely agreed-upon watershed event for the emergence of child abuse as a social problem was the publication of Dr. C. Henry Kempe's 1962 report, "The Battered-Child Syndrome," published by Kempe and colleagues.[32] The term "battered child syndrome" was introduced in the *Journal of the American Medical Association* as a diagnosis for *physical* injuries: it was used to describe the pattern of physical wounds inflicted upon children by abusive parents. Sexual abuse of children would not get recognized until January 1974 when President Nixon signed into law the Child Abuse Prevention and Treatment Act (CAPTA), which broadened the federal definition of child abuse from physical injury and neglect to include sexual abuse.[33]

The original model for the battering syndromes was battered woman's syndrome (BWS). In her 1979 book *The Battered Woman*, leading expert on the topic Lenore Walker, a clinical and forensic psychologist who has worked with Mones as a legal activist for juvenile rights, argues that prolonged exposure to the cycle of abuse has *psychological* effects and often produces in the subjects PTSD in which they no longer trust their own natural responses when under the threat of danger. Moreover, they lose their ability to predict the repercussions of their actions, experience learned helplessness—which causes abused people not to seek outside help—and exist in a state of hypervigilance and fear. Despite some differences between the response of adult women and that of children to exposure to chronic violence, researchers have noted the similarities in the *psychological* changes that occur after experiencing repeated abuse. The battering syndromes encompass cognitive disturbances, high arousal symptoms, and high avoidance symptoms.

Despite its association with BWS, which has been allowed in court to aid the jury in making a decision, albeit only in the last thirty years, BCS has had little acceptance in state courts. Whereas all fifty states recognize the *physical* manifestations of BCS, the *psychological* effects have not been legally validated. For example, in *Jahnke v. State* brother and sister Richard and Deborah Jahnke were convicted of the crime of voluntary manslaughter, which is a homicide committed in response to adequate provocation and which lacks malice aforethought (actual or implied intent to kill). Although this case captured the attention and moreover compassion of the country, the sentence was upheld by the court, which agreed that the Jahnkes did not show the requisite evidence for self-defense of actual or threatened assault for a lesser conviction or acquittal.

It would take almost close to a decade for a legislature to provide a battered person defense law. In 1991, the Texas legislature became the first in the country to provide a battered person defense law that applied to children as well as women, thus allowing evidence of family violence to be admitted when a woman or a child kills. Moreover, they allowed expert testimony to explain the characteristics and mentality of a battered child. Texas and later Washington were the first states to accept that some children who kill their parents are responding to legitimate threats against their lives and not exhibiting delinquent behavior.[34] They were the first to recognize that battered children should be accorded the same rights as battered women, and that consistent standards are essential to ensure that battered women and children receive fair adjudication.

In 1993, three years after Tom Lannert's death, BCS was used successfully for the first time as a defense for parricide. In *State v. Janes*, a landmark case for children's rights, the Washington Supreme Court "ruled that actual physical violence is not necessary to demonstrate imminent danger. Evidence of threatening behavior, gestures, or comments by the abuser is enough to show that the adolescent believed that he or she was in imminent danger."[35] And, it permitted the admission of battering evidence even when the battering episode substantially predated the killing: "The court acknowledged that children who suffer from prolonged abuse develop 'a very finely tuned antenna for impending violence [which] . . . picks up low-level cues that people who have not been traumatized would not see."[36] This was also the first time an appellate court ruled that the psychological syndromes related to battered women and children are based on the same principles, and thus such testimony for battered children should be admissible. Moreover, they acknowledged that abused children are entitled to the protection of self-defense. The Court held that "evidence of the battered child syndrome is admissible to prove self-defense, and expert testimony is allowed to help the trier of fact understand this 'little-known psychological problem.'"[37] In the decades following the landmark decision of *Janes*, however, not many other states have held that testimony regarding BCS should be admissible in a murder case. In 2013, "only eight of the 50 states in the United States specifically have legislation that pertains even broadly to BCS."[38]

> Since the mid-1990s, juveniles involved in murder have been typically prosecuted in adult court, where they face long sentences, and under today's laws, can still be sentenced to life without parole. Up until 2005, juvenile homicide offenders could be sentenced to death.[39]

When Lannert was being tried, the admissibility of BCS testimony was in its infancy and fraught with controversy as many feared that using it would allow these children to literally get away with murder. Convincing the court that Lannert acted in self-defense would have been the defense's best approach. Because Missouri did not recognize the validity of BCS, her public defender, McGraugh, sought to admit evidence of battered spouse syndrome at her trial. In his article, "Clemency: Doing Justice to Incarcerated Battered Children," then third-year law student at the University of Missouri-Columbia School of Law, Robert Hegadorn provides additional insight into why defense counsel take the approach of battering syndrome during trial. He explains that the typical method of parricides easily meets the legal definitions of first-degree murder: "The killing is commonly premeditated. The parent is 'almost always' slain in situations where a child is not immediately threatened and the parent has no opportunity to defend against attack."[40] In other words, the parent is not killed during an abusive act. Sometimes there is a triggering event that precedes the killing by about six months, or, in Stacey's case, just hours earlier when Tom raped Christy for the first time and fired a gun at Stacey's head. The child often feels like there is no other means of escaping further abuse except by taking life. Feeling a combination of fear, revenge, and self-defense, the child murders. Moreover, there is the "overkill factor": "the killing often appears to have been done in a most savage fashion, and only rarely 'is the parent killed with one clean shot; rather the parent is often shot, clubbed, or stabbed numerous times.' Afterwards, many parricides try to deny and cover up the killing, but later confess."[41] As Lannert states in her memoir, she shot at her father three times, tried to stage a break-in, but wound up admitting to the killing.

Honing in on what is at stake with BCS and parricide, Hegadorn states, "Without the admission of battered child syndrome evidence, a parricide defendant has little hope of demonstrating to a jury that his or her actions were in self-defense."[42] When Lannert was being prosecuted, Missouri case law held that a woman attempting to use evidence of battered spouse syndrome need not have been married to the alleged batterer, but this statute did not do much to help Stacey because its language excluded children from the coverage of battered syndrome, and it placed the burden on Stacey and her lawyer to properly demonstrate that she was acting in self-defense. And here's where it got very complicated: "Missouri case law requires a homicide defendant to show that he or she feared an *immediate* threat from the victim in order to be entitled to a jury instruction on self-defense."[43] In other words, Lannert needed to prove that she was in *immediate*—and not merely *imminent*—danger. As the Washington Supreme Court held in *State v. Janes*, these two words mean very different things. *Imminent* means ready to take place; near at hand; hanging threateningly over one's head; menacingly near. *Immediate*, however, means occurring, acting, or accomplished without loss of time; made or done at once. It is the court's job to determine if the triggering event is sufficiently close in time to allow the admission of evidence of battered spouse syndrome. The problem with this is that it fails to take into account the unique problems and perceptions of an abused-child parricide defendant and why, as some psychiatrists claim, the killing was "a sane reaction to an insane environment."[44] The big question in Lannert's case was if the jury would be given a chance to hear what led to the July 5 killing.

THE FACTS

Unfortunately, the jury did not get to hear about the time Tom first molested Stacey. As with most of the daughters in this study, the abuse started when Lannert was very young and followed a rather predictable pattern. Walker created a model called the "cycle theory of violence," which outlines the three phases in a cycle of abuse: a period of tension-building, an acute battering incident, and period of loving-contrition or absence of tension.[45] She defines someone as a battered woman if this cycle of abuse repeats at least twice.[46] For Lannert, the period of loving comes first, which partly explains why she so readily gave in to her father's desires. In 1980, when she was eight years old, Tom had his daughter kiss him, which escalated into oral sex.

Nor did the jury hear about the time Lannert was first raped. When she was nine-and-half-years old, Lannert experienced the start of many acute battering incidents. For proof, she received a scar on her left wrist, a mark she tried for most of her life to cover up unsuccessfully with clothes, makeup, and a watch. Much like Allison's account, Lannert explains in graphic details how her father took her virginity, which entailed him calling her offensive names and pinning her to the floor in front of their wood-burning stove.[47] In her effort to escape, she burnt her wrist on the stove. After jabbing his fingers into her, he thrust with his penis, delivering mind-numbing blows that made her dizzy. As he does this he uttered the first of many "I'll kill you."[48] Much like Pecola Breedlove, Lannert passed out and, also reminiscent of Pecola, she prayed to God. "The next day, my prayers had not been answered because I was still breathing," laments Lannert.[49]

Moreover, the jury did not learn about what happened on Lannert's eighteenth birthday. The abuse continued "unpredictably predictable" for another ten years, culminating in one of the most gruesome accounts on her eighteenth birthday.[50] By this point, she is told almost daily that she is "a worthless whore."[51] Also the 5'2", petite Stacey is no match to 5'9" Tom, who would balloon to three hundred pounds. On the day of her birthday, in the middle of an argument, Stacey asserts her independence and threatens to move out. Dismissing her words, Tom laughs and threatens with language similar to that of Daddy Glen and Harrison's father: "You're mine. You'll always be mine."[52] Growing jealous, Tom then violates his daughter, even going so far as cutting off her hair with a rusty pocketknife in a jealous effort to make her look unattractive. He does this after he slides the knife down her cheek from her ear to her lip. After blacking out, she wakes up to him kicking her in the ribs.

The jury did not hear how Tom was the initial aggressor. By July 1990, Tom, Stacey, and her sister are cycling between periods of tension-building and acute-battering incidents and they are using the word *kill* often. Stacey would threaten, "If you don't stop, I'll kill you."[53] She fantasized about her life without her father. Like most battered children, she became accustomed to an induced state of hypervigilance. On more than one occasion, Tom threatens to kill Stacey. As she notes in her memoir, Tom would "place the utensil holder on the counter to the left of the sink with the fork prongs and knife blades facing upward. When [Stacey's and Christy's] arms passed over the top of the fork prongs, he'd push them down so they'd scrape their skin."[54] Likewise, he would describe the ways he would barge in when Stacey was taking a bath and tell her he was going to electrocute her by tossing the radio in the tub. He said he would throw both daughters down the rickety wooden basement steps and break their necks. He'd make up stories to scare them like "I'll throw Christy down the steps and stab you and tell the police that you were trying to take my money to buy drugs."[55] When Stacey tried to join the Air Force as a way to escape her father's house, Tom told her that the sole-surviving-son rule applied to daughters, too, implying that he would kill Christy to get Stacey discharged from service. To prove his point, one night Tom tied Stacey to her bed with orange electrical cord and raped her with the gun she had just learned to use and had taught her sister how to in case they needed to defend themselves. Almost making good on his oft-repeated threat to kill her, he even pulled the trigger of the unloaded gun with it inside of her.

Furthermore, the jury did not learn of the events of July 4, including Tom raping Christy and shooting at Stacey. The holiday started with a happy Tom marinating pork steaks in the fridge, planning to barbecue. But by 1 pm, he was drunk and fighting with Christy. He threatened to kill the family dog for having an accident on the carpet. After a struggle in which the blinds in the front room were torn down and the phone cords were pulled out of the walls so the girls could not call for help, Tom took Christy to his bedroom, threw her across the room, slamming the door on Stacey's fingers. For the first time, Tom raped Christy, whom Stacey had spent her life protecting. After sending Christy away, Stacey stayed in the house, crying. Tom appeared in the doorway with the gun that would later kill him by his side. He fired the .22, hitting the wall a foot above Stacey's head. He then leaned the gun against the bookshelf and smiled, saying, "See how easy an accident can be?"[56] When Stacey led the detectives around the house after the killing, no one noticed the broken window blinds, cracked bedroom doors, the bullet holes above the couch where he shot at her, or the other signs of physical struggle.

Neither the jury nor Lannert's readers know why Tom resorted to such violent behavior. As with most of the books in this study, why the father abuses his daughter is never directly answered. Lannert hints at the social structures that encourage the daughter to align herself with the powerful father, often against the mother. And there are many times in the memoir when Lannert shows just how loving and caring her father can be in comparison to her mother. Tom worked as an actuary and, although he did not keep jobs for long, he "always had a job with good pay."[57] He regularly abused the family pets—kicked one of their dogs until her mother gave the dog away and intentionally ran over their cat with his family in the car.[58] So it is no surprise why on July 5 Stacey goes home to rescue her dog after cooling off from the afternoon fight. In an interview, Stacey acknowledges that alcohol and his failed marriage were contributing factors to why her father abused them: "Alcohol, feeling inadequate, losing jobs . . . I don't think he was sexually abused . . . emotionally, maybe."[59] She states that he never hurt them when he was sober but that she will probably never know why he did what he did.

Although Lannert spent much of her life trying to understand her father's motivation, the prosecution did not tarry in assessing her intentions in killing him. The prosecution, who could have filed charges ranging from manslaughter to first-degree murder, objected to the admission of expert testimony on the battered spouse syndrome before the defense was able to inject the issue of self-defense into the case. In her memoir, Lannert paints a vivid picture of the prosecution. In sum, these men embody "the Good Old Boys network."[60] As McGraugh was filing motions to get certain pieces of evidence about the abuse introduced to the jury, J. D. Evans was filing his own motions to prevent pieces of Stacey's past from reaching their ears.

Evans worked for the prosecuting attorney of St. Louis County, Robert McCulloch, the man "famous for being skeptical about sex crimes," who did not take the girls at their word.[61] This is the same man who refused to prosecute a high school principal accused of having sex with three of his students because the victims could offer no physical proof. The principal got just 120 days of time. McCulloch and the principal were both members of the Missouri Athletic Club and frequently met at the bar called the Edge, none other than Tom Lannert's favorite place to drink. Although it is unusual for elected officials to be involved in cases like Lannert's, McCulloch took an interest. He called her a "bald-faced liar" and believed that she killed her father in cold blood for his money.[62] He contended that the parricide was the result of a premeditated design to kill her father, and he blamed *The Courage to Heal Workbook* for planting false memories of abuse in Stacey.[63] "Mr. McCulloch believed that Thomas F. Lannert was a 'drunk and violent man, but that didn't make him a rapist.'"[64]

Although the prosecuting attorneys could have given Stacey a lighter charge, McCulloch wanted to punish her to the full extent of the law. In Missouri, juries are part of the sentencing process, and in Lannert's case, the jury was not provided with an alternative to the sentence of life without parole. According to McCulloch, Tom Lannert "never laid his hands on" Stacey, who maintains, "It didn't matter that Wendy, my former babysitter, and a psychologist testified that I was abused. It didn't matter that Detective Schulte believed I was abused. Schulte was never called to testify."[65] Schulte was the first official to talk with Stacey, and he had years of experience with sexually abused victims. Tellingly, the prosecution had him removed from the case.

The trial court agreed with the prosecution's objection and held that the events leading up to the homicide were too remote and insufficiently aggressive on Tom's part to establish immediate danger and to justify a self-defense instruction. Basically, the court rejected Lannert's position that a man who abused his daughter for ten years was the initial aggressor. They were unable to see that because Lannert was at a physical disadvantage, she struck when her abusive father was physically defenseless. Therefore, battered spouse syndrome did not have bearing on *State v. Lannert*. As she notes in her memoir, McGraugh "filed in vain to use self-defense in my case. That motion was denied because neither my sister nor I was in immediate danger when the crime took place. The victim—my father—had been sleeping."[66] And after Christy's rape, the sisters went to the state fair, drank, and ended the night by eating at the Olive Garden and going to a friend's house.

The defense's next option was to try for insanity. But as Heide notes, "despite the attention the insanity defense receives, it is seldom used and rarely successful."[67] "When it is successful, the defendant is hardly ever set free. Instead, he or she is almost always committed to a mental hospital for assessment of his or her present psychological condition."[68] The presumption of sanity exists in all jurisdictions, placing the burden of evidence on the defendant. At trial, Lannert's attorney was allowed to introduce some evidence of the long-term sexual abuse she suffered in an attempt to show mental disease or defect. In particular, they permitted expert evidence of abuse-induced PTSD and of some of the circumstances of Lannert's household. A court-appointed psychologist provided testimony as an expert witness and stated that Lannert suffered from PTSD. According to another expert, she had dissociative disorder, "a condition that caused [her] to lose memory, awareness, and functioning for periods of time. It meant [she] could detach from [her] body and leave reality to cope with abuse."[69] However, the prosecution responded by presenting their own experts, who testified that at the time of the killing Lannert was in full control of her actions and knew the difference between right and wrong. The jury, who did not know that Lannert rejected the plea bargain, deliberated for five hours and found that there was insufficient evidence of mental disease or defect to negate an element of the crime. In other words, they found Lannert guilty, and she began serving her life sentence in late 1992.

Despite Lannert's appeals, on March 11, 2003, the Honorable Catherine D. Perry, U.S. District Judge for the Eastern District of Missouri, "reluctantly" concurred with the jury that Stacey was not entitled to a self-defense instruction. However, she added that because of the abuse the sisters endured, she believed that "it is reasonable to conclude that Lannert's father was the true initial aggressor" and that "one could conclude that Lannert's altered state of mind led her to believe that her father, a relentless attacker, would hurt her or her sister again, perhaps on the night of his death."[70] In the final paragraph before Perry acknowledges that the Missouri courts have the authority to interpret the state's battered spouse syndrome statute, she indicates that the ambiguous time frame for self-defense worked against Lannert:

> The "absence of aggression or provocation on the part of the defender" element of the Missouri self-defense statute does not articulate a time frame during which the initial act of aggression and the act of self-defense must occur. It is therefore deeply troubling that the jury was not completely informed of the scope of the abuse Lannert suffered, her fear, or her rage that her sister may also have been victimized by their father. This evidence of battered spouse syndrome might have placed Lannert's actions in proper context, and may have allowed a jury to conclude that Lannert was not the initial aggressor on the night of her father's death, potentially resulting in a very different outcome than what she faces today.[71]

Because Lannert, convicted of parricide, was denied a chance to establish self-defense by offering expert testimony of BCS, her sentence was a miscarriage of justice. Her lawyer was unable to use the battering syndrome evidence to show how the effects of PTSD altered Stacey's perceptions and thereby met the required elements of self-defense. Therefore, Lannert was convicted of murder and sentenced to life in prison without parole. Smith observes that the average sentences handed down in parricide cases are "approximately fifteen to twenty years imprisonment."[72] These lengthy sentences are routinely imposed upon abused children and teenagers, like Lannert, driven to violence after years of severe abuse.

State v. Lannert raises questions about how our court system should proceed with child-abuse parricide cases. Should we extend the battering syndrome to include children and spouses? And should the admission of battering evidence be permitted even when a battering episode substantially predates the killing? Clearly, yes. Some rightly advocate that mitigating factors should be introduced in court to possibly reduce the charges or sentences, for example, classifying murder by a battered child as voluntary manslaughter. Some courts have developed creative sentences that incorporate both retribution and rehabilitation.[73] Others have proposed a more conservative system, using a partial excuse approach, which acknowledges that a nonconfrontational parricide is not justifiable self-defense and that the child is not legally insane and consequently devoid of all responsibility for the act, but it lessens the battered child's culpability for the death of an abusive parent, claiming that the effects of PTSD altered his or her state of mind at the time of the killing. Lengthy sentences are often unnecessary because most abused-child parricides rarely pose any threat of further criminal activity, and they respond favorably to psychiatric treatment and rehabilitation.

CPTSD

Although little has been written about treating parricide offenders, leading experts maintain that incarcerating them—certainly for life—is not the answer. Heide argues that these offenders should

> not be incarcerated in a prison, because prison psychological services are rarely adequate to deal with the depth of [their] problems. Institutional programs emphasize behavioral control and conformity to the institutional regime as a measure of progress and success, rather than individualized and specialized treatment of the youthful offenders.[74]

Prisons rarely give proper treatment, even when it is explicitly ordered. Parricide offenders should be placed in a structured therapeutic environment for a period of stabilization and receive mandatory counseling. "This environment might be a psychiatric hospital or clinic specializing in child abuse or the dysfunctional family, or a group treatment home with professional mental health staff."[75] Mones agrees, writing,

> Despite the apparently heinous nature of their crime, the majority of these kids pose no threat to society. If there is a risk, it is in incarcerat-

> ing them in a prison where they will be re-abused by other inmates and deprived of therapy. . . . The problems they suffer are particularly amendable to treatment.[76]

As she writes in her memoir, Lannert's ailments were not properly addressed in prison. For example, as her trial date drew closer, she states that she became more distressed. The prison system was quick to prescribe psych meds, like Vistaril, which made her feel like a zombie. She would get in trouble if she did not take her pills. Lannert notes that it was easier to medicate the prisoners rather than help them work through their problems. Moreover, she was not offered psychological counseling. The only times she saw licensed psychologists were when she needed to be analyzed for legal documents. As Lannert states, "those people wanted to know every detail of my life, but they did not offer support or advice."[77]

The prison system was ill-equipped to deal with traumatized individuals. The relationship of CPTSD and parricide is a significant one because PTSD has been offered as a framework for conceptualizing the effects of abuse. Heide notes that "understanding the extent of trauma and its effects is critically important in forensic assessment and in treating offenders."[78] In 1994, Mones acknowledged what he called "poly-abuse"—that most of these children are repeatedly traumatized mentally, physically, and sexually from a young age.[79] In "Psycholegal Considerations in Abuse-Motivated Parricides: Children Who Kill Their Abusive Parents," Kurt Bumby argued that the PTSD diagnosis is useful "in understanding the abused child or adolescent who has been subjected to the longstanding polyabuse that many youthful parricide perpetrators endure," but argues that it clearly does "not account for the diverse reactions of all abused children."[80] In her 2013 book, Heide uses the term *complex trauma* to describe what many of these abused children who kill parents endure, explaining that

> long-term childhood maltreatment can lead to complex PTSD, a chronic form of PTSD. In complex PTSD, trauma survivors commonly experience additional symptoms, for example, depression and dissociation. They tend to be impulsive and aggressive toward themselves or others, and they might suffer from chronic feelings of shame and self-blame. Individuals with complex PTSD often have difficulty maintaining long-term relationships and might have only superficial connections with others.[81]

Dissociation is a symptom of CPTSD. As Heide states, "given the intensity of [the] feelings, it was highly unlikely that [the person] could access the higher cortical processes of the brain associated with thinking, deliberation, and judgment and formulate the intent to hurt her father."[82] Many of these offenders "have complex PTSD as a result of their traumatic childhood experiences": "individuals with this disorder suffer from a combination of cognitive and physiological symptoms."[83] It is unlikely that Lannert and other youths like her experienced one traumatic event. Instead, the youth has probably been a victim or a witness to a *series* of incidents in which extreme violence was committed by the deceased parent. In addition to the repeated incidents, the homicide itself is likely to be another traumatic event the youth will re-experience.

Noting the irony of finding freedom behind bars, Lannert explains that she had "the most restorative, most complete rest I'd ever had in my entire life"—her first night in prison.[84] Typical of most people with CPTSD, Lannert admits to not knowing who she was for the first eighteen years of her life. It took going to prison to find herself. Lannert told a psychologist that she suffered from difficulty sleeping and from anxiety: "my anxiety levels stayed high at all times just in case."[85] When her parents were going through the divorce, Tom freely used her body. It was during this time that she stopped sleeping more than a few hours at a time because "danger was everywhere."[86] She also experienced dissociation and reports that she would "completely leave [her] small body when [the rapes] happened."[87] Throughout her memoir, she recounts just how desperate she was to be free from her father, attempting suicide twice in six months. She notes later in her book that she still hears his voice almost every night and experiences flashbacks during the day and night. In an interview with Kemp, Lannert says that she is "acutely aware of the destruction that occurs in the aftermath of sexual abuse."[88] Unlike most of the other daughters in this study, Lannert was diagnosed with PTSD. Her diagnosis, however, came late, as a result of her trial, thus delaying proper treatment.

As much as Lannert does not like psychiatric terms used in reference to her, after she heard the statement from the court-appointed psychologist, she says, it "definitely described me."[89] While in prison, she even wrote an article for the *Survivors of Incest Anonymous Newsletter* titled "Stone Walls" in which she opens up about her dissociation. As it was for Allison and Harrison, writing becomes an outlet for Lannert, certainly a healthier alternative to how the prison system deals with—or fails to deal with—CPTSD.

Her decision to go public with her story came later, however. After being told that all of her appeals would be denied, Lannert was encouraged to put together a clemency package and instructed that her only hope was to get public support behind her. Going public with her story was not something that came easily to Lannert, who has said that she has never been, and probably will never be, comfortable telling it. As she writes,

> I committed one of the worst crimes a person could commit—I took the life of someone in my family. Most people couldn't even begin to fathom why a teenage girl would do that. I did it because I was sexually

> abused, and I didn't know if I wanted to say that out loud to anyone ever again.[90]

Furthermore, Lannert states that healing and putting her life on paper were just as painful as living through the abuse and there were many days when she had to interrupt the writing of her memoir because it was too difficult.

However, shortly after being told that she would have to go public with her story, Kemp from *Glamour* called Lannert, requesting an interview. After January 2002, Lannert became somewhat of a talk-show star and was interviewed by then-reporter for the *Larry King Live* show Nancy Grace, along with Montel Williams and Oprah Winfrey. Lannert says that in front of the world, Oprah, who, along with Maya Angelou, served as an inspiration, validated her story. Recommending commutation, one of the jurors on Lannert's case, who said that the jury agreed that Lannert has been incestuously abused, submitted an affidavit for her clemency package, stating that she believed Lannert was serving a sentence too harsh for the crime, but that "the jury was not provided an alternative to the sentence of life without parole."[91] Even Detective Schulte was speaking out, publicly stating that Lannert was a victim of abuse and that her punishment did not fit her crime. For their efforts, on January 16, 2009, after serving eighteen years, Lannert's sentence was commuted.

What we can take away from *State v. Lannert* is that in all parricide cases, the jury should be allowed to consider whether the defendant acted in self-defense, which is accomplished only if the history of abuse is admitted at trial. Because the principles involving abuse are beyond the common knowledge of the average juror, an expert should be allowed to explain what effects the abuse has on the child's perceptions. For example, an expert is needed to explain that child-abuse parricides often experience numbing years before the homicide as a response to ongoing trauma in the home. This symptom of PTSD, which enables the child to endure sustained and severe conditions, is frequently misinterpreted after the homicide as an indication of callousness.

Although some evidence suggests that the reaction of the judicial system to abused youth who kill the victimizing parent is becoming more compassionate, more needs to be done. More states should legally recognize the *psychological* effects of BCS and admit testimony explaining its relevance in court cases such as this one. More states should adopt a more inclusive battered-child defense law that is far-reaching and more sympathetic than the current ones. It should allow the jury to hear about the acts of family violence committed by the deceased. And we need to medically recognize "the little-known psychological problem" of CPTSD, all of which can help courts and clinicians properly deal with Lannert and others who suffer from these disorders. Only then can we begin to ameliorate decades of judicial ignorance and only then can justice have a chance of being served. Although Lannert will not ever be able to get back the eighteen years she spent behind bars, these changes can help others like her live healthier and freer lives.

NOTES

1. Stacey Lannert and Kristen Kemp, *Redemption: A Story of Sisterhood, Survival, and Finding Freedom Behind Bars* (New York: Broadway, 2011). 202.
2. Louise Armstrong, Rocking the Cradle of Sexual Politics: What Happened When Women Said Incest (Reading, MA: Addison-Wesley Publishing, 1994), 198.
3. Lannert, *Redemption*, 191.
4. Ibid., 215.
5. Some might question why Lannert didn't bring her abuse to the authorities while it was happening. In "Incest: Sexual Abuse Begins at Home," Ellen Weber has an answer for why so many daughters like Lannert choose silence over pursuing legal action. For starters, they would be subject to repeating their humiliating and embarrassing details to a litany of people: "police, investigators, protective service workers, the district attorney, and, if she qualifies as a witness, to the defense attorney under cross-examination in open court." Weber, *Ms.*, April 1977, 65. Moreover, the abuser is usually "never brought to court because there is not enough evidence to prosecute." Ibid.
6. Kathleen Heide, *Why Kids Kill Parents: Child Abuse and Adolescent Homicide* (Columbus: Ohio State University Press, 1992), 72.
7. Kurt M. Bumby, "Psycholegal Considerations in Abuse-Motivated Parricides: Children Who Kill Their Abusive Parents," *The Journal of Psychiatry & Law* 22, no. 1 (1994): 56.
8. Ibid., 59.
9. Heide, *Why Kids Kill Parents*, 25.
10. Lannert, *Redemption*, 91.
11. Ibid.
12. Ibid., 215.
13. Quoted in Robert Hegadorn, "Clemency: Doing Justice to Incarcerated Battered Children," *Journal of the Missouri Bar* 55 (1999): 76.
14. Kathleen Heide, *Understanding Parricide: When Sons and Daughter Kill Parents* (Oxford: Oxford University Press, 2013), xiii.
15. Quoted in Heide, *Why Kids Kill Parents*, 6.
16. Heide, *Understanding Parricide*, 106.
17. Ibid.
18. Narina Nunez, Mindy J. Dahl, Connie M. Tang, and Brittney L. Jensen, "Trial Venue in Juvenile Cases: Mitigating and Extralegal Factors Matter," *Legal & Criminological Psychology* 12, no. 1 (2007): 34, 35.
19. Paul Mones, "Battered Child Syndrome: Understanding Parricide," *Trial* 30, no. 2 (1994): 26.
20. Jamie Heather Sacks, "A New Age of Understanding: Allowing Self-Defense Claims for Battered Children Who Kill Their Abusers," *Journal of Contemporary Health Law & Policy* 10, no. 1 (1994): 358–59.
21. Heide, *Understanding Parricide*, 122.
22. Ibid.
23. Lannert, *Redemption*, 7.
24. Quoted in Sacks, "A New Age," 352.
25. Mones, quoted in Heide, *Why Kids Kill Parents*, 17.
26. For a discussion of studies that found the societal consensus was to try these children in juvenile court, see Loretta J. Stalans and Gary T. Henry, "Societal Views of Justice for Adolescents Accused of Murder: Inconsistency between Community Senti-

ment and Automatic Legislative Transfers," *Law and Human Behavior* 18, no. 6 (1994): 675–96.

27. Bumby, "Psycholegal Considerations," 64.

28. Paul Mones, "When the Innocent Strike Back: Abused Children Who Kill Their Parents," *Journal of Interpersonal Violence* 8 (1993): 298.

29. Heide, *Understanding Parricide*, 125.

30. Heide, *Why Kids Kill Parents*, 55–56.

31. Heide, *Understanding Parricide*, 139.

32. Kempe was an instrumental figure in the child protection movement. In 1976, he launched the journal *Child Abuse and Neglect*, which was an important outlet for articles reporting on sexual abuse research. Joseph E. Davis, *Accounts of Innocence: Sexual Abuse, Trauma, and the Self* (Chicago: University of Chicago Press, 2005), 71.

33. It was not until 1978, when CAPTA was amended, that the term sexual abuse started to be clarified, as Joseph Davis remarks. "'Child abuse and neglect' means the physical or mental injury, sexual abuse, negligent treatment, or maltreatment of any child under the age of eighteen by a person who is responsible for the child's welfare under circumstances which indicate the child's health or welfare is harmed or threatened thereby." Davis, *Accounts of Innocence*, 281. What acts constitute sexual abuse, however, were not defined at first. Nor was sexual abuse defined in the vast majority of state reporting laws that were enacted in order to meet the funding requirements of the act. What constituted sexual abuse, in other words, was open to much interpretation.

34. Jessica L. Hart and Jeffrey L. Helms, "Factors of Parricide: Allowance of the Use of Battered Child Syndrome as a Defense," *Aggression and Violent Behavior* 8 (2003): 681.

35. Ibid.

36. Sacks, "A New Age," 375.

37. Ibid., 352.

38. Heide, *Understanding Parricide*, 148.

39. Ibid., 126.

40. Hegadorn, "Clemency," 71.

41. Ibid.

42. Ibid., 72.

43. Ibid.

44. Sacks, "A New Age," 349.

45. Lenore Walker, *The Battered Woman* (New York: Harper, 1979), 55.

46. Ibid., xv.

47. Lannert, *Redemption*, 74.

48. Ibid., 76.

49. Ibid., 77.

50. Ibid., 86.

51. Ibid., 6.

52. Ibid.

53. Ibid., 175.

54. Ibid., 137.

55. Ibid., 175–76.

56. Ibid., 183.

57. Ibid., 17.

58. For an understanding of the connection between sexual abuse and injury to animals, see Carol Adams's "Bringing Peace Home: A Feminist Philosophical Perspective on the Abuse of Women, Children, and Pet Animals" in which she argues that the torture of pets is used to establish a climate of terror. She explains the killing of pets as an attempt to establish domination over those constructed as inferior—adult female partners, children, and animals. Adams, "Bringing Peace Home: A Feminist Philosophical Perspective on the Abuse of Women, Children, and Pet Animals," *Hypatia* 9, no. 2 (1994): 76.

59. Quoted in Jeannette Cooperman, "A Conversation with Stacey Lannert," *St. Louis Magazine*, June 21, 2011.

60. Lannert, *Redemption*, 216.

61. Ibid. Tamara Haegerich and Bette Bottoms found that men like Robert McCulloch are not all that uncommon: "On average, many men view child sexual abuse as a less serious crime than women do and are significantly more likely to endorse what might be termed 'child sexual abuse myths' such as 'A child who does not display signs of distress probably has not been a victim of sexual assault.' Compared to women, men also tend to find child abuse victims less credible, and they are less likely to convict defendants accused of child sexual abuse." Haegerich and Bottoms, "Empathy and Jurors' Decisions in Patricide Trials Involving Child Sexual Assault Allegations," *Law and Human Behavior* 24, no. 4 (2000): 425.

62. Lannert, *Redemption*, 215.

63. As Joseph Davis mentions, *The Courage to Heal: A Guide for Women Survivors of Child Sexual Abuse* is a self-help book for adult survivors. It was not the first of its kind, but it has been "by far the most celebrated, the most discussed, and the most controversial." Davis, *Accounts of Innocence*, 143. Written by Ellen Bass and Laura Davis, neither of whom have formal psychological training although Davis herself is an incest survivor, the book has been heralded as "the Bible of the incest survivor movement." Ibid. It enjoyed extreme popularity, reportedly selling "750,000 copies in its first four years and was a favorite of therapists as well." Ibid. First published in 1988, it has had three subsequent editions, the last one being a twentieth-anniversary edition in 2008. Its accompanying workbook was also a bestseller (350,000 copies in print by 1994). It has not been without its critics, however, some of whom compared it to *Mein Kampf*. Ibid., 292. Many took issue with their assertion that "If you think you were abused and your life shows the symptoms, then you were." Qtd. in Davis, *Accounts of Innocence*, 151. By the third edition, Bass and Davis revised this statement to read "If you genuinely think you were abused and your life shows the symptoms, there's a strong likelihood that you were." Qtd. in Davis, *Accounts of Innocence*, 293. Not surprisingly, this book received the wrath of the False Memory Syndrome Foundation, who reported that a high percentage of accused parents said that their daughter was influenced by this book.

64. Lannert, *Redemption*, 216.

65. Ibid.

66. Ibid.

67. Heide, *Why Kids Kill Parents*, 57.

68. Ibid.

69. Lannert, *Redemption*, 217.

70. Lannert v. Jones, 321 F.3d 747, U.S. App. (8th Cir. March 11, 2003).

71. Ibid.

72. Quoted in Hegadorn, "Clemency," 82.

73. Bumby, "Psycholegal Considerations," 75.

74. Heide, *Understanding Parricide*, 326.

75. Heide, *Why Kids Kill Parents*, 143.

76. Mones, *When a Child Kills*, 320.

77. Lannert, *Redemption*, 206.

78. Heide, *Understanding Parricide*, 324.

79. Mones, "Battered Child Syndrome," 24.

80. Bumby, "Psycholegal Considerations," 55.

81. Heide, *Understanding Parricide*, 43.

82. Ibid., 140.

83. Ibid., 328.

84. Lannert, *Redemption*, 196.

85. Ibid., 86.

86. Ibid., 99.

87. Ibid., 98.

88. "A Conversation with Authors Stacey Lannert and Kristen Kemp."
89. Lannert, *Redemption*, 217.
90. Ibid., 272.
91. Quoted in Lannert, *Redemption*, 268.

Conclusion

Trauma in the Twenty-First Century

Toward the end of her memoir, Lannert says that she struggled more with forgiving herself than she did her father. And then she read a book that helped her: Maya Angelou's *I Know Why the Caged Bird Sings*. Lannert writes that the words of Angelou's memoir resonated with her; even the title changed her life.[1] Similar to what Allison said regarding Morrison's novel, Lannert saw so much of her own story in Angelou's. As Lannert puts it: "I was a caged bird, and I still had a voice. It dawned on me that my soul, my life, and my spirit could be beautiful despite the bars and fences."[2] It was this work that "helped [her] go easier" on herself.[3]

While I was in the middle of working on this book, I reread Angelou's *I Know Why the Caged Bird Sings* shortly after the author's death in late May 2014, and it brought back memories of hearing her speak in Tampa just six years before at an event to commemorate the life of Dr. Martin Luther King, Jr. I had read that Angelou and King had been good friends, and that he was assassinated on her fortieth birthday, resulting in her not celebrating her birthday for many years. I no longer remember all that the striking, 6-foot, deep-voiced Angelou shared with our audience that evening, but I do remember three things: (1) When she recited the poetry of others, Angelou did so from memory; when she shared the poetry she had written, she paused, put her glasses on, and read from the page. (2) She said she didn't trust anyone who didn't have a sense of humor. (3) She spoke about the time she was a victim of father-daughter incest and, as a result, went silent for many years.

After five additional volumes of autobiography and six books of poetry, it, her first book, published when she was forty-one, for which she is best remembered. In *I Know Why the Caged Bird Sings,* that tells her life story up to the age of seventeen, Angelou recounts her many traumatic events with much wit and grace including that her parents divorced when she was just three years old, and that she was raped by her mother's boyfriend, Mr. Freeman, at the age of seven on one of her visits to St. Louis. After the first time he molested her, Angelou is unsure of what happened and almost believes Freeman when he tells her that the bed is wet because she urinated on it. Longing for a father figure, much like Kathryn Harrison, she acknowledges conflicted feelings: "I didn't want to admit that I had in fact liked his holding me or that I had liked his smell or the hard heart-beating."[4] Although Freeman threatened her to remain silent or else he would kill her and her brother, Angelou finally told, and Freeman was arrested. She testified against him in court, which made the defendant feel like she was the one on trial. "You mean to say this man raped you and you don't know what he was wearing?" Freeman's lawyer questioned and "snickered as if [Angelou] had raped Mr. Freeman."[5] He goes on to ask, "Do you know if you were raped?" which elicits laughter from the courtroom.[6] When asked if that was the first time Freeman touched her, Angelou pauses and thinks, "Mr. Freeman had surely done something very wrong, but I was convinced that I had helped him to do it. I didn't want to lie, but the lawyer wouldn't let me think, so I used silence as a retreat."[7] When pressed for an answer, Angelou finally replies "No."[8]

As in Lannert's memoir, the justice system described in *Caged Bird* does not live up to its name. The Missouri court sentenced Freeman to one year and one day, "but he never got a chance to do his time. His lawyer (or someone) got him released that very afternoon," Angelou explains.[9] Later that same day, Freeman was found kicked to death in a lot behind a slaughterhouse—most likely by Angelou's maternal uncles. Freeman's pleading looks in the courtroom, along with Angelou's own shame, compelled her to lie, and after she learns that he is murdered, she believes that her words are responsible. She thinks that she "forfeited [her] place in heaven forever."[10] Angelou's response to the trauma was to become virtually mute: she couldn't—or wouldn't—speak to the public for more than half a decade, stating: "My 7-and-a-half-year-old logic deduced that my voice had killed him, so I stopped speaking for almost six years." She later recalled, "I was a volunteer mute. I had voice but I refused to use it. . . .When I heard about his murder, I thought my voice had killed a man and so it wasn't safe to speak."[11]

She often cited this silent period as a time when she became poignantly aware of the written word. As Angelou says, "And then I started reading, really reading, at about 7 ½, because a woman in my town took me to the library, a black school library. . . . And I read every book, even if I didn't understand it."[12] Her love of literature eventually helped restore language to her. As she recounts in *Caged Bird*, it is Mrs. Bertha Flowers, a beautiful black woman, who breaks Angelou's self-imposed silence by asking her to read aloud. The first words Angelou speaks after her long spell of muteness are those of Charles Dickens.

Her account of the sexual abuse, along with her depiction of black life in the Jim Crow South during the Depression, is, like Morrison's novel, not easy reading. In stark language and with poetic command, she bears witness to the brutality of racism, having grown up between St. Louis, where she was born, and the then-racially segregated tiny town of Stamps, Arkansas, one of America's poorest regions, where her grandmother lived. It is the story of how her parents essentially abandoned her and her brother and how she was homeless for a stint; it ends with her becoming a mother at the age of seventeen, giving birth to her first and only child, Guy Angelou. He was the result of a loveless one-night stand undertaken largely in a spirit of exploration; the father did not speak to Angelou after her fourth month of pregnancy. But, as she notes in her memoir with irony regarding her sexual encounter with Guy's father, "Thanks to Mr. Freeman nine years before, I had had no pain of entry to endure."[13] For her frank treatment of these issues and her emerging womanhood, the book has been banned numerous times and occasionally attacked for its "'manipulative' melodrama" and facile or solipsistic style.[14]

But in this story of struggle, a narrative of survival emerges. In one of the more humorous chapters of the book, a fifteen-year-old Angelou tells of the time she spent the summer with her father, "Daddy Bailey," in southern California. The vacation goes as follows. Meeting her father's girlfriend, Dolores Stockland, at the train station, Angelou muses that the young Dolores must have been horrified at her prospective stepdaughter who was nearly six-foot and "not even pretty," a far cry from the picture she was shown by Daddy Bailey of the eight-year-old Angelou, who was as "cute as buttons."[15] Angelou learns many things on that visit that upset her expectations of her father, starting with the fact that he "lived in a trailer park on the outskirts of a town that was itself the outskirts of town."[16] One of his weekly routines consisted of traveling across the border to buy Mexican food. On this particular day, he takes Angelou along. And their foreign adventure consists of Daddy Bailey getting intoxicated so much so that Angelou, who has never driven before, has to twist and turn her father's Hudson home along the roads besides the steep mountain. At the border town's guard's station, Angelou causes an accident, which her father fixes with smooth talking and left over tequila.

As the scene unravels, Angelou gains insight into what kind of person her father really is. About the man who "never spoke" but "orated," she writes, "It seemed hard to believe that he was a lonely person, searching relentlessly in bottles, under women's skirts, in church work and lofty job titles for his 'personal niche,' lost before birth and unrecovered since."[17] Much like Ellison's Trueblood, Daddy Bailey had the misfortune of being "born in a cotton field."[18] When given the ultimatum between choosing his girlfriend and his daughter, Daddy Bailey picks his girlfriend and leaves Angelou in the company of his friends. Thinking her disappearance would be a welcomed relief to her father, not to mention to Dolores, Angelou chooses homelessness over trying to make the situation work with her father. This scene can be read as Angelou leaving behind Daddy Bailey, repudiating the patriarch and all it stands for.

Although she dropped out of school at the age of fourteen, Angelou would go on to become San Francisco's first female streetcar driver, speak at least six languages, and work as a newspaper editor in Egypt and Ghana. She was the first black person and the first woman to recite a poem at a presidential inauguration: she read "On the Pulse of Morning," a cautiously optimistic poem of racial reconciliation, at fellow Arkansas native Bill Clinton's first inauguration in 1993. She was among the first black women to enjoy mainstream success. In addition to receiving honorary doctorates, several elementary schools have been named for her. She counted as her friends Malcolm X, Nelson Mandela, Oprah Winfrey, and Toni Morrison.

In 1970, the same year *The Bluest Eye* was released, the publication of *Caged Bird* was both "daring and historic."[19] Author Tayari Jones wrote, "She told a story that wasn't allowed to be told. Now, people tell all sorts of things in memoir, but when she told the truth, she challenged a taboo—not for shock value, but to heal us all."[20] Legend has it that friend and fellow-writer James Baldwin wanted Angelou to write down her story. Still grieving King's death, she attended a party at author and cartoonist Jules Feiffer's house. Feiffer was so taken by Angelou that he mentioned her to Random House editor Bob Loomis, who persuaded her to write a book by daring her into it, saying that it was "nearly impossible to write autobiography as literature."[21] As white women's—let alone black women's—lives were rarely thought worthy of autobiography, Angelou accepted the challenge. She replied "I'll start tomorrow."[22]

"A childhood victim of rape, shamed into silence, eventually told her story through one of the most widely read memoirs of the past few decades," one of the obituaries reads.[23] Perhaps needless to say, Maya Angelou, like Stacey Lannert, Kathryn Harrison, Bone Boatwright, and Dylan Farrow, found her voice. As Nicole Diver had done by uttering the statement, "Am I going through the rest of life flinching at the word *father*?" Angelou turns the linguistic key toward healing with the publication of her first memoir.[24] She, like Ellison and Morrison, uses her rape to explore the oppression of her black community. And much like Morrison, Angelou shows the victimization of the daughter and focuses on the act itself and what had groomed her for the abuse.

Like Pecola Breedlove, Angelou came of age in a world that saw her as ugly, unloved, and unworthy, as not good enough. The humanity of a young girl was not readily acknowledged. All of culture—even education, religion, and toys—conspired to devalue females. The cycle of violence and abuse seemed inevitable. Almost forty-five years after its initial publication, *Caged Bird* shares more than a publication year with Morrison's first novel. *The Bluest Eye* was rejected a dozen times, which suggests that few people were interested in the life of a young girl—especially a black one. Today both books are controversial staples of high school English classes. In addition to pointing out the toxic effects of racial self-loathing and the girls' attempts to dismantle dominant illustrations of beauty, both books include graphic episodes of abuse tempered by humor and show how incest and rape are used as instruments of terror to regain power and privilege lost. And as all of the books in this study show, they indicate what the perceptive narrator of *The Bluest Eye* notes after Pauline Breedlove loses her front tooth: "there must have been the conditions, the setting that would allow it to exist in the first place."[25] Although these words are said in the context of Pauline and her rotting tooth, they take on new meaning in the context of the whole story, the tale of a daughter who is raped by her father and who suffers from trauma caused by exposure to multiple stressors. When viewed in this light, that statement reinforces Morrison's point that there is something wrong with a society that produces fathers who rape their own daughters. I think it's safe to say that Angelou won the bet with Loomis and transformed her life experiences into literature, crafting one of the first autobiographical works to break the silence surrounding father-daughter incest.

In the mid- to-late 1970s, around the time Morrison and Angelou published their first books, it was clear that the psychological community needed a new diagnosis for patients suffering from severe, chronic, and sometimes irreversible syndromes following exposure to catastrophic events. Before this time, rough efforts had been made to diagnose traumatic stress as early as the mid-nineteenth century and progressed through the years, ranging from "combat fatigue" to "gross stress reaction" to "temporary situational disorder" and other nomenclatures sprinkled in between. As I explained in my introduction, the third edition of the *DSM* introduced PTSD in 1980. PTSD was initially classified as a fear disorder defined by three clusters of symptoms: re-experiencing of fear memories (intrusive memories), avoidance of trauma reminders (amnesia, withdrawal, avoidance of situational reminders), and hyperarousal symptoms (sleep disturbance, heightened startle response). At that time, one of the criteria used to diagnose the disorder was defined as "a recognizable stressor that would evoke significant symptoms of distress in almost anyone."[26] During the 1970s, the conventional thinking was that rape, war, and holocaust were rare, and so the American Psychiatric Association added the phrase "generally outside the range of usual human experiences."[27]

By the time of the *DSM-IV* in 1994, when an explosion of works on father-daughter incest was being published, sufficient data indicated that traumatic exposure is not unusual but a relatively common occurrence, especially for women in civilian life. The potential stressor events were expanded to encompass a greater number, including being diagnosed with a life threatening disease, learning about the sudden death of a family member or close friend, and experiencing child sexual abuse. Although foreshadowed in the *DSM-III-R*, the *DSM-IV* stipulated that the intense emotional reactions—fear, helplessness, horror—had to be present in traumatized individuals as a result of the event. The timing, however, was unclear and later subjected to different interpretations, with some saying trauma may happen during the event and others arguing that it can happen after the event.

In 2006, the *DSM-5* Task Force was created to undertake the latest revision process. The first meeting of the *DSM-5* Anxiety and Dissociative Disorders Work Group was held October 6–7, 2008. There were fifteen members, including the chair, Katherine Phillips. As the group deliberated the changes, they sought public comment three times. Essentially, they debated the following questions: Should the stressor criterion be revised? Should other diagnostic criteria be revised, and, if so, which ones? Should other proposed posttraumatic syndromes also be included in the *DSM-5*?

After much spirited debate, the Work Group made the following changes to the PTSD construct.[28] Because PTSD did not fit neatly into the anxiety disorder niche to which it had been assigned since *DSM-III*, nor was it best categorized as either a stress-induced fear-circuitry disorder or as an internalizing disorder, a new chapter in the *DSM-5* metastructure was created and named "Trauma and Stress-Related Disorders" (TSRD). Modifications were made to the stressor criteria and to the symptom clusters. The three major PTSD symptom clusters (re-experiencing, avoidance/numbing, and arousal) were revised to four clusters (re-experiencing, arousal, avoidance, and persistent negative changes in both cognition and mood). The number of symptoms in PTSD increased from seventeen to twenty, and changes were made to those tied to the traumatic event. Two new PTSD subtypes were added: Posttraumatic Stress Disorder for Children 6 Years or Younger and Prominent Dissociative Symptoms (either experiences of feeling detached from one's own mind or body, or experiences in which the world seems unreal, dreamlike, or distorted).

Although the *DSM-5* expanded some of its criteria for PTSD, and for all it did to further our understanding of the disorder, it failed to recognize CPTSD. The most common exemplar of complex trauma is prolonged trauma of an interpersonal nature, as we see in childhood sexual abuse and father-daughter incest. The unique trademark of complex trauma has been described as a compromise in the individual's self-development in childhood, when self-definition and self-regulation are being formed. Survivors of prolonged, especially childhood, abuse often experience altered consciousness and develop complex deformations of identity.

Fitzgerald, who knew intimately the effects of traumatic stress, once said, "In the real dark night of the soul it is always three o'clock in the morning."[29] In her memoir, Lannert notes that she was all too acquainted with the darkness. She encourages all to break the silence and "to bring sexual abuse out of the darkness and into the light."[30] Acknowledging CPTSD in the *DSM*, we can help these victims find healing by unveiling societal and psychological problems of father-daughter incest. It's time the psychological community catch up with the complex trauma of father-daughter incest, which the literary world has been bearing witness to for the last century.

NOTES

1. Stacey Lannert and Kristen Kemp, *Redemption: A Story of Sisterhood, Survival, and Finding Freedom Behind Bars* (New York: Broadway, 2011), 256.
2. Ibid.
3. Ibid.
4. Maya Angelou, *I Know Why the Caged Bird Sings* (1969; New York: Random House, 1997): 76.
5. Ibid., 81.
6. Ibid.
7. Ibid., 82.
8. Ibid., 83.
9. Ibid.
10. Ibid., 84.
11. "Obituary: Maya Angelou," BBC News, May 28, 2014.
12. "Maya Angelou Obituary," Legacy.com, May 28, 2014.
13. Angelou, *Caged Bird*, 275.
14. "Maya Angelou Obituary," Legacy.com.
15. Angelou, *Caged Bird*, 220.
16. Ibid., 221.
17. Ibid., 222, 226.
18. Ibid., 226.
19. Todd Leopold, Ashley Fantz, Moni Basu, and Faith Karimi, "Legendary Author Maya Angelou Dies at Age 86," CNN.com, June 19, 2014.
20. Quoted in Leopold et al., "Legendary Author Maya Angelou."
21. "Maya Angelou Obituary," Legacy.com.
22. Margalit Fox, "Maya Angelou, Lyrical Witness of the Jim Crow South, Dies at 86," *New York Times*, May 28, 2014.
23. "Maya Angelou Obituary," Legacy.com.
24. F. Scott Fitzgerald, *Tender Is the Night* (1934; New York: Scribner's, 1982), 290.
25. Toni Morrison, *The Bluest Eye* (1970; New York: Plume, 1994), 116.
26. Matthew J. Friedman, Patricia A. Resick, Richard A. Bryant, and Chris R. Brewin, "Considering PTSD for DSM-5," *Depression and Anxiety* 28 (2011): 752.
27. Quoted in Ibid.
28. It should be noted that not just the PTSD revisions, but also the entire DSM-5 elicited passionate debates both within and outside the psychiatric community, which some found "unnecessarily contentious." Steven Welch, Cherisse Klassen, Oxana Borisova, and Holly Clothier, "The DSM-5 Controversies: How Should Psychologists Respond?" *Canadian Psychology* 54, no. 3 (2013): 166. Some criticized the emphasis on biology at the expense of psychological and social factors. For example, they found the focus on biomarkers to be too limiting when diagnosing major disorders such as schizophrenia, bipolar disorder, and major depression. Even former president of the APA, Steven S. Sharfstein, stated that "as a profession, we have allowed the biopsychosocial model to become the bio-bio-bio model." Qtd. in Ibid., 170. Overall, the DSM-5 has been criticized for multiplying the number of psychiatric diagnoses and for medicalizing normal human behavior and experience.
29. F. Scott Fitzgerald, *The Crack-Up*, ed. Edmund Wilson (New York: New Directions, 1964), 344.
30. Lannert, *Redemption*, 311.

Bibliography

Adams, Carol J. "Bringing Peace Home: A Feminist Philosophical Perspective on the Abuse of Women, Children, and Pet Animals." *Hypatia* 9, no. 2 (1994): 63–84.

Allison, Dorothy. *Bastard Out of Carolina*. New York: Plume, 1992.

———. *Skin: Talking About Sex, Class & Literature*. Ithaca: Firebrand, 1994.

———. *Trash*. New York: Plume, 1988.

———. *Two or Three Things I Know for Sure*. New York: Dutton, 1995.

Alther, Lisa. "Blaming the Victim." *Women's Review of Books* 14, no. 10/11 (1997): 33–34.

American Psychiatric Association. *Diagnostic and Statistical Manual of Mental Disorder*. 3rd ed. Washington D.C.: APA, 1980.

———. *Diagnostic and Statistical Manual of Mental Disorder*. 3rd ed.-revised. Washington D.C.: APA, 1987.

———. *Diagnostic and Statistical Manual of Mental Disorder*. 4th ed. Washington D.C.: APA, 1994.

———. *Diagnostic and Statistical Manual of Mental Disorder*. 5th ed. Washington, D.C.: APA, 2013.

Andermahr, Sonya. *Trauma Narratives and Herstory*. Basingstoke: Palgrave Macmillan, 2013.

Angelou, Maya. *I Know Why the Caged Bird Sings*. 1969. New York: Random House, 1997.

Armstrong, Louise. *Kiss Daddy Goodnight: A Speak-Out on Incest*. New York: Pocket Books, 1978.

———. *Rocking the Cradle of Sexual Politics: What Happened When Women Said Incest*. Reading, MA: Addison-Wesley Publishing, 1994.

Atwood, Joan D. "When Love Hurts: Preadolescent Girls' Reports of Incest." *The American Journal of Family Therapy* 35 (2007): 287–313.

Awkward, Michael. "'The Evil of Fulfillment': Scapegoating and Narration in *The Bluest Eye*." In *Toni Morrison: Critical Perspectives Past and Present*, edited by Henry Louis Gates Jr. and K. A. Appiah, 175–209. New York: Amistad, 1993.

Bailey, Peggy Dunn. "Female Gothic Fiction, Grotesque Realities, and *Bastard Out of Carolina*: Dorothy Allison Revises the Southern Gothic." *Mississippi Quarterly* 63, no. 1–2 (2010): 269–90.

Baker, Houston A. "To Move Without Moving: An Analysis of Creativity and Commerce in Ralph Ellison's Trueblood Episode." In *The Critical Response to Ralph Ellison*, edited by Robert J. Butler, 73–93. Westport: Greenwood, 2000.

Balaev, Michelle. *The Nature of Trauma in American Novels*. Evanston: Northwestern University Press, 2012.

Banks, Russell. *The Sweet Hereafter*. New York: Harper Collins, 1991.

Barnes, Elizabeth, ed. *Incest and the Literary Imagination*. Gainesville: University Press of Florida, 2002.

Bass, Ellen. *The Courage to Heal: A Guide for Women Survivors of Child Sexual Abuse*. 3rd ed. New York: Harper, 1994.

Bass, Ellen, and Laura Davis. *The Courage to Heal: A Guide for Women Survivors of Child Sexual Abuse*. New York: Harper, 1988.

Bell, Vikki. *Interrogating Incest: Feminism: Foucault and the Law*. London: Routledge, 1993.

Bellamy, Joe David. "An Interview with Colin and Kathryn Harrison." *The Iowa Review* 37, no. 1 (2007): 157–76.

Benjamin, Shanna Greene. "There's Something about Mary: Female Wisdom and the Folk Presence in Ralph Ellison's *Invisible Man*." *Meridians* 12, no. 1 (2014): 121–48.

Bennett, Paula. "The Mother's Part: Incest and Maternal Deprivation in Woolf and Morrison." In *Narrating Mothers: Theorizing Maternal Subjectivities*, edited by Brenda O. Daly and Maureen T. Reddy, 125–38. Knoxville: University of Tennessee Press, 1991.

Berman, Jeffrey. *The Talking Cure: Literary Representations of Psychoanalysis*. New York: New York University Press, 1985.

Bigsby, Christopher. *Writers in Conversation*. Vol. 1. Norwich: Arthur Miller Centre for American Studies, 2000.

Biss, Eula. "The Voice Box: Our Opera of High and Low." *Columbia: A Journal of Literature and Art* 45 (2008): 150–64.

Bisson, J. I. "What Happened to Harmonization of the PTSD Diagnosis? The Divergence of ICD11 and DSM5." *Epidemiology and Psychiatric Sciences* 22, no. 3 (2013): 205–07.

Blazek, William. "'Some Fault in the Plan': Fitzgerald's Critique of Psychiatry in *Tender Is the Night*." In *Twenty-First-Century Readings of* Tender Is the Night, edited by William Blazek and Laura Rattray, 67–84. Liverpool: Liverpool University Press, 2007.

Blouch, Christine, and Laurie Vickroy, eds. *Critical Essays on the Works of American Author Dorothy Allison*. Lewiston: Edwin Mellen Press, 2004.

Boker, Pamela A. "Beloved Illness: Transference Love as Romantic Pathology in F. Scott Fitzgerald's *Tender Is the Night*." *Literature and Medicine* 11, no. 2 (1992): 294–314.

Bolonik, Kera. "About Kathryn Harrison." *Ploughshares* 35, no. 2/3 (2009): 174–77.

Bouson, J. Brooks. *Embodied Shame: Uncovering Female Shame in Contemporary Women's Writings*. Albany: State University of New York Press, 2009.

———. *Quiet as It's Kept: Shame, Trauma, and Race in the Novels of Toni Morrison*. Albany: State University of New York Press, 2000.

Bradley, Adam. *Ralph Ellison in Progress: From* Invisible Man *to* Three Days Before the Shooting . . . New Haven: Yale University Press, 2010.

Brown, Laura. "Not Outside the Range: One Feminist Perspective on Psychic Trauma." In *Trauma: Explorations in Memory*, edited by Cathy Caruth. 100–12. Baltimore: Johns Hopkins University Press, 1995.

Brownmiller, Susan. *Against Our Will: Men, Women, and Rape*. New York: Simon and Schuster, 1975.

Bruccoli, Matthew J. *The Composition of* Tender Is the Night*: A Study of the Manuscripts*. Pittsburgh: University of Pittsburgh Press, 1963.

Bruccoli, Matthew J., and Margaret M. Duggan, eds. *Correspondence of F. Scott Fitzgerald*. New York: Random, 1980.

Bryer, Jackson R., and Cathy W. Barks, eds. *Dear Scott, Dearest Zelda: The Love Letters of F. Scott and Zelda Fitzgerald*. New York: St. Martin's, 2002.

Bumby, Kurt M. "Psycholegal Considerations in Abuse-Motivated Parricides: Children Who Kill Their Abusive Parents." *The Journal of Psychiatry & Law* 22, no. 1 (1994): 51–90.

Burton, Mary E. "The Counter-Transference of Dr. Diver." *ELH* 38, no. 3 (1971): 459–71.

Butler, Jess. "For White Girls Only? Postfeminism and the Politics of Inclusion." *Feminist Formations* 25, no.1 (2013): 35–58.

Butler, Robert J. Introduction to *The Critical Response to Ralph Ellison*, edited by Robert J. Butler, xix–xl. Westport: Greenwood, 2000.

Butler, Sandra. *Conspiracy of Silence: The Trauma of Incest*. San Francisco: New Glide Publications, 1978.

Carpenter, Faedra Chatard. "Addressing 'The Complex'-ities of Skin Color: Intra-Racism and the Plays of Hurston, Kennedy, and Orlandersmith." *Theatre Topics* 19, no. 1 (2009): 15–27.

Caruth, Cathy. *Unclaimed Experience: Trauma, Narrative, and History*. Baltimore: Johns Hopkins University Press, 1996.

Champagne, Rosaria. *The Politics of Survivorship: Incest, Women's Literature, and Feminist Theory*. New York: New York University Press, 1996.

Claxton, Mae Miller. *Conversations with Dorothy Allison*. Jackson: University Press of Mississippi, 2012.

Cline, Sally. *Zelda Fitzgerald: Her Voice in Paradise*. New York: Arcade, 2002.

Cloutier, Jean-Christophe. "The Comic Book World of Ralph Ellison's *Invisible Man*." *Novel: A Forum on Fiction* 43, no. 2 (2010): 294–319.

Cokal, Susann. "Caught in the Wrong Story: Psychoanalysis and Narrative Structure in *Tender Is the Night*." *Texas Studies in Literature and Language* 47, no. 1 (2005): 75–100.

Conner, Marc C. "Introduction: Aesthetics and the African American Novel." In *The Aesthetics of Toni Morrison: Speaking the Unspeakable*, edited by Marc C. Conner, ix–xxviii. Jackson: University Press of Mississippi, 2000.

"A Conversation with Authors Stacey Lannert and Kristen Kemp." *Amazon.com*, November 14, 2014.

Cooperman, Jeannette. "A Conversation with Stacey Lannert." *St. Louis Magazine*, June 21, 2011.

Cowley, Malcolm. "Introduction to the Revised Edition." In *Critical Essays on F. Scott Fitzgerald's* Tender Is the Night, edited by Milton R. Stern, 102–9. Boston: G. K. Hall, 1986.

Cvetkovich, Ann. "Sexual Trauma/Queer Memory: Incest, Lesbianism, and Therapeutic Culture." In *Incest and the Literary Imagination*, edited by Elizabeth Barnes, 329–57. Gainesville: University Press of Florida, 2002.

Daly, Brenda. "When the Daughter Tells Her Story: The Rhetorical Challenges of Disclosing Father–Daughter Incest." In *Survivor Rhetoric: Negotiations and Narrativity in Abused Women's Language*, edited by Christine Shearer-Cremean and Carol L. Winkelmann, 139–65. Toronto: University of Toronto Press, 2004.

Davis, Joseph E. *Accounts of Innocence: Sexual Abuse, Trauma, and the Self*. Chicago: University of Chicago Press, 2005.

Demetrakopoulos, Stephanie. "On Morrison's Bleak Vision and Its Redemption." In *Toni Morrison's* The Bluest Eye, edited by Harold Bloom, 64–67. New York: Infobase Publishing, 2010.

Di Prete, Laura. *"Foreign Bodies": Trauma, Corporeality, and Textuality in Contemporary American Culture*. New York: Routledge, 2006.

Doane, Janice, and Devon Hodges. *Telling Incest: Narratives of Dangerous Remembering from Stein to Sapphire*. Ann Arbor: University of Michigan Press, 2001.

Dockterman, Eliana. "Dylan Farrow on Woody Allen Allegations Backlash." *Time.com*, February 18, 2014.

Donaldson, Scott. "The Seduction of Dr. Diver." *The Hopkins Review* 8, no. 1 (2015): 5–21.

———. "A Short History of *Tender Is the Night*." In *Writing the American Classics*, edited by James Barbour and Tom Quirk, 177–208. Chapel Hill: University of North Carolina Press, 1990.

Douglas, Kate. "'Blurbing' Biographical: Authorship and Autobiography." *Biography* 24, no. 4 (2001): 806–26.

Duvall, John N. "Naming Invisible Authority: Toni Morrison's Covert Letter to Ralph Ellison." *Studies in American Fiction* 25, no. 2 (1997): 241–53.

———. *Race and White Identity in Southern Fiction: From Faulkner to Morrison*. New York: Palgrave, 2008.

Eakin, Paul John. "Breaking Rules: The Consequences of Self-Narration." *Biography* 24, no. 1 (2001): 113–27.

Eberstadt, Mary. "Pants on Fire! Who Really Believes Kathryn Harrison's Incest Tale?" *Weekly Standard*, March 24, 1997, 31–32.

Ellis, James. "Fitzgerald's Fragmented Hero: Dick Diver." In Tender Is the Night: *Essays in Criticism*, edited by Marvin J. LaHood, 127–37. Bloomington: Indiana University Press, 1969.

Ellison, Ralph. "The Influence of Folklore on 'Battle Royal.'" In *The Story and Its Writer: An Introduction to Short Fiction*, Compact Seventh Edition, edited by Ann Charters, 864–65. Boston: Bedford, 2007.

———. *Invisible Man*. 1952. New York: Vintage, 1995.

———. *Juneteenth: A Novel*, edited by John F. Callahan. New York: Random House, 1999.

———. *Three Days Before the Shooting: The Unfinished Second Novel*, edited by John F. Callahan and Adam Bradley. New York: Modern Library, 2010.

"False Memories." *Recovered Memory Project: Case Archive, Commentary, and Scholarly Resources* (blog). Brown University Blogs. 2010. blogs.brown.edu/recoveredmemory/.

Faludi, Susan. *Backlash: The Undeclared War Against American Women*. New York: Crown Publishers, 1991.

Feng, Pin-Chia. *The Female* Bildungsroman *by Toni Morrison and Maxine Hong Kingston*. New York: Peter Lang, 1998.

Fetterley, Judith. "Who Killed Dick Diver? The Sexual Politics of *Tender Is the Night*." *Mosaic* 17, no. 1 (1984): 111–28.

Fischer, Nancy L. "Oedipus Wrecked? The Moral Boundaries of Incest." *Gender and Society* 17, no. 1 (2003): 92–110.

Fitzgerald, F. Scott. *The Crack-Up*, edited by Edmund Wilson. New York: New Directions, 1964.

———. *Tender Is the Night*. 1934. New York: Scribner's, 1982.

Ford, Jane M. *Patriarchy and Incest from Shakespeare to Joyce*. Gainesville: University Press of Florida, 1998.

Forward, Susan, and Craig Buck. *Betrayal of Innocence: Incest and Its Devastation*. Los Angeles: J. P. Tarcher, 1978.

Fraiberg, Selma. "Two Modern Incest Heroes." *Partisan Review* 28 (1961): 646–61.

French, Marilyn. *Our Father*. Boston: Little, Brown, 1994.

Freud, Sigmund. "The Aetiology of Hysteria." In *Collected Paper*, vol. 1, translated by Joan Riviere, 183–219. London: Hogarth, 1950.

———. "An Autobiographical Study." In *The Standard Edition of the Complete Psychological Works of Sigmund Freud*, vol. 20, translated by James Strachey, 7–70. London: Hogarth, 1959.

———. *The Standard Edition of the Complete Psychological Works of Sigmund Freud*, vol. 1, translated by James Strachey. London: Hogarth, 1957.

Friedel, Tania. "The Transformational Power of Shame: Masturbation, Religion, and White Trash Myths in *Bastard Out of Carolina*." In *Critical Essays on the Works of American Author Dorothy Allison*, edited by Christine Blouch and Laurie Vickroy, 29–54. Lewiston: Edwin Mellen Press, 2004.

Friedman, Matthew J. "Finalizing PTSD in *DSM-5*: Getting Here from There and Where to Go Next." *Journal of Traumatic Stress* 26 (2013): 548–56.

Friedman, Matthew J., Patricia A. Resick, Richard A. Bryant, and Chris R. Brewin. "Considering PTSD for *DSM-5*." *Depression and Anxiety* 28 (2011): 750–69.

Frost, Laura. "After Lot's Daughters: Kathryn Harrison and the Making of Memory." *Auto/Biography Studies* 14, no. 1 (1999): 51–70.

Fryer, Sarah Beebe. *Fitzgerald's New Women: Harbingers of Change*. Ann Arbor: UMI Research Press, 1988.

Gaitskill, Mary. *Two Girls, Fat and Thin*. New York: Poseidon, 1991.

Gates, Henry Louis, Jr. *Figures in Black: Words, Signs, and the "Racial" Self*. New York: Oxford University Press, 1987.

Gerrard, Nicci. "A Family Affair: Father, We Have Sinned . . . " *The Observer Review*, April 13, 1997, 6.

Giles, Jeff. "A Father. A Daughter. A Kiss Wasn't Just a Kiss." *Newsweek*, February 17, 1997, 62.

———. "The Father Won't 'Kiss' and Tell." *Newsweek*, April 28, 1997, 81.

Graff, E. J. "Dorothy Allison: Novelist Out of Carolina." *Poets and Writers Magazine*, Jan-Feb. 1995: 40–49.

Griffin, Susan. "Rape: The All-American Crime." 1971. In *Women: A Feminist Perspective*, edited by Jo Freeman, 24–39. Palo Alto: Mayfield, 1975.

Haegerich, Tamara M., and Bette L. Bottoms. "Empathy and Jurors' Decisions in Patricide Trials Involving Child Sexual Assault Allegations." *Law and Human Behavior* 24, no. 4 (2000): 421–48.

Harkins, Gillian. *Everybody's Family Romance: Reading Incest in Neoliberal America*. Minneapolis: University of Minnesota Press, 2009.

———. "Telling Fact from Fiction: Dorothy Allison's Disciplinary Stories." In *Incest and the Literary Imagination*, edited by Elizabeth Barnes, 283–315. Gainesville: University Press of Florida, 2002.

Harrison, Kathryn. *The Kiss: A Memoir*. New York: Avon, 1997.

———. *Thicker Than Water*. New York: Random, 1991.

Hart, Jessica L., and Jeffrey L. Helms. "Factors of Parricide: Allowance of the Use of Battered Child Syndrome as a Defense." *Aggression and Violent Behavior* 8 (2003): 671–83.

Hart, Lynda. *Between the Body and the Flesh: Performing Sadomasochism*. New York: Columbia University Press, 1998.

Hays, Peter L. "The Incest Theme in *Invisible Man*." *Western Humanities Review* 23 (1969): 335–39.

Hegadorn, Robert. "Clemency: Doing Justice to Incarcerated Battered Children." *Journal of the Missouri Bar* 55 (1999): 70–83.

Heide, Kathleen. *Understanding Parricide: When Sons and Daughters Kill Parents*. Oxford: Oxford University Press, 2013.

———. *Why Kids Kill Parents: Child Abuse and Adolescent Homicide*. Columbus: Ohio State University Press, 1992.

Heilbrun, Carolyn G. "Contemporary Memoirs: Or, Who Cares Who Did What to Whom?" *The American Scholar* 68, no. 3 (1999): 35–42.

Henderson, D. James. "Incest." In *Comprehensive Textbook of Psychiatry*, vol. 2, 2nd ed., edited by Alfred M. Freedman, Harold I. Kaplan, and Benjamin J. Sadock, 1530–39. Baltimore: Williams & Wilkins, 1975.

Henke, Suzette A. *Shattered Subjects: Trauma and Testimony in Women's Life-Writing*. New York: St. Martin's, 1998.

Herman, Judith. "Complex PTSD: A Syndrome in Survivors of Prolonged and Repeated Trauma." *Journal of Traumatic Stress* 5, no. 3 (1992): 377–91.

———. "CPTSD is a Distinct Entity: Comment on Resick et al. (2012)." *Journal of Traumatic Stress* 25 (2012): 256–57.

———. *Trauma and Recovery*. New York: Basic, 1992.

Herman, Judith Lewis, and Lisa Hirschman. *Father–Daughter Incest*. Cambridge: Harvard University Press, 1981.

Hersey, John. "'A Completion of Personality': A Talk with Ralph Ellison." In *Speaking for You: The Vision of Ralph Ellison*, 285–307. Washington, D. C.: Howard University Press, 1987.

Hill, Michael D., and Lena M. Hill. *Ralph Ellison's* Invisible Man*: A Reference Guide*. Westport: Greenwood, 2008.

Hipchen, Emily. "Genetic Sexual Attraction and the Creation of Fatherhood: Making Daddy (Infamous) in *The Kiss*." *The Journal of the Midwest Modern Language Association* 42, no. 2 (2009): 5–22.

Hollibaugh, Amber. "Telling a Mean Story." *The Women's Review of Books* (July 1992): 16–17.

hooks, bell. "Reconstructing Black Masculinity." In *The Masculine Masquerade: Masculinity and Representation*, edited by Andrew Perchuk and Helaine Posner, 69–88. Cambridge: MIT Press, 1995.

———. *We Real Cool: Black Men and Masculinity*. New York: Routledge, 2004.

———. *The Will to Change: Men, Masculinity, and Love*. New York: Atria Books, 2004.

Horeck, Tanya. "'Let Me Tell You a Story': Writing the Fiction of Childhood in Dorothy Allison's *Bastard Out of Carolina*." *New Formations* 42 (2000): 47–56.

Horvitz, Deborah. *Literary Trauma: Sadism, Memory, and Sexual Violence in American Women's Fiction*. Albany: State University of New York Press, 2000.

———. "'Sadism Demands a Story': Oedipus, Feminism, and Sexuality in Gayl Jones's *Corregidora* and Dorothy Allison's *Bastard Out of Carolina*." *Contemporary Literature* 39, no. 2 (1998): 238–61.

Houston, Pam. "Pam Houston Talks with Toni Morrison." In *Toni Morrison: Conversations*, edited by Carolyn Denard, 228–59. Jackson: University Press of Mississippi, 2008.

Howard, Jennifer. "Ralph Ellison's Never-Ending Novel." *The Chronicle Review*, May 9, 2010.

Irving, Katrina. "'Writing It Down So That It Would Be Real': Narrative Strategies in Dorothy Allison's *Bastard Out of Carolina*." *College Literature* 25, no. 2 (1998): 94–107.

Jackson, Lawrence. *Ralph Ellison: Emergence of Genius*. New York: Wiley, 2002.

Jarenski, Shelly. "Invisibility Embraced: The Abject as a Site of Agency in Ellison's *Invisible Man*." *MELUS* 35, no. 4 (2010): 85–109.

Jetter, Alexis. "The Roseanne of Literature." *New York Times Magazine*, December 17, 1995, 54–57.

Johns, Gillian. "Jim Trueblood and His Critic-Readers: Ralph Ellison's Rhetoric of Dramatic Irony and Tall Humor in the Mid-Century American Literary Public Sphere." *Texas Studies in Literature and Language* 49, no. 3 (2007): 230–64.

Joseph, Tiffany. "'Non-Combatant's Shell-Shock': Trauma and Gender in F. Scott Fitzgerald's *Tender Is the Night*." *NWSA Journal* 15, no. 3 (2003): 64–81.

Karlyn, Kathleen Rowe. *Unruly Girls, Unrepentant Mothers: Redefining Feminism on Screen*. Austin: University of Texas Press, 2011.

Kempe, C. Henry, Frederic N. Silverman, Brandt F. Steele, William Droegemueller, and Henry K. Silver. "The Battered-Child Syndrome." *Journal of the American Medical Association* 181, no. 1 (1962): 17–24.

Klotman, Phyllis. "Dick-and-Jane and the Shirley Temple Sensibility in *The Bluest Eye*." *Black American Literature Forum* 13, no. 4 (1979): 123–25.

LaCapra, Dominick. *Writing History, Writing Trauma*. Baltimore: Johns Hopkins University Press, 2001.

Langer, Adam. "Star Power." In *Toni Morrison: Conversations*, edited by Carolyn C. Denard, 206–13. Jackson: University Press of Mississippi, 2008.

Lannert, Stacey, and Kristen Kemp. *Redemption: A Story of Sisterhood, Survival, and Finding Freedom Behind Bars*. New York: Broadway, 2011.

Lannert v. Jones. 321 F.3d 747. U.S. App. (8th Cir. March 11, 2003).

Lanser, Susan Snaider. *Fictions of Authority: Women Writers and Narrative Voice*. Ithaca: Cornell University Press, 1992.

Laub, Dori. "Bearing Witness or the Vicissitudes of Listening." In *Testimony: Crises of Witnessing in Literature, Psychoanalysis, and History*, edited by Shoshana Felman and Dori Laub, 57–74. New York: Routledge, 1992.

Lee, Amanda Charlene. "Forgotten Child: *Bastard Out of Carolina* and the History of Child Sexual Abuse." *Proteus* 30, no. 1 (2014): 17–23.

Lehan, Richard D. "Tender Is the Night." In Tender Is the Night: *Essays in Criticism*, edited by Marvin J. LaHood, 61–85. Bloomington: Indiana University Press, 1969.

LeMahieu, Michael. "An Interview with Dorothy Allison." *Contemporary Literature* 51, no. 4 (2010): 651–76.

Leopold, Todd, Ashley Fantz, Moni Basu, and Faith Karimi. "Legendary Author Maya Angelou Dies at Age 86." *CNN.com* June 19, 2014.

Leys, Ruth. *Trauma: A Genealogy*. Chicago: University of Chicago Press, 2000.

Marshall, Elizabeth. "The Daughter's Disenchantment: Incest as Pedagogy in Fairy Tales and Kathryn Harrison's *The Kiss*." *College English* 66, no. 4 (2004): 403–26.

"Maya Angelou Obituary." *Legacy.com* May 28, 2014.

Mayfield, Sara. *Exiles from Paradise: Zelda and Scott Fitzgerald*. New York: Delacorte, 1971.

Mayo, James. "Morrison's *The Bluest Eye*." *The Explicator* 60, no. 4 (Summer 2002): 231–34.

McNally, Richard J. *Remembering Trauma*. Cambridge: Belknap, 2003.

Megan, Carolyn. "Moving Toward Truth: An Interview with Dorothy Allison." *The Kenyon Review* 16, no. 4 (1994): 71–83.

Meiselman, Karin. *Incest: A Psychological Study of Cause and Effects with Treatment Recommendations*. San Francisco: Josey-Bass, 1978.

Michlin, Monica. "Narrative as Empowerment: *Push* and the *Signifying* on Prior African-American Novels on Incest." *Études Anglaises* 59, no. 2 (2006): 170–85.

Milford, Nancy. *Zelda: A Biography*. New York: Harper, 1970.

Mones, Paul. "Battered Child Syndrome: Understanding Parricide." *Trial* 30, no. 2 (1994): 24-29.

———. *When A Child Kills: Abused Children Who Kill Their Parents*. New York: Pocket Books, 1991.

———. "When the Innocent Strike Back: Abused Children Who Kill Their Parents." *Journal of Interpersonal Violence* 8 (1993): 297–99.

Morrison, Toni. *The Bluest Eye*. 1970. New York: Plume, 1994.

———. Interview by Stephen Colbert. *The Colbert Report*. Comedy Central, November 19, 2014. Television.

———. "10 Questions for Toni Morrison." *TIME.com*. TIME, May 7, 2008.

Natterman, Udo. "Nicole Diver's Monologue: A Close Examination of a Key Segment." *Massachusetts Studies in English* 10, no. 4 (1986): 213–28.

Nunez, Narina, Mindy J. Dahl, Connie M. Tang, and Brittney L. Jensen. "Trial Venue Decisions in Juvenile Cases: Mitigating and Extralegal Factors Matter." *Legal & Criminological Psychology* 12, no. 1 (2007): 21–39.

"Obituary: Maya Angelou." *BBC News* May 28, 2014.

O'Connell, Patricia A. "Kathryn Harrison: Her Harrowing Psychological Novels Are Fiction, But Seem Vividly Real." *Publisher's Weekly*, March 1, 1993, 33–34.

O'Meally, Robert O. *The Craft of Ralph Ellison*. Cambridge: Harvard University Press, 1980.

Orth, Maureen. "Mia Farrow and Eight of Her Children Speak Out on Their Lives, Frank Sinatra, and the Scandals They've Endured." *Vanity Fair*, October 2, 2013.

———. "Mia's Story." *Vanity Fair*, November 1992.

Paglia, Camille. *Sex, Art, and American Culture*. New York: Vintage, 1992.

Pederson, Joshua. "Speak, Trauma: Toward a Revised Understanding of Literary Trauma Theory." *Narrative* 22, no. 3 (2014): 333–53.

Penny, Laurie. "The Woody Allen Case Reminds Us that It's the Accuser Who Invariably Ends up on Trial." *New Statesman*, February 7–13, 2014.

Peterson, Nancy. "Introduction: Reading Toni Morrison—From the Seventies to the Nineties." In *Toni Morrison: Critical and Theoretical Approaches*, 1–15. Baltimore: Johns Hopkins University Press, 1997.

Pollak, Ellen. *Incest and the English Novel, 1684–1814*. Baltimore: Johns Hopkins University Press, 2003.

Powers, Elizabeth. "Doing Daddy Down." *Commentary* 103, no. 6 (1997): 38–41.

Pratt, Minnie Bruce. "Dorothy Allison." *Progressive* 59, no. 7 (1995): 30–34.

Prigozy, Ruth. "From Griffith's Girls to Daddy's Girl: The Masks of Innocence in *Tender Is the Night*." *Twentieth Century Literature* 26, no. 2 (1980): 189–221.

Rampersad, Arnold. *Ralph Ellison: A Biography*. New York: Knopf, 2007.

Rank, Otto. *The Incest Theme in Literature and Legend*. 1912. Baltimore: Johns Hopkins University Press, 1992.

Resick, Patricia A., Erika J. Wolf, Shannon Wiltsey Stirman, Stephanie Y. Wells, Michael K. Suvak, Karen S. Mitchell, Matthew W. King, and Michelle J. Bovin. "Advocacy Through Science: Reply to Comments on Resick et al. (2012)." *Journal of Traumatic Stress* 25 (2012): 260–63.

Resick, Patricia A., Michelle J. Bovin, Amber L. Calloway, Alexandra M. Dick, Matthew W. King, Karen S. Mitchell, Michael K. Suvak, Stephanie Y. Wells, Shannon Wiltsey Stirman, and Erika J. Wolf. "A Critical Evaluation of the Complex PTSD Literature: Implications for *DSM-5*." *Journal of Traumatic Stress* 25 (2012): 241–51.

Rich, Adrienne. *Of Woman Born: Motherhood as Experience and Institution*. New York: Norton, 1976.

Robson, Kathryn. *Writing Wounds: The Inscription of Trauma in Post-1968 French Women's Life-Writing*. New York: Rodopi, 2004.

Rohrberger, Mary. "'Ball the jack': Surreality, Sexuality, and the Role of Women in *Invisible Man*." In *Approaches to Teaching Ellison's* Invisible Man, edited by Susan Resneck Parr and Pancho Savery, 124–32. New York: MLA, 1989.

Roiphe, Katie. "Making the Incest Scene." *Harper's*, November 1995, 65, 68–71.

Root, Maria. "Women of Color and Traumatic Stress in 'Domestic Captivity': Gender and Race as Disempowering Statuses." In *Ethnocultural Aspects of Posttraumatic Stress Disorder: Issues, Research, and Clinical Applications*, edited by Anthony J. Marsella, Matthew J. Friedman, Ellen T. Gerrity, and Raymond M. Scurfield. 363–87. Washington, DC: American Psychological Association, 1996.

Rush, Florence. "The Freudian Coverup." Featured Reprint. *Feminism & Psychology* 6, no. 2 (1996): 261–76.

Russell, Diana E. H. *The Secret Trauma: Incest in the Lives of Girls and Women*. New York: Basic, 1986.

Sacks, Jamie Heather. "A New Age of Understanding: Allowing Self-Defense Claims for Battered Children Who Kill Their Abusers." *Journal of Contemporary Health Law & Policy* 10, no. 1 (1994): 349–81.

Sanchez-Hucles, Janis, and Patrick Hudgins. "Trauma across Diverse Settings," In *Encyclopedia of Women and Gender: Sex Similarities and Differences and the Impact of Society on Gender*, L-Z, vol. 2, edited by Judith Worell, 1151–68. San Diego: Academic, 2001.

Sapphire. *Push*. New York: Knopf, 1996.

Saunders, Catherine E. "Makers or Bearers of Meaning? Sex and the Struggle for Self-Definition in Ralph Ellison's *Invisible Man*." *Critical Matrix* 5, no. 1 (1989): n.p.

Schappell, Elissa. "Toni Morrison: The Art of Fiction." In *Toni Morrison: Conversations*, edited by Carolyn C. Denard, 62–90. Jackson: University Press of Mississippi, 2008.

Shearer-Cremean, Christine, and Carol L. Winkelmann. Introduction to *Survivor Rhetoric: Negotiations and Narrativity in Abused Women's Language*, edited by Christine Shearer-Cremean and Carol L. Winkelmann, 3–22. Toronto: University of Toronto Press, 2004.

Showalter, Elaine. "Rethinking the Seventies: Women Writers and Violence." *The Antioch Review* 70, no. 1 (2012): 162–76.

Showden, Carisa R. "What's Political about the New Feminisms?" *Frontiers: A Journal of Women Studies* 30, no. 2 (2009): 166–98.

Smethurst, James. "'Something Warmly, Infuriatingly Feminine': Gender, Sexuality, and the Work of Ralph Ellison." In *A Historical Guide to Ralph Ellison*, edited by Steven C. Tracey, 115–42. Oxford: Oxford University Press, 2004.

Smiley, Jane. *A Thousand Acres*. New York: Knopf, 1991.

Spillers, Hortense. "'The Permanent Obliquity of an In(pha)llibly Straight': In the Time of the Daughters and the Fathers." In *Changing Our Own Words: Essays on Criticism, Theory, and Writing by Black* Women, edited by Cheryl A. Wall, 127–49. New Brunswick: Rutgers University Press, 1989.

Stalans, Loretta J., and Gary T. Henry. "Societal Views of Justice for Adolescents Accused of Murder: Inconsistency between Community Sentiment and Automatic Legislative Transfers." *Law and Human Behavior* 18, no. 6 (1994): 675–96.

Stanton, Robert. "'Daddy's Girl': Symbol and Theme in *Tender Is the Night*." *Modern Fiction Studies* 4 (1958): 136–42.

Stein, Karen F. *Reading, Learning, Teaching Toni Morrison*. New York: Peter Lang, 2009.

Steinberg, A. H. "Fitzgerald's Portrait of a Psychiatrist." In Tender Is the Night: *Essays in Criticism*, edited by Marvin J. LaHood, 138–43. Bloomington: Indiana University Press, 1969.

Stepto, Robert B. "'Intimate Things in Place': A Conversation with Toni Morrison." In *Toni Morrison: Critical Perspectives Past and Present*, edited by Henry Louis Gates Jr. and K. A. Appiah, 378–95. New York: Amistad, 1993.

———. "Literacy and Hibernation: Ralph Ellison's *Invisible Man*." In *Speaking for You: The Vision of Ralph Ellison*, edited by Kimberly Benston, 360–85. Washington, D.C.: Howard University Press, 1987.

Stern, Milton R. Introduction to *Critical Essays on F. Scott Fitzgerald's* Tender Is the Night, edited by Milton R. Stern, 1–20. Boston: G. K. Hall, 1986.

Straker, Gillian. "Continuous Traumatic Stress: Personal Reflections 25 Years On." *Peace and Conflict: Journal of Peace Psychology* 19, no. 2 (2013): 209–17.

Strong, Marilyn. "Talking Trash with Dorothy Allison." *San Francisco Focus*, June 1994: 61-98.

Surányi, Ágnes. "*The Bluest Eye* and *Sula*: Black Female Experience from Childhood to Womanhood." In *The Cambridge Companion to Toni Morrison*, edited by Justine Tally, 11–25. Cambridge: Cambridge University Press, 2007.

Sylvander, Carolyn W. "Ralph Ellison's Man and Female Stereotypes." *Negro American Literature Forum* 9, no. 3 (1975): 77–79.

Tally, Justine. "Introduction: 'All Necks are on the Line.'" In *The Cambridge Companion to Toni Morrison*, edited by Justine Tally, 1–7. Cambridge: Cambridge University Press, 2007.

Tate, Claudia. "Notes on the Invisible Women in Ralph Ellison's *Invisible Man*." In *Speaking for You: The Vision of Ralph Ellison*, edited by Kimberly Benston, 163–72. Washington, D.C.: Howard University Press, 1987.

Tavernier-Courbin, Jacqueline. "The Influence of France on Nicole Diver's Recovery in *Tender Is the Night*." In *French Connections: Hemingway and Fitzgerald Abroad*, edited by J. Gerald Kennedy and Jackson R. Bryer, 215–32. New York: St. Martin's, 1998.

Taylor, Kendall. *Sometimes Madness Is Wisdom: Zelda and Scott Fitzgerald: A Marriage*. New York: Ballantine, 2001.

Thurman, Wallace. "Harlem Facets." 1927. In *The Collected Writings of Wallace Thurman: A Harlem Renaissance Reader*, edited by Amritjit Singh and Daniel M. Scott III, 35–39. New Brunswick: Rutgers University Press, 2003.

Tokarczyk, Michelle. *Class Definitions: On the Lives and Writings of Maxine Hong Kingston, Sandra Cisneros, and Dorothy Allison*. Selinsgrove: Susquehanna University Press, 2008.

Valenti, Jessica. "Choosing Comfort Over Truth: What It Means to Defend Woody Allen." *The Nation*, February 3, 2014.

van der Kolk, Bessel A. Afterword to *Treating Complex Traumatic Stress Disorders: An Evidence-Based Guide*, edited by Christine A. Courtois and Julian D. Ford, 455–66. New York: Guilford, 2009.

———. *Psychological Trauma*. Washington D.C.: American Psychiatric Press, 1987.

Wagner-Martin, Linda. *Toni Morrison and the Maternal: From* The Bluest Eye *to* Home. New York: Peter Lang, 2014.

———. *Zelda Sayre Fitzgerald: An American Woman's Life*. New York: Palgrave, 2004.

Walker, Lenore. *The Battered Woman*. New York: Harper, 1979.

Weber, Ellen. "Incest: Sexual Abuse Begins at Home." *Ms.*, April 1977, 64–67.

Weide, Robert B. "The Woody Allen Allegations: Not So Fast." *The Daily Beast*, January 27, 2014.

Weiss, Daniel S. "Introduction to the Special Feature on Complex PTSD." *Journal of Traumatic Stress* 25 (2012): 239–40.

Welch, Steven, Cherisse Klassen, Oxana Borisova, and Holly Clothier. "The *DSM-5* Controversies: How Should Psychologists Respond?" *Canadian Psychology* 54, no. 3 (2013): 166–75.
West, James L. W. III. "F. Scott Fitzgerald and American Psychiatry: A New Letter." *American Imago* 68, no. 1 (2011): 59–65.
———. "The Internal Chronology of *Tender Is the Night*." *The Papers of the Bibliographical Society of America* 104, no. 4 (2010): 527–537.
Whitehead, Anne. *Trauma Fiction*. Edinburgh: Edinburgh University Press, 2004.
Wilson, Elizabeth. "Not in This House: Incest, Denial, and Doubt in the White Middle Class Family." *Yale Journal of Criticism* 8, no. 1 (1995): 35–58.
Wolcott, James. "Dating Your Dad." *New Republic*, March 31, 1997, 32–36.
World Health Organization. *The ICD-10 Classification of Mental and Behavioral Disorders: Clinical Descriptions and Diagnosis Guidelines*. Geneva: WHO, 1992.
Wray, Matt, and Annalee Newitz. *White Trash: Race and Class in America*. New York: Routledge, 1997.
Wypijewski, JoAnn. "Woody, Dylan & Doubt." *The Nation*, March 10, 2014.
Yoshikawa, Mako. "The New Face of Incest? Race, Class, and the Controversy over Kathryn Harrison's *The Kiss*." In *Incest and the Literary Imagination*, edited by Elizabeth Barnes, 358–76. Gainesville: University Press of Florida, 2002.
Young, Harvey, and Jocelyn Prince. "Adapting *The Bluest Eye* for the Stage." *African American Review* 45, no. 1–2 (Spring/Summer 2012): 143–55.

Index

About the Author

Christine Grogan is senior lecturer of English at The Pennsylvania State University–University Park and the current president of the Katherine Anne Porter Society. She holds a PhD in literature from the University of South Florida. She has published articles on Azar Nafisi's *Reading Lolita in Tehran,* Calixthe Beyala's *Your Name Shall Be Tanga,* and the short stories of Zelda Fitzgerald.

Lightning Source UK Ltd.
Milton Keynes UK
UKHW010655180520
363372UK00003B/293